Hurricane of Fire

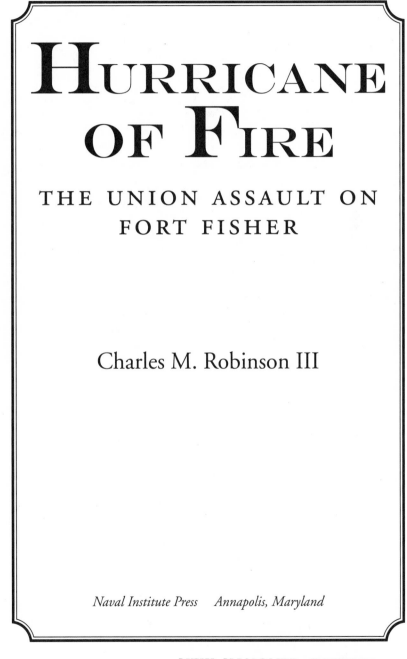

Hurricane of Fire

THE UNION ASSAULT ON FORT FISHER

Charles M. Robinson III

Naval Institute Press   Annapolis, Maryland

Library of Congress Cataloging-in-Publication Data
Robinson, Charles M., 1949–
    Hurricane of fire : the Union assault on Fort Fisher /
Charles M. Robinson III.
        p.   cm.
    Includes bibliographical references and index.
    ISBN 1-55750-720-1 : alk. paper
    1. Fort Fisher (N.C. : Fort)—Siege, 1864–1865.
I. Title.
    E477.28.R63   1998
    973.7'37–dc21   97-46090

Printed in the United States of America on acid-free paper ∞
98 99 00 01 02 03 04 05   9 8 7 6 5 4 3 2
First printing

Frontispiece: Naval bombardment of Fort Fisher during the
second attack, January 1865 (reprinted from Johnson and Buel,
Battles and Leaders of the Civil War)

To Norman Delaney

CONTENTS

ILLUSTRATIONS

AUTHOR'S NOTE

IN THE DECADES immediately following the American Civil War, the two battles of Fort Fisher figured prominently in magazine articles and war anthologies. In that era, when many of the survivors were still alive and memories were fresh, the combined army-navy operation against this most fearsome of all Confederate forts was considered a major achievement of the war. But as time passed and the veterans died, it was relegated to a sidebar of history. Occurring simultaneously with Gen. U. S. Grant's operations against Richmond, it was lost in the vast drama of the Confederate collapse. And as the fort itself eroded into the sea, it was almost forgotten. One rarely read of it except as a page or two in a general history of the war, in books on blockade-running, in regional histories, or in graduate dissertations.

With the publication of Rod Gragg's *Confederate Goliath: The Battle of Fort Fisher* in 1991, the fort and the great battles fought there began to regain their proper role in the history of the war. This book is not an attempt to duplicate Gragg's work, which examines virtually every aspect of the final days of the fort, in December 1864 and January 1865. Instead, I have attempted to show the part it played in the whole sweep of blockade operations on the Atlantic Coast during the four years of the war— how Fort Fisher came to be, why it was important, why the Union waited so long to take action, and the significance of the fort's fall on the outcome of the war.

I have told the story primarily from a naval point of view, because of the two services the navy was most concerned with Fort Fisher. In dealing with the final battle, I have not dwelt on the army effort, which Gragg has covered so well, but have concentrated instead on the great and terrible assault across more than a mile of open beach by ill-armed, ill-trained sailors and marines. In particular, I have tried to do justice to the marines, who I believe have been unjustly blamed for more than 130 years for the failure of the assault.

I also hope that I have been able to change the perception of Rear Adm. Samuel Phillips Lee's role in the story of Fort Fisher. Most histories state that Lee was replaced as commander of the North Atlantic Blockading Squadron because he was not aggressive enough to undertake an operation of that magnitude. I believe the evidence shows the exact opposite—that Lee lobbied and cajoled the Navy Department for two years to seize the fortifications on the Cape Fear River, only to have command taken from him for political reasons just as the government finally assented to the project.

The reader may feel that I have used an excessive number of quotes, especially in the chapters dealing with the battle. Perhaps so. But I personally believe no one can tell of the frustration in having to sit idly offshore and watch the fort grow in size and strength from one day to the next, or describe the awful grandeur of the naval assault better than those who were there.

Many people and institutions helped make this book possible, and at the risk of leaving some out, I would like to acknowledge them:

Montana—Crow Agency: Little Bighorn Battlefield National Monument.

North Carolina—Chapel Hill: Richard A. Shrader, Southern Historical Collection, Wilson Library, University of North Carolina. Kure Beach: E. Gehrig Spencer, Manager, Fort Fisher State Historic Site. Durham: William R. Erwin, Jr., Senior Reference Librarian, Special Collections Library, Duke University. Raleigh: North Carolina Department of Cultural Resources, Division of Archives and History.

Pennsylvania—Carlisle: United States Army Military History Institute, Carlisle Barracks.

Virginia—Williamsburg: Margaret Cook, Earl Gregg Swem Library, College of William and Mary.

Washington, D.C.—Library of Congress. National Archives.

I wish to make special mention of Alicia Patino and Rubén Coronado, Interlibrary Loan Department, University Library, University of Texas–Pan American, Edinburg, Texas. Without their help in obtaining many rare and obscure titles (often within a few days of my request), this project would have been impossible.

Thanks also to Paul Wilderson, executive editor, and the staff of the Naval Institute Press for their advice and encouragement.

Grateful acknowledgment is extended to the following publishers and holding institutions for permission to publish material under their custodianship:

Manuscripts and Rare Books Department, Swem Library, College of William and Mary, Williamsburg, Virginia—William Lamb Papers.

North Carolina Department of Cultural Resources, Division of Archives and History, Raleigh, North Carolina—Charles Pattison Bolles Papers, P.C. 44; William Henry Chase Whiting Papers, P.C. 195.

Special Collections Library, Duke University, Durham, North Carolina— Catherine Jane (McGeachy) Buie Papers; James J. Cleer Papers; Enoch Greenleafe Parrott Papers; William Read, Jr., Papers; Charles Steedman Papers.

Southern Historical Collection, University of North Carolina Library, Chapel Hill—Battle Family Papers, #3223-A; Macon Bonner Papers, #3758-Z; Samuel Cooper Papers, #2482-Z; Joseph Fernald Papers, #4280.

Had there been no fleet to assist the army at Fort Fisher the Federal infantry could not have dared to assault it until its land defenses had been destroyed by gradual approaches.

COLONEL WILLIAM LAMB, *Commanding Officer, Fort Fisher, North Carolina*

In no campaign of the war did such great achievements upon land result from the operations of so small a force of men. . . . Yet this small Federal force, co-operating with the navy, assaulted and captured one of the strongest defensive works erected in these modern times, after a seven hours' fight.

EDSON J. HARKNESS, *Union survivor*

Hurricane of Fire

PROLOGUE

THE NORTH CAROLINA COAST from Cape Fear to Cape Hatteras is known as the Graveyard of the Atlantic. The curve of the coast, the sudden right angle to the west at Cape Fear, and the flow of rivers striking the ocean currents create hidden shoals stretching miles out to sea. The winters may be temperate one day and bitterly cold the next, with damp winds, storms, and blinding fog. In the summers, the coastline is exposed to vicious hurricanes sweeping across the ocean from near Africa.

For a month, in December 1864 and January 1865, there was a storm of a different kind—a hurricane of fire and steel, as the United States mounted a land-sea assault never before equaled in the history of the world. This was the attack on the Confederate stronghold of Fort Fisher, a maze of earthworks, bomb shelters, and gun emplacements protecting the city of Wilmington.

For four years, Fort Fisher was the Achilles' heel of the Union blockade. As long as it stood, Wilmington would remain open. The odds were overwhelmingly in favor of the blockade-runners that came and went virtually on schedule, openly defying the Federal fleet. In short, because of Fort Fisher, the blockade of Wilmington simply did not work, and it was an easy matter to transport incoming matériel to the front in Virginia.

Although Federal naval authorities early in the war grasped the need to take Fort Fisher, their army counterparts did not. Their reasons, stated or otherwise, were numerous. One was an obsession with Charleston, South Carolina, a port of less strategic significance but far greater emotional interest. Because the war had started in Charleston, that city had become a fetish for the North, and in 1863 all resources for a coastal invasion were diverted in a wasteful and futile attempt to capture it. By the middle of 1864, however, Federal planners had come to realize that if the war were to end soon, Fisher would have to be taken.

When the North finally moved against Fort Fisher and Wilmington, the Confederacy was crumbling. Most of the country was either occupied or isolated, and the Federal armies had the approaches to Richmond under siege. Modern historians, given the vantage of more than 130 years of hindsight, question whether an expedition against Fort Fisher at that point was even significant to the outcome of the war. But to those at the time, the question was not so simple. As long as Wilmington remained open, food coming through the blockade would reach Lee's beleaguered army, and that army could continue the war. Confederate leaders hoped a prolonged war would exhaust the North and bring about an armistice that would allow the South to maintain its independence. While their Northern counterparts did not doubt the outcome of the war, they dreaded its continuation and meant to conclude it as rapidly as possible. To do so, they had to deny food to the Confederate armies. This meant capturing Fort Fisher, closing Wilmington, and disrupting the blockade traffic.

From the beginning it was obvious that the navy would play a major role in the capture of the fort. In the earliest days, when the defenses were still rudimentary, one Federal admiral proposed sending a landing party to take and hold the position until relieved by troops. The validity of his proposal is apparent when one sees that the Confederate defenders feared just such an action. It is also apparent that when naval coastal bombardment forces were diverted to places like Charleston, it took pressure off the Confederates, who used the time to strengthen the fort until it gave the impression of virtual impregnability. When it finally came, the attack that took the fort was successful largely because naval gunnery had reduced the defenses to the point that troops could push into the works, and because a naval assault diverted attention from the main force.

The events of that last, terrible day made a profound impression, not only on strategic planners, but on ordinary sailors and soldiers. It created a special bond between former enemies who had seen the inside of hell. Less than ten years after the battle, an anonymous author observed: "The ranks of those who fought at Fort Fisher grow thinner and weaker. How many of those who still survive, with health broken down by hardship and disease, in obscurity, and forgotten, have little pleasure but in memories of the past! Often they recall them, and always with kindly thoughts of the old enemy who fought them so long and well."[1] Like the hurricanes of nature, this hurricane carried such devastating force that the mere act of survival was itself a victory.

1

NORTH CAROLINA AND SECESSION

IT WAS SUNDAY AFTERNOON, January 15, 1865. The day was cold and clear, and the Atlantic Ocean was calm in front of Fort Fisher, North Carolina. For more than forty-eight hours, the largest fleet ever assembled by the United States Navy had hammered the fort day and night with the heaviest bombardment in history. On the first day, the Confederate defenders had watched as surfboats ferried thousands of Union soldiers ashore under cover of the navy guns. Now, on the third day, the boats were landing an assault force of two thousand Union sailors and marines.

Fort Fisher's commanding officer, Col. William Lamb, had spent more than two years preparing for this day. From a weak, virtually unarmed series of sandbank gun emplacements, he had created what was generally considered the most formidable defensive work in the South. At the beginning of 1865 it constituted a string of earthworks and protected gun chambers, magazines, and bombproof shelters a mile long on its sea face and half a mile wide the land side, the whole bristling with forty-four heavy-caliber guns.[1] The land face was its vulnerable spot, for as Lamb himself pointed out, Fort Fisher was built for defense against a naval assault.[2]

This was the Union's second attempt to take the fort. Only three weeks earlier, after another navy pounding, Union soldiers had attacked the land face but were pulled back by their own commanders. The failure humiliated the North and brought recriminations among both Union and Confederate officers. The much-vaunted naval bombardment prior to the assault had caused very little actual damage, and the Union soldiers charged into a storm of heavy cannon fire. Yet they did make it to the parapet at Fort Fisher's weakest point, and many Union officers were convinced that only the timidity of their generals prevented them from carrying the day. The navy, of course, agreed, and the accusations became so vehement that the U.S. Congress's Joint Committee on the Conduct of the War announced an investigation of the fiasco.

On the Confederate side, Lamb and his superior, Maj. Gen. William Henry Chase Whiting, believed that only Providence had saved them. Fort Fisher was short on ammunition and seriously undermanned. Reinforcements promised from Virginia had not arrived, and their own departmental commander, Gen. Braxton Bragg, offered no support.

Now, once again, Lamb was facing a massive onslaught against his defenses. This time, his situation was far more serious. The Union navy's gunfire had improved dramatically during the last three days. The fort was seriously damaged, and many of its guns were knocked out. On the land face he had only one heavy gun still capable of firing. It was as if one of the great hurricanes that periodically strike the North Carolina coast had swept through Fort Fisher, tearing away at its earthworks, knocking its guns off their carriages and platforms, and leaving it helpless. When the assault came—and Lamb knew it would be within the hour—he would have to place his hope on musket, bayonet, and electrically fired land mines planted in the plain in front of the fort—assuming the wires to the mines had not been cut by shells churning up the beach.

The Union ships ceased fire. After the constant roar of guns and the explosion of shells overhead, a brief silence descended, interrupted by the breaking of the waves as they came ashore. Suddenly the quiet was shattered by the shriek of steam whistles on dozens of warships. Up the beach, the cheering blue mass of sailors and marines started toward Fort Fisher.

Lamb ordered his men to open fire with two small fieldpieces and the one remaining big gun on the land face. Grape and canister tore into the Union ranks. Then, when the blue jackets reached the palisade in front of the fort, the storm of fire and lead broke in full fury as Confederate rifle-men poured volley after volley on them.

For the Union navy, the assault of January 15 marked the end of long frustration. Although Wilmington, North Carolina's largest city and chief seaport, was officially blockaded, Fort Fisher's looming presence made it virtually an open port. Already this had prompted the recall of one admiral, and the Navy Department had been accused of everything from indifference to collusion with the South. The real indifference, however, came from the army and the political arm of the government, neither of which could—or would—understand the fort's importance to Confederate supply. The men who ran the navy had to wait until the soldiers and politicians realized the seriousness of this hole in the blockade.[3]

The blockade itself had been proclaimed by Abraham Lincoln on April 19, 1861, five days after the battered Union garrison evacuated Fort Sumter. Initially covering the Southern coast from South Carolina to Texas, it ostensibly had two reasons—because the Federal government was unable to collect revenue on seaborne cargo arriving in the Confederate States, and for the "prevention and punishment of piracy" against U.S. shipping by Southern vessels operating under letters of marque from the Confederate government. Yet the name by which the blockade became known, Anaconda, was a clear statement of the Federal government's actual goal.[4] Devised by Maj. Gen. Winfield Scott, general in chief of the Union army, and named for a large South American snake that suffocates its prey, Anaconda called for suffocating the South by cutting off its external commerce.

Scott was one of the few who realized from the outset that a conventional war of armies would last for years rather than weeks or months, as most people preferred to believe. He was also one of the few army officers who recognized the value of combined operations with the navy, drawn from his own experiences in the Mexican War. His rationale was simple. The Southern economy was agrarian. It produced raw materials and consumed manufactured products. The industrial base to sustain a war did not exist, and the outbreak of the hostilities would halt the flow of goods from the industrialized North. The blockade was designed to isolate the Confederacy from the world so that it would be unable to obtain manufactured goods, particularly implements of war. Thus, Scott hoped to avoid a prolonged conflict that would require a massive call for troops and crushing national debt in the North, as well as devastate the South and embitter its people for generations.[5]

Under the plan, naval flotillas supported by troops would seize the Mississippi and deny the Confederacy access to the West. Squadrons along the Gulf and Atlantic Coasts would stop overseas trade. Aside from isolating the South, a properly implemented blockade in conjunction with imaginative army command would give the North mobility, allowing raids along the coast and forays into the interior, as well as permitting the Union army to choose the time and place of a major offensive. Unfortunately, shortsighted army command, interference by Northern armchair strategists in high political circles, and the determination of the Southern people negated any hope of the short, relatively uncomplicated police action envisioned at the outset by General Scott.[6]

During its first days the blockade did not concern North Carolina, which had remained in the United States when its Southern neighbors withdrew. Economically, the state had little to gain from secession. Its soil was not conducive to large-scale cotton production, and unlike South Carolina, Georgia, and Alabama, there was no significant elite class whose wealth was based on cotton. The most labor-intensive crop was rice grown by a few large plantations in the coastal areas. Even in that region the main product was naval stores—pine tar, turpentine, and resin, produced from the state's vast forests and vital to the maintenance of the wooden ships of the period. The bulk of North Carolina's agriculture centered around small farms producing cattle, vegetables, and grains such as corn, wheat, and bran. Their proprietors had no paramount economic interest in slavery and no real desire to involve themselves in preserving the system of bonded labor. Thus, despite a small but vocal secessionist element, most North Carolinians opposed leaving the Union.[7]

Like most white Southerners, many North Carolinians did believe the Federal government was strengthening itself at the expense of rights they had won in the Revolutionary War and enshrined in the Constitution. Nevertheless, the majority seemed to feel that some sort of solution could be achieved within the framework of the federal Union. Even the election of Lincoln, who was unpopular with virtually every political faction in the state, was not viewed as grounds for a rupture with the United States.

In Raleigh, the state's capital, Gov. William H. Ellis personally sympathized with the secessionists, but his official stance was caution. He did, however, advocate a reorganization of the militia, and on that all factions agreed; the unstable political situation in Washington and among the surrounding states made it imperative that North Carolina be in a position to defend itself. In December 1860 and January 1861, the two houses of the state's general assembly approved $300,000 for the purchase of arms and ammunition.[8]

The secession of South Carolina on December 20 brought demonstrations of support in Wilmington, but elsewhere in the state many believed South Carolina's action would make it all the more difficult for the other Southern states to regain their rights. Throughout much of North Carolina, many agreed with one mountaineer from the western part of the state, who supposedly said, "Let South Carolina nullify, revolute, secess, and BE DAMNED!"[9] But there was one point on which everyone concurred: the Federal government had no right to forcibly return a seceded state to the Union.

Once South Carolina took the initial step, other states began to follow. Secession sentiment began to grow in North Carolina as well, and even the Unionists agreed that if attempts at peaceful compromise failed, their state should also withdraw. Given these circumstances, and the fear of a Federal backlash once Lincoln was inaugurated, attention turned to the four Federal military installations in the state: the Fayetteville Arsenal on the easternmost edge of the Piedmont, and Forts Caswell, Johnston, and Macon on the Atlantic Coast.[10]

Fort Caswell and Fort Johnston guarded the Cape Fear River, navigable by deep-water vessels as far as Wilmington, and by river steamers another hundred miles to Fayetteville. Fort Johnston, begun by the British colonial administration in 1745 and reconstructed by the United States from 1794 to 1809, fronted the Cape Fear near its mouth at Smithville.[11] Not a defensive work, it was actually a cantonment with barracks, officers' quarters, and support structures around a parade ground. Two miles to the southwest on Oak Island, Fort Caswell was a pentagonal casemated masonry fort built from 1827 to 1838. Designed with strong defensive perimeters, it commanded both the Atlantic and the Cape Fear. Fort Macon, a casemated masonry fort similar to Caswell and built from 1826 to 1834, guarded the approaches to the port at Beaufort, some ninety miles northeast of the Cape Fear.[12]

The three forts had been deactivated several years earlier and were now occupied only by ordnance sergeants who functioned as caretakers. Nevertheless, their locations made them more immediately important than the Fayetteville Arsenal. If the Federal government regarrisoned them, they could become bases from which to subjugate North Carolina and forcefully keep it in the Union fold. The North Carolinians' fears were aggravated when the government dispatched 250 troops by sea to reinforce Fort Sumter in Charleston Harbor. A few days later a Raleigh newspaper reported that the revenue cutter *Forward* was heading south with troops to reoccupy Fort Caswell.

The people of Wilmington were especially nervous. Even if the lame-duck administration of President James Buchanan did not reoccupy Caswell and Johnston, the city's business and political leaders believed that once in office, Lincoln would turn the forts into major strongpoints and could, if he so desired, close off the seaborne commerce that was the basis of their city's existence.[13]

Wilmington secessionists telegraphed Raleigh asking Governor Ellis's permission to occupy Forts Johnston and Caswell. When the governor refused, they boarded the train to the capital and made their case in person. Ellis, however, stood his ground; despite his personal feelings, North Carolina was still part of the United States, and Federal property would be respected.[14]

Frustrated, the Wilmingtonians acted on their own. In the early hours of January 9, 1861, the recently organized Cape Fear Minute Men, under the command of Maj. John J. Hedrick, sailed downriver to Smithville, where they seized Fort Johnston from its caretaker, Ordnance Sergeant James Reilly. Although Reilly was a Southern sympathizer, he demanded and received a receipt for the military stores at the post, and duly reported the seizure to the adjutant general in Washington. Fifteen men were left at Fort Johnston, while the remainder, now joined with the local Smithville Guards, continued on to Oak Island and took possession of Fort Caswell from Ordnance Sergeant Frederick Dardingkiller, who likewise demanded and was given a receipt.[15]

Governor Ellis reacted immediately, ordering the forts restored to their caretakers. Then he sent a message to President Buchanan which, while apologetic for the incident, bluntly asked whether the president actually planned to regarrison the forts. Secretary of War Joseph Holt replied that the forts would be defended if attacked. On the other hand, he said Buchanan did not intend to regarrison them, because he did not fear for the safety of Federal installations in North Carolina. Even so, Ordnance Sergeant William Alexander at Fort Macon, which was not molested during the takeovers at Johnston and Caswell, was nervous enough to request a revolver. The federal Ordnance Department replied that none was available.[16]

Soon after Lincoln's inauguration, Governor Ellis received a telegram from a citizen in Washington stating, "It is believed that the North Carolina forts will immediately be garrisoned by Lincoln."[17] No such steps were taken, and the change of government had no particular impact on North Carolina until April 15, when Lincoln responded to the bombardment of Fort Sumter by declaring a national levy of 75,000 troops to reestablish Federal authority in the South.[18] When North Carolina was notified of its quota, most remaining Union sympathies evaporated. Throughout the state, even the Unionists resolved that they would not support an effort to uphold Federal authority by military force.[19] Ellis spoke for former Unionists as well as ardent secessionists when he advised Lincoln's secretary of war, Simon Cameron, "I can be no party to this wicked violation of the laws of the country, and to this war upon the liberties of a free people. You can get no troops from North Carolina."[20]

Convinced that reconciliation was hopeless, the governor then ordered the seizure of Forts Caswell, Johnston, and Macon. At Caswell and Johnston, Sergeants Dardingkiller and Reilly once again surrendered their keys. Volunteers from Beaufort, anticipating the governor's order by one day, had already taken Fort Macon from Sergeant Alexander. People in the streets of Wilmington began wearing badges and rosettes calling for secession, and many citizens of Northern birth quietly left.[21]

On April 27, Lincoln reacted to these events and similar demonstrations in Virginia by extending the blockade north to the Virginia Capes. So far as he was concerned, North Carolina and Virginia had now joined the insurrection, even though they had not yet seceded.[22]

Ellis, likewise, considered the breach with the Union to be a fact, and said as much in a letter to Confederate president Jefferson Davis on the day Lincoln extended the blockade.[23] Nevertheless, concerned with legalities, the governor convened a special session of the general assembly and began placing the state on a war footing. The assembly met on May 1, 1861, and ordered a convention to determine the state's future. On May

20 that convention voted to formally withdraw from the Union and to ratify the Provisional Confederate Constitution.[24]

Even before the general assembly met, Ellis had appointed Maj. William Henry Chase Whiting inspector general of the state's armed forces. A career officer who had resigned from the U.S. Army earlier in the year, Chase Whiting was born in Biloxi, Mississippi, and maintained a Southern outlook throughout his life. Yet oddly enough, he was of New England descent; both his parents were from Massachusetts, and his father, Lt. Col. Levi Whiting, was descended from Puritans who settled in Boston in 1636. True to their heritage, the parents sent the Southern-born Chase to school in Boston and later to Georgetown, where he graduated first in his class. From there he went to West Point, likewise graduating first in the class of 1845, with the highest marks ever attained up until that time; his classmates included FitzJohn Porter, E. Kirby Smith, and Gordon Granger.

Upon graduation, Chase Whiting entered the Corps of Engineers, serving in the South and in California until 1861. During 1856 and 1857 he was assigned to the Cape Fear, where he married Kate D. Walker, member of a prominent family in Wilmington and Smithville. Thereafter, he considered Wilmington home.[25]

With secession imminent and a Federal reaction expected, Whiting's duty was to assist in preparing the state for war. The most critical area was the coast with its system of sounds—great sea lochs that penetrate deep into North Carolina's interior. Protected from the Atlantic by a chain of barrier islands known as the Outer Banks, these sounds could offer sheltered anchorages, coaling stations, and depots for the Federal fleet should the United States choose to take them. Inside the barrier, navigable rivers flow into the sounds from the state's interior, and canals and the Great Dismal Swamp provide access to the waters of Virginia. As one Union officer's wife later wrote to a friend, "North Carolina seems to be all water."[26]

The state was most vulnerable along these waterways, and logic dictated immediate preparations for defense. To protect the passages through the Outer Banks, construction began on fortifications at Ocracoke and Hatteras. Farther south, the garrisons at Forts Macon and Caswell were substantially reinforced. In Wilmington, the local Committee of Safety authorized one of its members to visit South Carolina and try to secure the loan of such guns and carriages as that state might be able to spare. Anticipating North Carolina's secession, the Confederate government had, on April 30, authorized the transfer of twenty 13-pounder fieldpieces to the state for protection of the land faces of Macon and Caswell, and elsewhere along the coast.[27]

The state's efforts received a major setback with the unexpected death of Governor Ellis in late May. Although his successor, Henry T. Clark, was equally aware of North Carolina's vulnerability to seaborne attack, he lacked Ellis's political influence in Richmond, and his requests for assistance in the state's defense were ignored. The Confederate government itself was in the process of organizing, often with conflicting priorities, and amid the chaos no one appeared to realize the seriousness of Clark's position until it was too late.[28]

North Carolina got some reprieve because the Federal government was slow to react. The United States had been caught woefully unprepared for war and initially had neither the military strength nor the fleet necessary for an attack on the Southern coast. Likewise, the blockade existed mainly on paper because the U.S. Navy lacked fast, shallow-draft ships adequate for prolonged coastal duty. Nevertheless, the mere announcement of a blockade was enough to adversely affect the South. Ships no longer called at Southern ports, curtailing the imports on which the region depended. Prices rose and merchants began to operate on a cash-only basis.[29] As the Northern effort became more effective, Augustus Charles Hobart-Hampden, on leave from the Royal Navy and running the blockade under the alias of "Captain Roberts," commented on "the very great inconvenience and distress that was entailed on the South through the want of almost every description of manufacture. . . . [W]hen they were shut out by land and by sea from the outer world, their raw material was of but little service to them. This fact tended, more than is generally believed, to weaken the Southern people in the glorious struggle they made for what they called and believed to be their rights."[30] One of these distressed cities was Wilmington, where the blockade began on July 21, 1861, when the *Daylight,* a small merchant steamer converted to a warship, arrived off the Cape Fear inlets.[31]

2

THE NORTHERN THRUST

DURING THE SUMMER OF 1861, the Northern effort to blockade and penetrate the Confederacy appeared pointless. A thrust into Virginia had been thrown back by the Southern victory at First Manassas. The Confederates held a solid line of defense from just below Alexandria, Virginia, down the Potomac to the Atlantic, then south along the Atlantic to the Gulf of Mexico, west along the Gulf Coast, and up the Mississippi, Cumberland, and Tennessee Rivers. In short, the areas vital to the Southern cause were completely enveloped in a protective shield of fortified waterways.

To deal with the problem, the U.S. Department of the Navy convened a blockade board consisting of representatives of the navy, army, and Coast Survey to study the existing defenses of Southern harbors and the best means of approach. The members also examined reports of Confederate fortification efforts and thus were able to form some idea of the areas the South considered most essential. Since the Confederacy now was expending substantial labor on the approaches to Hatteras Inlet in North Carolina, the board turned its attention there.[1]

Hatteras Inlet leads into Pamlico Sound, one of the inland seas penetrating the interior. Much of the local population was, if not hostile to the

Confederacy, at least indifferent. It was obvious to the board that if the blockade was to be effective, the United States had to control eastern North Carolina.[2]

The first target was the town of Hatteras, at that time second to Wilmington as the state's leading port, and which the Confederates were rushing to fortify. Two earthen forts, designated Hatteras and Clark, were under construction near the inlet, to cover the channel with a cross fire. They augmented the "mosquito fleet," five steamers hastily purchased by the state and manned with soldiers and area residents hurriedly trained on the ships' indifferent armament and equipment. Nevertheless, these steamers worried the Federal government by dashing out into the Atlantic and capturing Northern merchant ships. Merchants, shipowners, and insurers demanded action from Washington.[3]

The Federal move against Hatteras became the first major naval expedition of the war. A squadron under Commodore Silas H. Stringham sailed from Hampton Roads on August 26, transporting about nine hundred troops under Maj. Gen. Benjamin F. Butler. At 10 A.M. on August 28 the warships opened fire, and shortly before noon troops began moving ashore in surfboats. Despite heavy seas, the action was a success; Fort Clark was in Federal hands by late that afternoon, and Fort Hatteras surrendered the following day. The United States had regained a toehold in North Carolina, while the impact on the Confederates was the loss of 670 men, a thousand stand of arms, thirty-five cannon, two forts, and what one Federal officer called "the best sea entrance to the inland waters of North Carolina; and the stoppage of a favorite channel through which many supplies had been carried for the use of the Confederate forces."[4]

The impact on both sides was felt immediately. The loss of Hatteras severely damaged the prestige of Confederate arms. Albemarle and Pamlico Sounds were effectively bottled up, and the North had a base for further operations. Coming so soon after the Union defeat at Manassas, the victory gave a much-needed boost to the North. Yet it was incomplete; had the government provided Butler and Stringham with more men and ships, they could have pushed far deeper into North Carolina. As it was, they could only leave enough forces to hold Hatteras.[5]

Although Washington failed to follow up the victory at Hatteras, elsewhere the North was not idle. In November a combined land-sea assault commanded by Rear Adm. Samuel F. Du Pont and Brig. Gen. Thomas West Sherman reduced the earthen fortifications on Hilton Head, South Carolina, allowing the Union to seize the strategic anchorage at Port Royal. From there, Du Pont moved south and took control of the northeastern coast of Florida, effectively closing Jacksonville, Ferdinandina, and St. Augustine, as well as Tybee Island, which guarded the approaches to Savannah.[6]

The Florida ports were effectively closed. Although Savannah remained open, commerce was seriously curtailed, reducing the bulk of the Confederacy's Atlantic commerce to Charleston, Wilmington, and Beaufort, North Carolina.[7] The loss of Port Royal gave the U.S. Navy a convenient depot to resupply the squadrons blockading those ports without having to steam all the way back to Hampton Roads. Taking advantage of the momentum, the new Federal general in chief, Maj. Gen. George B. McClellan, proposed a second thrust into North Carolina.

Like General Scott, whom age and ill health had forced into retirement, McClellan understood the advantage of combined army-navy operations. He believed massed confrontations of armies were pointless so long as the South was capable of reinforcement and supply. If, on the other hand, Federal troops were transported along the Southern waterways, they could choose their point of attack, slash into the interior, and disrupt supply lines, particularly the railroads on which the Confederate war effort depended. This, in turn, might force the Confederate armies to divide into smaller forces to defend sections of railroad. Thus they could be defeated piecemeal and an early conclusion brought to the war.[8]

The move against North Carolina was but one phase of McClellan's overall plan to close in on the Confederacy by permanently occupying three points: the North Carolina sounds, Savannah, and New Orleans. With footholds on the North and South Atlantic Coasts and on the Mississippi, the Union forces could then strike out in any of several directions up and down the coast and into the interior. The choice of targets was particularly sound because Wilmington, Savannah, and New Orleans were three of only six Southern ports with interstate rail connections, and Wilmington had the only interstate line leading directly to the war front in Virginia.[9]

Describing his immediate goal, McClellan wrote:

The general purposes of this expedition were to control the navigation of the sounds on the North Carolina coast, thus cutting off the supplies of Norfolk by water, and at the same time covering the left flank of the main army when operating against Richmond by the line of the James river, the reduction of New Berne [*sic*], Beaufort, and Wilmington, which would give us the double advantage of preventing blockade-running at those points and of enabling us to threaten or attack the railways near the coast, upon which Richmond largely depended for supplies.[10]

Beaufort, one of McClellan's objectives, was a colonial city on the northeast side of Topsail Inlet, facing the newly established town of Morehead City on the south side. Together they constituted the South's first deepwater port below Norfolk, and given Morehead City's rail connections to New Bern and the interior, they held major potential as a harbor for both sides.[11]

Topsail Inlet was protected by Fort Macon on Bogue Island at the entrance to the harbor. After North Carolina declared for the Confederacy, efforts began in earnest to prepare the post for war. The sand hills beyond the fort were leveled to provide a clear field of vision and fire for five hundred yards. Heavy guns, carriages, ammunition, and stores were brought in, and the work itself was considerably strengthened.[12] By September 1861, when Union blockaders began hovering off Topsail, morale was high although the enthusiasm of the garrison far exceeded its training or experience. In other words, despite all efforts, Fort Macon was woefully unprepared for a determined assault.[13]

Ninety miles southwest of Beaufort, Wilmington is situated on the east bank of the Cape Fear about twenty miles up from the East or New Inlet to the river. Dating from the middle of the eighteenth century, the city was a port of entry and a shipping point for North Carolina tobacco and naval stores. During the Revolutionary War it was occupied by the British, and the house purportedly used as headquarters by the Earl of Cornwallis, the British military commander, is preserved as a museum.

Geography favored Wilmington for a major role in the war. The city is 225 miles due south of Richmond, and the Wilmington and Weldon Railroad, a target of McClellan's proposed thrust, provided direct connections to both the Confederate capital and the war front. Only a narrow strip of ocean separated the city from British ports in Bermuda and the Bahamas. As the war progressed and blockade-running became increasingly special-

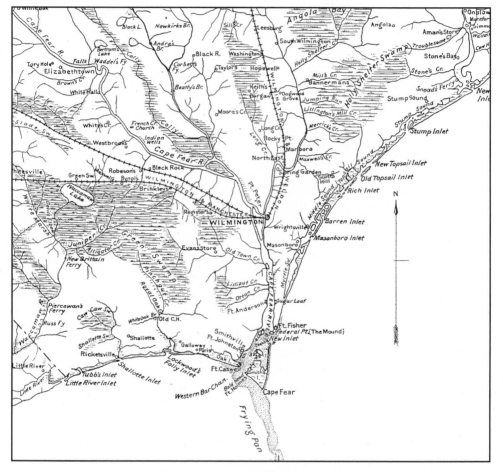

APPROACHES TO WILMINGTON

Reprinted from *Official Records of the Union and Confederate Navies in the War of the Rebellion*

ized, goods from Europe were transported to St. George's or Nassau, where they were loaded on specially designed or purchased ships for the dash to Wilmington. Reaching North Carolina waters, the blockade-runner could chose the most convenient of two inlets into the Cape Fear River. The inlets were separated by Smith's Island, at the end of which was Cape Fear itself. Extending out from the cape into the Atlantic was Frying Pan Shoals, a twenty-five-mile-long sandspit just below the surface. A shallow-draft blockade-runner could skim over the shoals and into one of the inlets, leaving the captain of a pursuing gunboat to watch in helpless frustration.

Describing the situation, the *Richmond Dispatch* commented:

> It is a matter of absolute impossibility for the Federals to stop our blockade-running at the port of Wilmington. If the wind blows off the coast, the blockade fleet is driven off. If the wind blows landward, they are compelled to haul off to a great distance to escape the terrible sea which dashes on a rocky coast without a harbor within three days' sail. The shoals on the North Carolina Coast are from five to twenty miles wide; and they are, moreover, composed of the most treacherous and bottomless quicksands. The whole coast is scarcely equaled in the world for danger and fearful appearance, particularly when a strong easterly wind meets the ebb tide.[14]

Blockade-runners tried to time their departures for Wilmington in order to reach the Cape Fear inlets at night, when there was little or no moon. If they arrived off schedule, they would stand well out to sea until dark, then slip past the anchored blockade fleet and run for the river, hugging the coast just outside the line of breakers, which would muffle the sound of their paddle wheels until they reached one of the inlets.

The war brought boom times to the city, as cotton was shipped in from throughout the Southeast, piling up in warehouses and on the docks waiting shipment to Europe. A specially designed steam-driven press on the west bank of the river compressed bales into the smallest possible size to get the maximum number into the cramped holds of the blockade-runners.

Wartime commerce combined with blockade-induced shortages to create profiteering. Those with gold snapped up whatever was available, leaving the average person with inflated paper money unable to buy even ordinary dry goods. In this cutthroat atmosphere of deprivation and lavish spending, Wilmington society became decadent. Many of the old families moved into the interior, and those that remained were reclusive, abandoning the social amenities to those whom Augustus Charles Hobart-Hampden described as "adventurers of all descriptions; some who came to sell cotton; others to buy, at enormous prices, European goods brought in by blockade-runners. These goods they took with them to the interior; and, adding a heavy percentage to the price, people who were forced to buy them paid most ruinous prices for the commonest necessaries of life."[15]

Despite Wilmington's importance, it took a long time for the Confederates to realize the need for strong defenses. The entrances to the Cape Fear were virtually unprotected except for Fort Caswell, which covered Old Inlet, the western entrance and main channel of the river, and Fort Johnston (called Fort Pender by the Confederates) at Smithville.

Fort Johnston was worthless without substantial engineering and reconstruction. Although Fort Caswell was designed for defense, like Fort Macon it had been allowed to deteriorate over the years. Initially the Southerners found only two guns mounted at Caswell, and these were useless because their carriages were rotted. In fact, the fort was indefensible. Nevertheless, the North Carolinians set to work, and by summer they had mounted twenty-two guns and constructed a supporting work, designated Fort Campbell, about half a mile down the island to cover the beach.[16]

Despite its deficiencies, Fort Caswell at least protected Old Inlet, but New Inlet was virtually defenseless at the time of secession. Soon after North Carolina left the Union, troops under Maj. Charles P. Bolles began constructing two sand batteries on the peninsula between the Cape Fear and the Atlantic at New Inlet. The larger battery was constructed for heavy-caliber columbiads set forty feet apart "with a massive traverse between them," according to Bolles. The batteries would be connected by a covered curtain wall for infantry.

When the work was finished, Bolles was sent to Oak Island to build earthworks below Fort Caswell, and his battery at New Inlet was occupied by the Wilmington Light Infantry under Capt. William DeRosset. No armament had been placed in the fort, which DeRosset named Battery Bolles, and the only guns available were two 24-pounders mounted in the larger work—a far cry from the columbiads that the battery was designed to hold. In short, New Inlet essentially remained undefended, and here Wilmington and the Cape Fear were particularly vulnerable.[17]

If the weakness of the Cape Fear defenses was lost on the Confederates, it was very evident to the Union's blockade board. Only four days after the capture of Fort Hatteras, the board began discussing the possible seizure of Wilmington and destruction of the rail system by landing troops at New Inlet. Nothing was done for the time being, although the navy continued to urge the army to at least occupy the entrance to the river as the only way to effectively close Wilmington.[18]

With McClellan's proposed thrust into North Carolina, however, it appeared the North might now be ready to remedy the situation. Maj. Gen. Ambrose Burnside was given command of the Federal troops and would operate in conjunction with the North Atlantic Blockading Squadron under Flag Officer Louis M. Goldsborough. McClellan ordered Burnside to capture Roanoke Island and New Bern, then move against Beaufort and Fort Macon. From there, he was to seize the railroad as far west as Goldsboro, North Carolina, where "a great point would be gained . . . by the effectual destruction of the Wilmington and Weldon Railroad." After achieving those goals, McClellan said, "the next point of interest would probably be Wilmington, the reduction of which may require that additional means shall be afforded you."[19]

Burnside's force of some fifteen thousand men began sailing out of Hampton Roads just before midnight on January 11, 1862. Bad weather and the necessity to deepen the channel at Hatteras Inlet delayed the arrival off Roanoke until February 5, but eventually everything was in place. Two days later the ships began bombarding the Confederate defenses, and most troops were landed by midnight. The Confederate works were stormed on February 8. By the end of the day Roanoke Island was secured, the garrisons surrendered, and most Confederate gunboats scuttled by their crews to prevent capture.[20]

Two days later, the navy cornered and destroyed the irritating "mosquito fleet" at Elizabeth City, and by February 12 the Federal fleet was patrolling the entrance to the harbor at Edenton on Albemarle Sound. In only four days, the combined army-navy expedition had taken control of northeastern North Carolina. Now, however, it faced a hostile population. Whereas earlier many local citizens had remained loyal to the Union or at least neutral, looting and wanton destruction by Federal troops galvanized opposition to the North.[21]

After resting his men, Burnside moved against New Bern, an important port and rail center on the Neuse River. Goldsborough, having been recalled to Hampton Roads to deal with the threat from the ironclad ram *Virginia* (ex-*Merrimack*), left the naval arm under the command of Comdr. Stephen Rowan. Transports with eleven thousand soldiers, accompanied by fourteen gunboats, steamed up the Neuse toward New Bern on March 12. The gunfire from the fleet kept the Confederate forces pinned down, allowing Burnside's troops to move in close to the defenses, and the city fell on the fourteenth. Dozens of Southern vessels and thousands of barrels of rosin, pitch, and turpentine were destroyed.[22]

The Confederates, anticipating McClellan's intention to disrupt the Wilmington and Weldon Railroad at Goldsboro, rushed troops from Virginia and reorganized the command structure in the Department of North Carolina. Yet as the Confederates strengthened the defenses around Goldsboro, Burnside turned toward Beaufort and Fort Macon. His reasoning was sound. With Fort Macon knocked out, the South would lose the excellent harbor at Beaufort, while the North would gain yet another convenient depot for the blockade. Before moving, the Federals destroyed the track between New Bern and Goldsboro, and that, along with a new line of fortifications, strengthened their position at New Bern. But the move against Beaufort meant the all-important Wilmington and Weldon Railroad remained intact at Goldsboro, and Goldsboro remained in the hands of an enemy whose ability to defend it was daily growing.[23]

The seizure of Hatteras, aggravated by sporadic Federal probes into the area, unnerved the citizens of Beaufort, and false alarms, combined with monotonous diet and bad water, undermined morale at Fort Macon.[24] When Burnside moved into North Carolina, the Confederate command correctly guessed he would attack New Bern before Beaufort, because New Bern would give him a central location from which he could strike in any of several directions. Consequently, ordnance bound for Fort Macon was rerouted to New Bern, and troops were pulled away from the Beaufort defenses and sent to New Bern. When that city fell, Fort Macon was weakened to the point where it could no longer withstand a prolonged siege—if indeed it ever could have.[25]

Morale at Fort Macon dropped even more with news of the fall of Fort Donelson, Tennessee, soon after the loss of Roanoke Island. The blockade of Beaufort further tightened on March 19, when steam cruisers arrived to augment the sailing vessels and auxiliary craft already on station. The guns

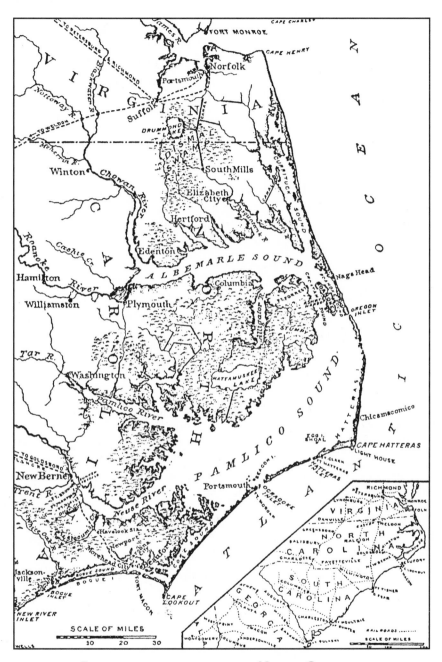

EARLY COASTAL OPERATIONS IN NORTH CAROLINA

Reprinted from Johnson and Buel, *Battles and Leaders of the Civil War*

at Fort Macon began firing to warn off the Federal ships, reducing the fort's supply of powder and shot. The same day, a battalion of Rhode Island infantry marched down the Atlantic and North Carolina Railroad from New Bern, while two Union regiments embarked on transports. Morehead City was occupied on March 22, and Beaufort fell four days later. Although Fort Macon still prevented the Union from using the harbor, the post was now isolated.[26]

The siege of Fort Macon functioned like a textbook operation. Union forces landed on Bogue Island on March 29 and erected siege works behind the sand hills beyond the area leveled by the Confederates, isolating the fort from the mainland, while the Federal fleet cut off any access from the sea. Fighting broke out between Union forces and Confederate pickets on April 8. In the days that followed, the U.S. troops, protected by covering fire from the navy, were able to move within a mile of the fort and set up batteries behind sand hills. Naval gunfire kept the fort's gunners off the ramparts, and by April 23 the Confederates had absolutely no communications with the outside world. A general bombardment began on the morning of the twenty-fifth, breaching the walls and disabling seventeen guns. The next morning, Fort Macon surrendered.[27]

The fall of Beaufort reduced the South's major Atlantic ports to Wilmington and Charleston. Admiral Du Pont, whose jurisdiction as commander of the South Atlantic Blockading Squadron included Charleston, believed he had access to that city reasonably under control. But he advised the Navy Department "to look out for *Wilmington,* for they will go from Charleston there."[28]

The Federal government, however, had other priorities. With the destruction of the ironclad *Virginia,* the Union navy controlled the James River as far as Drewry's Bluff, and McClellan launched his Peninsula campaign to take Richmond. Convinced the city's fall was imminent, Assistant Secretary of the Navy Gustavus Vasa Fox instructed Goldsborough to hold off on Wilmington until the Confederate capital was taken. Then he could move against the Cape Fear defenses.[29]

General Burnside, meanwhile, hoped to use the Atlantic and North Carolina Railroad to transport troops and supplies into the interior to take Goldsboro and further isolate Wilmington.[30] Admiral Goldsborough, however, did not intend to share glory with the army. Preparing to move against Wilmington on his own, he ordered Comdr. Oliver S. Glisson in *Mount Vernon* to take the small work under construction at New Inlet and, if successful, test the defensive capabilities of Fort Caswell. If Caswell proved too strong for *Mount Vernon* alone, Goldsborough felt the ironclads *Monitor* and *Galena* could batter the fort into submission. To give himself an even greater edge, he had the *Susquehanna* armed with two 100-pounder Parrott guns.[31]

Although Fox believed Goldsborough could take Fort Caswell with naval forces alone whenever he felt inclined to do so, the admiral never got the chance to prove it, for the ironclads were unavailable and the *Susquehanna* with its heavy guns was pulled away to cover the army on the Peninsula.[32] It was a moot point in any case, because if the navy bogged down before the Cape Fear defenses, Burnside was hardly in a position to assist. At New Bern and again at Morehead City, Burnside found that the Confederates had removed most locomotives and rolling stock, leaving him with a critical shortage that was not remedied until June, when new equipment arrived. Before he could finalize preparations for a new advance, however, he and the bulk of his forces were summoned to Virginia, where McClellan's Peninsula campaign had been fought to a complete standstill. Richmond did not fall, Wilmington and Goldsboro remained in Confederate hands, and the Wilmington and Weldon Railroad was intact.[33]

Fox, however, remained optimistic. Richmond aside, he was convinced that complete Federal control of the Mississippi River was imminent (in actuality it took another year), after that Mobile would fall (which took another two years), and then, Fox said, "Goldsborough will certainly take Caswell, which leaves Charleston for the closing act, so far as the Navy is concerned."[34]

Goldsborough did not take Caswell, and Burnside did not take Wilmington. They can be forgiven, for Goldsborough no longer had the resources, and as Burnside stood poised and ready to move, the fortunes of war intervened against him. This does not, however, excuse the United States from failure to take advantage of the gains up to that point. The defenses of the Cape Fear were notoriously weak, particularly at New Inlet. The perfectly coordinated actions between army and navy had allowed the Union to capture and occupy much of the North Carolina coast, as well as the entire northeastern part of the state, with relative ease and minimal losses. The Wilmington and Weldon was within a cavalry dash of the Union-held areas, and indeed over the next eighteen months three raids were made on the line, two of which resulted in the destruction of rolling stock and several miles of track. Each time the line was repaired and service restored, although the raids strained resources and eroded the railroad's efficiency.[35]

Yet the United States did not follow up on these raids and completely knock out the railroad. Nor did Federal troops board ships at Beaufort for the ninety-mile dash down the coast to the Cape Fear while New Inlet was still weak and Fort Caswell could have been invested and taken in the same manner as Fort Macon. Had they tried they doubtless would have succeeded, because the area had become practically the Union backyard. This was emphasized by no less than Gen. Ben Butler, who was arguing for a reduction in the Union garrisons in North Carolina. "Holding Hatteras and Fort Macon," he noted, "we hold the whole North Carolina coast save Wilmington, which somehow we cannot blockade."[36] One must ask why Wilmington was spared.

Part of it was shortsightedness in the army command. After the Peninsula campaign, McClellan was replaced as general in chief by Maj. Gen. Henry Wager Halleck, a traditionalist who expected great armies to slam against each other in battles of Napoleonic proportions. In his mind, combined operations with the navy wasted manpower and equipment and drew troops away from what he considered their primary duty—to mass together as a barrier between the Confederates and Washington.[37] Any notion of a move against Wilmington was scrapped, prompting the disillusioned McClellan to remark, "Had I remained in chief command I should have proceeded to its capture as soon as practicable after the fall of Fort Macon."[38]

Even if Halleck had been interested in Wilmington, political considerations gave priority to Charleston. To the Northern public, Wilmington was merely a spot on a map; South Carolina was the birthplace of secession, and Charleston was where the war began. Even as Fox discussed the capture of Wilmington, he wrote Du Pont, "We should be inclined to skip Fort Caswell if you consider it imperative, for the fall of Charleston is the fall of Satan's Kingdom."[39]

Allowing for political considerations and tunnel vision in the army, there is a third possible reason for the failure to attack Wilmington—that certain elements in the North actually wanted the port to continue functioning unmolested. It has long been established that Northern business interests were heavily involved in illegal trade with the South.[40] Hobart-Hampden, who was in a position to know and had no particular grievance with either side, remarked that some blockade-runners were actually fitted out in New York. Northern domination of trade with the Confederacy through neutral countries was also noted by Raphael Semmes, captain of the famed Confederate warship *Alabama,* who saw it firsthand in Cuba, Mexico, and Texas.[41]

There was a constant flow of U.S. goods through Nassau, and the American consul there had no doubts that it was all bound for the South. Some cargo was shipped in foreign hulls directly from New York and Boston to the Bahamas, while vessels under the U.S. flag would put in briefly at Canadian ports for the sake of appearance, then sail south to Bermuda or Nassau. Thomas Dudley, the ever vigilant U.S. consul in Liverpool, complained that beef from Cleveland and pork from Cincinnati were landed in Great Britain for transshipment to Bermuda. Blockade-runners captured by Federal warships carried cargoes that left little doubt Philadelphia was also involved.[42]

Nassau cargo might go to Wilmington, Charleston, or, early in the war, to northeast Florida or Savannah. But the obvious destination for Bermuda cargo was Wilmington, which, at 674 miles, was the closest available Confederate port. By 1863, Acting Rear Adm. Samuel Phillips Lee, who replaced Goldsborough as commander of the North Atlantic Blockading Squadron, reported that the Confederate government had established "a regular agency at Bermuda and uses the port of Wilmington as the principal depot of supplies. It is a matter of notoriety that regular trips are made between the two ports."[43] In the city itself, a resident recalled, "It seemed singular to us that the United States should so long neglect to close the only port [in] almost all of the Confederacy into which every 'dark of the moon' there ran a half dozen or so swift blockade-runners, freighted with cannon, muskets, and every munition of war—medicines, cloth, shoes, bacon, etc."[44]

Such a situation could exist only with sanction from high levels in the U.S. political and military structure. While the Federal government did permit a certain amount of clandestine commerce in Southern cotton to keep the Northern mills supplied, and also to allow enough to reach Great Britain to reduce the possibility of British intervention on behalf of the

South, the trade went far beyond the official blind eye. From September 1861 to April 1865, the South exported 780,000 bales of cotton to the North by smuggling alone, of which 172,000 bales were sent by sea. Between 1862 and 1865, about 60 percent of the cotton consumed by the North was grown in the South, and Confederate cotton exports to the United States were double the fabled cotton exports to Great Britain.[45] Among the names connected with the trade was Ben Butler, who was accused in an unsubstantiated letter of getting a rake-off directly from the Wilmington traffic.[46]

In view of these circumstances, one cannot ignore the possibility that Wilmington remained open to blockade-runners in part because certain Northern economic interests would have been damaged if it were closed. And those interests had enough political power to keep the port open until sheer military necessity—and the diminished importance of the Wilmington and Weldon Railroad—dictated otherwise.[47]

3

{ FORT FISHER }

SINCE BEFORE RECORDED HISTORY, Old Inlet was the only mouth to the Cape Fear River. From this entrance the river turned due north, forming a peninsula between itself and the Atlantic. This peninsula was (and is) known as Federal Point, although during the war it was called Confederate Point. Cape Fear itself is a headland once located at the extreme end of the point. In 1761, however, a hurricane cut a channel—the New Inlet—through the lower portion of the point and formed Smith's Island, with the cape at its southeast end. A century later, the deeper Old Inlet remained the main channel, but its approaches were guarded by treacherous shoals that frequently shifted as the river current swirled about Cape Fear and met the Atlantic. As one Confederate soldier in Fort Caswell noted, "Our greatest protection is in the 'Bar': a vessel drawing more than fourteen feet cannot cross."[1] New Inlet, with a more stable bar, could be negotiated by light- and medium-draft vessels, and so became vastly more important during the war.

A signal station was necessary so the pilots would know where to round Confederate Point, and whether it was safe to approach. It was also imperative to fortify the point with heavy artillery, not only to protect Wilm-

MAJ. GEN. W. H. C. WHITING
Courtesy of the North Carolina Division of Archives and History

ington but to keep Federal gunboats at a safe distance; blockade-runners often were spotted during their nocturnal attempts to slip into the river, and long-range gunfire from shore might determine whether a ship reached the inlet or was beached or captured.

The loss of Beaufort emphasized the vulnerability of the Cape Fear, and on November 8, 1862, William Henry Chase Whiting, the former state inspector general and now a Confederate brigadier general, was sent to command the District of Wilmington. Two days later, Col. T. S. Rhett, the army's inspector of ordnance, assured North Carolina's new governor, Zebulon Vance, that "Wilmington will not be forgotten." President Davis added his own reassurances to the governor, stating, "The vigilance of deepest interest watches affairs in North Carolina. We will try to anticipate the enemy."[2]

Much had happened in the almost two years since Chase Whiting resigned from the U.S. Army. After North Carolina seceded, he entered Confederate service and performed with distinction at First Manassas, where he received a field promotion to brigadier general on President Davis's orders. He was also at Seven Pines, the Shenandoah, Gaines Mill, and Malvern Hill before returning to the Cape Fear.

Despite his success, Whiting came to Wilmington under a cloud. Touchy and opinionated, he had refused command of a brigade from his native Mississippi. His bluntly worded rejection offended the president, himself a Mississippian who had commanded that state's troops during the Mexican War. Davis went to great lengths to humiliate him, even attempting to reduce him in rank. The intervention of Gen. Joseph E. Johnston managed to save Whiting's position, but Davis remembered the incident.[3]

Assuming his new command, Whiting began assessing his position based on service in the major Southern ports during his tenure with the U.S. Army Corps of Engineers. He was particularly apprehensive because of a recent Northern drive against Tarboro and Weldon, and made contingency plans for removing large stores of salt from Wilmington. Although the Union troops ultimately fell back without attaining their goal, spies in New Bern sent word that an expedition against Wilmington was contemplated by running down the sounds from Beaufort.[4]

In a letter to Secretary of War George W. Randolph, Whiting said the three most important ports remaining in the Confederacy were Charleston, Mobile, and Wilmington. While the loss of Charleston would be a serious blow to Confederate prestige both at home and abroad, the city was not as important strategically as Wilmington or Mobile. The latter cities had the most access to the interior for transportation and communication. If lost, they would give the North the easiest passage into the South, driving a wedge between the Confederate armies in the East and West and further splitting the country. The fall of Wilmington and Mobile would also cancel any strategic value Charleston might have, Whiting contended, because the city would be effectively isolated from the rest of the Confederacy.

Unfortunately, he continued, Wilmington and Mobile were more vulnerable than Charleston, and Wilmington presented special problems.[5] The situation within the city was chaotic because of a devastating outbreak of yellow fever brought in from the West Indies by one of the blockade-runners. He advised his superiors, "I anticipate trouble from the enemy, who, aware of the undefended condition of this important place, are likely to strike before we can collect our resources."[6]

More serious than the epidemic, however, was the geography of the Cape Fear. Whiting told Secretary Randolph that the very same features that made it so helpful to blockade-runners—two entrances to the river separated by Smith's Island—prevented troops stationed at the inlets from assisting each other if either was attacked. Likewise, if the works were attacked separately, the supporting forces would be divided. "The fall of one, though so far apart, will necessarily result in that of the other," Whiting wrote, "and thus, without mutually assisting in the defense of either, the safety of either of these important positions depends on the other."

Another problem was that the Cape Fear ran almost parallel to the Atlantic as far as Wilmington. So while the city was twenty-one miles upriver from Fort Fisher (as the expanded Battery Bolles at New Inlet was now called) and twenty-eight miles from Fort Caswell, it was only six miles in a direct line from the ocean. In view of events so far, Whiting believed a Union thrust down the sounds from Beaufort was still probable. If Wilmington was taken, the Cape Fear forts would be isolated and "must fall without resistance."

After laying out various ways such a Union attack could be thwarted, Whiting concluded by stating he needed at least ten thousand men to do it: "If this cannot be had we must trust to God in what we have, small as it is, and the blindness of the enemy. Why [the Union] neglected this place and struck at New Berne [sic] is more than I can tell."[7]

Secretary Randolph referred Whiting's letter to Maj. Gen. G. W. Smith, whose responsibility included the Department of North Carolina. Smith had no troops to spare, but he sent an extract of the letter to General Lee in Virginia, although he doubted Lee could provide them either. Remarking on Whiting's dilemma, a War Department clerk in Richmond noted in his diary, "There is no repose for us!"[8]

Battery Bolles had been renamed Fort Fisher in memory of Col. Charles Fisher of the 6th North Carolina Regiment, who was killed at First Manassas in 1861. From Major Bolles's two small, inconsequential batteries, the fort had gradually expanded according to no particular plan until, in July 1862, it was about a hundred yards long. Under various commanders, the armament had grown to seventeen guns, but only two 8-inch columbiads were actually effective for coastal defense.[9]

The turning point came on July 4, when Col. William Lamb assumed command. He was not happy with what he found, noting, "It was composed of several detached earth-works, with a casemated battery of sand and palmetto logs, mounting four guns with only one heavy gun in the works. The frigate *Minnesota* could have destroyed the works and driven us out within a few hours."[10] Although two ironclads, *North Carolina* and *Raleigh,* were then under construction in Wilmington to assist with the defenses, they were far from ready.

Faced with a fort that was virtually worthless for its intended purpose, Lamb set to work. Ironically, the man who would construct the South's greatest fortification was not an engineer by training. Only twenty-seven at the time he assumed command, William Lamb was born in Norfolk, Virginia, to a prominent local family. After attending schools in Virginia and Connecticut, he entered the College of William and Mary, where he graduated first in the class of 1855 with a law degree. Only twenty at the time, he was not old enough to legally practice law in Virginia, so he acquired part ownership of the *Southern Argus* newspaper in Norfolk and became its editor. Two years later, he married Sarah Ann Chaffee of Providence, Rhode Island. Despite her Northern birth, "Daisy," as her husband called her, became as ardent a Confederate as any soldier who served at Fort Fisher.

Lamb's military career began when he was appointed captain of a local rifle company, and he attended the hanging of John Brown following Brown's ill-fated attack on Harpers Ferry in 1859. After the war began in earnest, he became a major and was named quartermaster of the Wilmington District, on the staff of the then-commander, Brig. Gen. Joseph R. Anderson. He subsequently was given command of Fort St. Philip, overlooking the river by Orton Pond midway between Old Inlet and Wilmington, and covering the site of the abandoned colonial settlement of Brunswick Town. While serving at Fort St. Philip, Lamb was elected colonel of the 36th North Carolina Regiment, a position he would hold simultaneously with his post commands until the end of the war.[11]

As he later would do at Fort Fisher, Lamb turned a miscellaneous set of earthworks at Fort St. Philip into a formidable bastion better known by its permanent name, Fort Anderson.[12] Although Anderson was smaller than Fisher would ultimately become, Lamb's hand is evident, for both forts followed the same "L"-shaped plan, with heavy earthen traverses separating the gun chambers so that, in the event of attack, each gun chamber could become a self-contained fort. Today, the well-preserved works

COL. WILLIAM LAMB
Reprinted from Johnson and Buel, *Battles and Leaders of the Civil War*

of Fort Anderson are a far better indication of Lamb's natural ability as an engineer than the scattered, heavily eroded, and much-restored remains of Fort Fisher.

Lamb received his appointment as commander of Fort Fisher about noon on July 4 and immediately reported to New Inlet. By sunset he had completely inspected the defenses. Discouraging as it was, he saw its potential. "I determined at once to build a work of such magnitude that it could withstand the heaviest fire of any guns in the American Navy. I had seen the effect of eleven inch shell, and had read about the force of the fifteen inch shell, and believed that their penetrating power was well ascertained and could be provided against."[13]

By now, military engineers had realized the value of earthen fortifications over masonry. During the siege of Fort Brown, Texas, sixteen years earlier in the Mexican War, Mexican cannonballs had buried themselves harmlessly in the earthworks, and the fort held out for six days with only two deaths until it was relieved.[14] It is probable that Lamb, like most men of his generation, was aware of the bombardment of Fort Brown, because much had been made of its heroic defense at the time. But his own writings indicate that he was profoundly impressed by the Malakoff Tower, a gigantic earthwork guarding Sevastopol on the Black Sea that held off combined land-sea assaults by Great Britain and France for almost a year during the Crimean War.[15] Lamb had remarked on the fall of the Malakoff in 1855, and in December 1861 he purchased a book on the Crimean War that contained detailed plans and specifications of the Sevastopol defenses. The earthworks at the Malakoff, then, would be the model for Lamb's reconstruction of Fort Fisher.[16]

The fort, as Lamb envisioned it, would be "built solely with the view of resisting the fire of a fleet."[17] That purpose was brought forcibly to his attention the morning after he took command, when he saw a Union blockader anchored off the bar less than two miles from the fort and well within gun range.

"I asked if she was not unusually close in, and was answered no," Lamb wrote. He then observed that the ship could fire into the fort without warning, and was told that Federal warships occasionally did open fire on construction details and drive them away from their work. Lamb announced that would not happen again, and ordered his guns to open fire on the blockader. "The astonished enemy slipped his cable and retreated as fast as possible, and from that day to the final attack no blockader anchored within range of our guns and no working party was ever molested, not even when hundreds were congregated together in constructing the mounds."[18]

To expedite construction, Lamb drafted five hundred black laborers to supplement the garrison troops already at work. The palmetto logs were replaced by heavy timbers, then covered with fifteen to twenty feet of sand. The sand was sodded over and planted with sea grass.[19]

Fortune favored Lamb. Shortly before he took command, the blockade-runner *Modern Greece* grounded off the Cape Fear while being chased by a Federal warship. Much of the cargo was later salvaged, including a battery of 12-pounder Whitworth rifled cannon. These guns fired a 3-inch hexagonal projectile with a slight twist conforming to the rifling grooves in the barrel; this gave them remarkable range and accuracy. Lamb, who according to one Confederate officer was "anxious to try them," had the guns set up and "calculated the distance to one of the blockaders and giving the gun a proper elevation fired and struck her in the side, the distance being 4 miles. [A]s a matter of course, [the Federals] finding their guns could not reach, they retired still further to seek protection from 'King Neptune.'"[20]

Accuracy aside, the Whitworth projectile was not large enough to cause anything beyond superficial damage. The officers of the blockading fleet were far more concerned with the accelerated pace of the Cape Fear defenses. The works were becoming more than a simple nuisance; they were formidable and effective. On October 11 the Federal gunboat *Maratanza* ventured too close to Oak Island, and a shore battery near Fort Caswell opened fire. A shell struck the *Maratanza* on the port quarter, killing two men and wounding five.[21]

On November 17 the *Daylight* chased a British brig running the blockade, and although the brig grounded near Fort Fisher, the fort's guns held off the *Daylight* so that she could not destroy the blockade-runner. The same day, a landing party consisting of a lieutenant, two midshipmen, and ten seamen from the USS *Cambridge* managed to destroy a grounded blockade-runner near Masonboro Inlet twelve miles northeast of Fort Fisher, but was captured by Confederate pickets.[22]

This was an early example of what the Federal blockaders would have to face over the next two and a half years with Lamb in command at Fort Fisher. The blockade-runners trusted him implicitly, knowing that he would be watching with guns ready during the times they were most likely to come in. "Many a smart vessel did his skill and activity snatch from the very jaws of the blockaders," British blockade-runner Thomas E. Taylor later wrote. "He came to be regarded by the runners as their guardian angel; and it was no small support in the last trying moments of a run to remember who was in Fort Fisher."[23]

The grateful captains generally remembered to bring luxury items for Lamb and his family. Daisy Lamb once wrote her mother in Rhode Island that in only two days the family had received white sugar, rum, pickles, cheese, sardines, limes, pineapples, toilet soap, beef tongues, claret, and various bottles of fortified wines. While these may have been common enough in the North, they were virtually unheard of in the Confederacy and, when available, brought exorbitant prices. "I think we are in the most comfortable place we could possibly find during the war," Daisy remarked, "there are so many blockade runners come in here every week."[24]

One thing she could not get, either locally or through the blockade, was decent furniture for her quarters, a small, garrison-built house known as "The Cottage," located on the Wilmington Road, outside of the defensive perimeter of the fort. Discussing the furniture problem, she told her mother, "[I] am going to have some made at the fort, of course of pine— and very rough—but I presume the place will look real neat and comfortable, when it is all done."[25]

While Daisy worried about housekeeping and her husband pondered the Union blockaders, work was progressing on the fort itself. Describing the project, Lamb wrote:

> Between the gun-chambers, containing one to two guns each (there were twenty heavy guns on the land-face), there were heavy traverses, exceeding in size any known to engineers, to protect from an enfilading fire. They extended out some twelve feet from the parapet, and were twelve feet or more in height above the parapet, running back thirty feet or more. The gun-chambers were reached from the rear by steps. In each traverse was an alternate magazine or bomb-proof [shelter], the latter ventilated by an air-chamber. Passageways penetrated the traverses from the interior of the work, forming additional bomb-proofs for the relief of the guns.[26]

Lamb was not alone in his efforts. After General Whiting took command of the District of Wilmington, construction crews erected defensive works all along the river and around the city itself, turning the lower Cape Fear into one gigantic fortress. Whiting and Lamb worked particularly well together, and the general no doubt advised the young colonel on the design of Fort Fisher, adding his training and long experience as an engineer to Lamb's natural talent.[27]

Nor was Old Inlet neglected. The Confederate Engineer Bureau ruled out as impractical the notion of strengthening Fort Caswell by constructing additional casemates, recommending instead that the walls be built up with earthen parapets and traverses and sodded over. The garrison set to work. Triangular pens of heavy timber were constructed around the guns, with more timber across the top so that the gun was completely enclosed except for a port. The entire chamber was then covered with railroad iron and reinforced with sandbags. Soon the old brick walls were hidden behind fifteen feet of sand, and from the sea at least, Caswell took on much

FORT FISHER LAND FACE, SHOWING THE HIGH TRAVERSES WITH GUN
CHAMBERS IN BETWEEN AND THE STOCKADE
Courtesy of the North Carolina Division of Archives and History

the same appearance as Fort Fisher. Not quite a mile down the beach, Fort Campbell had sixteen guns and two mortars. A small work, Battery Shaw, with a single 10-inch columbiad, was located between Caswell and Campbell. Fort Holmes was established on Smith's Island, facing Caswell across Old Inlet.[28]

There was a sense of urgency to the work, for the threat of attack always seemed near. These fears were not entirely groundless, because whatever the influence of blockade-running economics in the Federal War Department, the navy wanted something done. At Admiral Lee's behest, Lt. Comdr. Daniel Braine undertook the dangerous job of conducting two surveys of the Western Bar by Fort Caswell, and found ten feet of water at low tide. Lee also offered rewards for captured Cape Fear pilots imprisoned at Fort Lafayette, New York, who would volunteer to take the monitors to North Carolina, and eventually secured the services of three.[29]

These efforts appeared likely to pay off in December 1862, following Burnside's defeat at Fredericksburg. Lincoln needed a victory somewhere, and Secretary of the Navy Gideon Welles wanted that victory to be the capture of Wilmington. The army, eager to redeem itself after Fredericksburg, was willing. In a joint operation reminiscent of that which had already taken so much of eastern North Carolina, the Union commander in the state, Maj. Gen. John Foster, was prepared to cut the railroad near

Goldsboro and block Confederate reinforcements from Virginia, then move to Tarboro and destroy any Confederate gunboats that might be under construction, and from Tarboro attack Wilmington in a coordinated effort with the navy.[30]

On the navy's part, the depth at the entrance to the Cape Fear precluded a run past the forts using large warships with heavy broadsides, as had been done at New Orleans and Port Royal. But delivery of a second generation of monitors was imminent, and U.S. naval authorities hoped to use these, together with the original *Monitor* and the ironclad *Passaic,* to force a passage. This, they believed, would be a good trial run for the monitors.[31]

Admiral Lee felt the sheer nature of the monitors—a new type of weapon, low, shadowy, and seemingly shellproof—would have a psychological effect on the Cape Fear's defenders. Even before Fredericksburg, he had given the matter some thought. In a confidential letter to Fox on December 11, he wrote: "A powerful force awes, & makes the result certain—it provides for accidents, grounding, torpedoes &c. If two or three more [monitors] can be sent it is all the better for the work in hand & for that ahead further South. . . . The more of these . . . the better for all interests. *It is they alone who will have to deal with Fort C[aswell],* with its doubtless heavy ordnance, obstructions, etc."[32]

Fox liked the plan, but preferred New Inlet. He believed that while the monitors might get past Fort Caswell, there were not enough of them to actually reduce it. Instead, he felt a bombardment of Fort Fisher while it was still abuilding would drive out the defenders, allowing a landing party to get ashore, seize the batteries, and spike the guns. Then Wilmington could be held until the army arrived. Barring this, he said the monitors would have to run past the forts, destroy the ships and port facilities of Wilmington, then put back out to sea, a prospect he felt entailed considerable risk with no long-term effect.[33]

It was typical of Fox to consider all the pros and cons of an operation and come up with the most logical answer. A native of Saugus, Massachusetts, Fox was a former naval officer, steamship officer, and businessman with a reputation as a superb organizer. He was also well connected; his wife's brother-in-law was Montgomery Blair, Lincoln's postmaster general. Even before Lincoln took office, the powerful Blair had advanced Fox as a consultant to the War Department, and on arriving in Washington he sub-

U.S. ASSISTANT SECRETARY OF THE NAVY GUSTAVUS VASA FOX
Reprinted from *Diary of Gideon Welles*

mitted a plan to relieve the garrison at Fort Sumter. Ultimately approved after Lincoln's inauguration, the plan failed because of cabinet-level jealousies and bureaucratic incompetence, and Fox arrived in Charleston just in time to witness the bombardment of Sumter.

Fox joined the Navy Department as a clerk in May 1861, and proved so useful that three months later Congress created the office of assistant secretary for him. He was largely responsible for the naval actions that led to the seizure of Port Royal and New Orleans, and was an early proponent of John Ericsson's revolutionary *Monitor*.

At the end of 1862, Fox was forty-one years old, powerful, egotistical, and vindictive. Welles found him irritating, but realized he was indispensable; he handled the multitude of details, allowing Welles to tackle the all-absorbing job of running the department.[34]

For all his talent and his careful consideration of this project, Fox had one blind spot—the depth of the water. Admiral Lee never indicated that the monitors could run past the defenses of either inlet. Instead, he apparently intended to use their heavy guns to reduce the forts by offshore bombardment because the shoals made the inlets too shallow for the ironclads to pass. To his disgust, however, Fox refused to accept his advice or the soundings shown on the charts of the Cape Fear.

"There is plenty of water," Fox insisted, and justified his position by repeating an ongoing but never substantiated rumor that the deep-draft Confederate raider *Nashville* had managed to enter the Cape Fear and steam to Wilmington.[35] Assuming the *Nashville* had entered Wilmington, Fox and his planners believed she had a light draft of eleven feet. The *Monitor* drew ten and a half feet; the monitor *Montauk,* eleven and a half; and the monitor *Passaic* could be reduced to eleven when coaled for only seven days' steaming. Capt. John Bankhead of the *Monitor* argued, however, that even if the bar did allow eleven feet, as everyone believed, it was completely exposed to the wind and sea, and swells averaging two feet on a clear day could slam the ironclads down on the bar.

With New Inlet ruled out for the time being, attention turned once again to Old Inlet. Here, however, there were many variables to be considered— possible obstructions, torpedoes in the river, and whether the monitors could actually reduce Fort Caswell before running out of ammunition.[36]

While the navy fretted, General Foster had already begun a preliminary probe to hold up his end of the expedition. Opening his drive on December 11, he moved as far as the Neuse River, where he burned the Wilmington and Weldon bridge and destroyed several miles of track. Satisfied that he had blocked Confederate reinforcements from that direction, and that the attack on Wilmington was feasible, he withdrew to New Bern and asked for 12,000 additional troops. He hoped to have 20,000 men by January 5 so that he could begin his expedition in earnest.

On December 15, Admiral Lee received formal orders for an operation against the Cape Fear. He would have the ironclads *Monitor, Passaic,* and *Montauk* and two gunboats for an attack through New Inlet. The only problem was the bar, because soundings conducted at different times showed the depth to be variable, and the continuous swell threatened even the light-draft *Monitor.*[37] Then, to make matters worse, the *Monitor* herself, under tow from Hampton Roads to the Cape Fear, sank in a storm on New Year's Eve. Her loss not only weakened Lee's strength by one ironclad, it also showed the inherent weakness of the monitors as a type—they simply were not seagoing ships, and if anything went wrong in winter weather off Cape Fear, they could be in serious trouble.

The Confederates were not idle during this period, and General Whiting was shrewd enough to anticipate the enemy. In the closing weeks of 1862 and throughout all of 1863, there were alarms as the North massed troops and transports in Hampton Roads and Beaufort for various operations. Invariably, it seemed that Wilmington was the logical target. The North Carolina Militia was mobilized, and on January 11, 1863, James A. Seddon, latest in the long line of Confederate secretaries of war, advised Governor Vance, "We send every man to North Carolina who can be spared from points not vital."[38]

The following day, headquarters in Wilmington sent a message to Colonel Lamb at Fisher and Lt. Col. Washington Gwathmey at Caswell: "From information received here it is probable the enemy will move to attack this place, both by land and sea. . . . Have everything ready to receive them."[39] The information was correct, for Admiral Lee was not willing to let the matter drop without some sort of demonstration.

The preliminaries began on January 13, when five U.S. steam gunboats bombarded Fort Caswell. Believing the assault imminent, Whiting ordered Colonel Gwathmey to "hold your position to the last extremity." If it became evident that the fort would fall, Gwathmey was to blow it up and destroy as much as possible, after which he could retreat without blame. Assuming there would also be an assault on Fort Fisher, Whiting told Lamb, "Fight as well as you have labored and I have no fears for the result."

Whiting presumed that once the steamers had softened the defenses, monitors would force their way into the inlets and pound the forts with reasonable impunity. Yet he, like his Union counterparts, had overestimated this second generation of monitors. By now, Fox was aware that the heavy ironclads drew too much water to run into the river, and that shoal waters might in fact force them to keep several miles out to sea. Days earlier, he had decided not to try them against Wilmington, but instead to send them on to Du Pont at Charleston. Without the monitors, the bombardment of Fort Caswell soon tapered off, and it later became apparent that the Union army was again probing toward Goldsboro rather than Wilmington.[40]

Assessing the situation from his vantage point at Port Royal, and removed from the immediate clamor, Admiral Du Pont wrote his wife: "The operation against Wilmington . . . was one of those chaotic conceptions, produced by the desire of the President and others 'to strike a blow' somewhere. Very well! I understand that—but one would suppose that somebody would sit down and study out how the blow was to be given."[41]

4

THE CHARLESTON EFFECT

ALTHOUGH ADMIRAL LEE still hoped he could take Fort Caswell and garrison it from his flagship *Minnesota* until Federal troops arrived, Welles already had decided to abandon the project, at least for the time being. As early as January 5, he was prepared to write off Wilmington and turn his attention toward Charleston. The *Monitor,* on which he had pinned much of his hopes, was gone, and the new monitors were of no use at the entrance to the Cape Fear. Without direct naval support, General Foster was unwilling to move against Wilmington.[1]

Fox now was beginning to regard Wilmington as far more important to the Confederate political and military effort than Charleston, but he admitted there was a "popular clamor" to move against the latter city.[2] The North had effectively ended Confederate maritime trade from South Carolina to Florida, and despite the crippling effect of the blockade, Charleston remained the one gap in that cordon.

Welles first raised the possibility of attacking Charleston the previous September, when he learned the new class of monitors was nearing completion. Here again was the theory that the ironclad warships could run past the harbor defenses and, once inside, bombard the city into submission, as Adm. David G. Farragut had done with conventional warships at New Orleans. At the time this might have been possible. The defenses consisted primarily of Fort Sumter, Fort Moultrie, the near-worthless Castle Pinckney, and a few shore batteries. But, as Du Pont observed when Welles gave him the job of taking Charleston, New Orleans is on a river where a fleet actually can run past shore defenses and keep going until opposite the city itself. Charleston, on the other hand, is at the end of a cul-de-sac, and with the perimeter properly fortified, enemy ships inside the harbor would be at the mercy of the shore installations.[3]

During the first two years of the war, the city dominated Southern maritime commerce, and after the fall of New Orleans it became the Confederacy's main seaport. In Liverpool, Consul Dudley contended that its capture would be the death blow to the South, discouraging the foreign interests that aided the Confederacy.[4] The quick seizure of Port Royal was a demonstration of the great tactical skill available in the U.S. Navy and, as Union admiral David D. Porter later observed, it created "a stampede all along the coast, which indicated the moral effect of Dupont's victory on the Southern people."[5] Du Pont and his army counterpart at Port Royal, Gen. Thomas Sherman, believed the victory at Port Royal should be followed by prompt action to close the entire coast, starting with Savannah and running up the inland passages linking that city with Charleston. Even if the cities themselves could not be taken, they would be useless as seaports.

Du Pont and Sherman were preparing for the first phase of a move against Savannah—an attack on the defending Fort Pulaski—when Sherman was replaced by Maj. Gen. David Hunter. From that point on, the failure of the army to support any effort beyond Pulaski, and the failure of Welles to press for support, probably cost the United States the chance to seize Charleston and hamstring the Confederacy early in the war.[6]

The South, thus given another reprieve, used it wisely. In September 1862, the brilliant Gen. Pierre G. T. Beauregard assumed command in Charleston and, like Lamb and Whiting on the Cape Fear, began overhauling the city's defenses. The armament of Fort Sumter was strengthened, and new earthworks were raised surrounding the harbor and on Morris Island south of the channel opposite Fort Moultrie. Moultrie itself was built up with earthen embankments. Mindful of the inland passages that had been so attractive to Du Pont and Sherman, Beauregard threw up earthworks covering them. By 1863, any effort to take Charleston would be long and bloody.[7] Unfortunately, it was not until that year that the North finally was ready to move against the city.

Although Du Pont had misgivings, he believed the attack could succeed—assuming, of course, that the navy would work in conjunction with ground troops attacking from the land side. Welles, however, had determined on a purely naval attack, hoping to impress the watching British and French governments with the power of the new monitors and undermine any thoughts they might have of recognizing the Confederacy. On January 6, 1863, he advised Du Pont that the capture of Charleston "rests solely upon the success of the naval force." Du Pont was floored at the proposal, particularly after a test run against the Savannah defenses showed monitors were ineffective against earthworks without ground support. But Welles was adamant.[8]

The decision having been made, Du Pont began preparations. He no doubt knew that the Charleston project now had top priority, and neither Welles nor Fox would allow it to be undermined by any other operation. But Du Pont despised Fox and could not resist needling the assistant secretary about the failure of the Wilmington effort.

Expressing concern over having enough ironclads to resist the fire from the Charleston forts, Du Pont indicated that he feared the army might seek to redeem itself by drawing the monitors away for another attempt against Wilmington. He told Fox: "I trust in God you are not going to let Foster inveigle you into any Wilmington operation until we are through here. Let the army go on if it pleases with that system of dissemination which has well nigh ruined it and us, but keep it out of the Navy." He added that during the move against Wilmington in January, he had taken the diversion of the monitors "patiently though pressed all round [at Charleston] by rebel rams."[9]

The letter irritated Fox, who responded, "Lee offered to attack Wilmington with the first two [ironclads] whilst the others were preparing for you, and we gave him the *Passaic* and the old *Monitor,* which unfortunately sunk, breaking up the whole affair." He added he had refused to divert the monitors to other squadron commanders, despite their pleas and despite the fact that the Confederates were completing their ironclads more rapidly than the North. In fact, Fox pointed out, one of the ironclads under construction at Wilmington reportedly had been completed and was now lying at Fort Caswell; the blockading squadron at Old Inlet had no defense against it.[10] Perhaps realizing that he had pushed too far over the Wilmington affair, Du Pont let the matter drop.

The attack on Charleston began on April 7 when seven monitors, the ironclad frigate *New Ironsides,* and the double-turret ironclad *Keokuk* attempted to run past Fort Sumter. Heavy fire from Sumter, Fort Moultrie, and the shore batteries, aggravated by channel obstructions, swells, and strong, erratic tides, rendered the effort futile and exposed the ships to concentrated fire from the defenses. The ships themselves were unable to return fire at a comparable rate, because the slow-rotating mechanisms of the turrets added substantially to the reload time. After two hours of heavy and accurate pounding from shore, the monitors withdrew.

Although Du Pont planned to resume the bombardment the following day, damage reports forced him to cancel the operation. All the ironclads were battered. The *Keokuk* was so badly damaged that she sank a day later, and several monitors were effectively knocked out of action. The naval planners were forced to recognize that, for all their innovative armor, ironclads alone could not take a heavy artillery pounding for the length of time needed to destroy the forts and batteries.[11]

Du Pont ultimately asked to be relieved, and Welles, who was already planning to replace him, complied. Admirals John Dahlgren and Andrew Foote both had their supporters in high political places, and the secretary shrewdly decided to accommodate both—Foote would command the South Atlantic Blockading Squadron, while Dahlgren would have independent command of the naval forces directed against Charleston. Conveniently for the navy, Lincoln had recently sacked General Hunter, and in his place Halleck appointed Maj. Gen. Quincy Gillmore, who, like the general in chief himself, was an engineer. Gillmore had a simple, straightforward plan—the occupation of Morris Island, which would allow "a portion or all of the blockading fleet to lie inside the bar" and effectively close the harbor. It would also provide army artillerists a position from which to bombard and demolish Fort Sumter, clearing the way for the monitors to push through the channel and demand the surrender of the city.[12]

Despite his aversion to combined operations, General Halleck understood the plan and liked it. So did Fox, who convinced Welles to work with the army. Admirals Dahlgren and Foote met with Gillmore on June

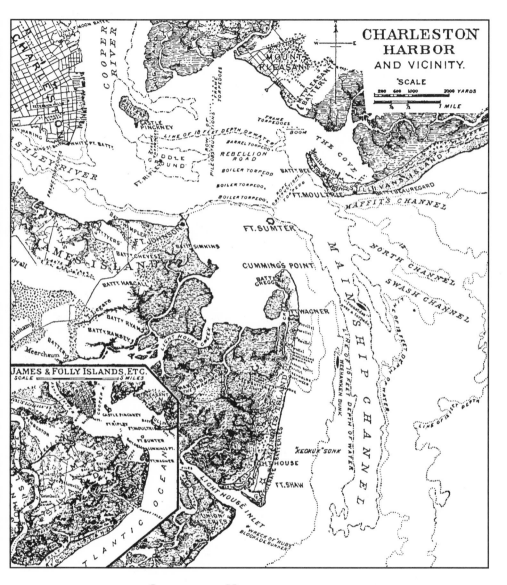

CHARLESTON HARBOR AND VICINITY
Reprinted from Johnson and Buel, *Battles and Leaders of the Civil War*

3 to work out details. Nine days later, Gillmore assumed command of the Department of the South with the specific task of destroying Fort Sumter and giving the navy access to Charleston.[13]

On the surface, Gillmore's choice of Morris Island defied logic. The key to Charleston's outer defenses was nearby James Island, and knowing this, General Beauregard had placed most of his troops there. Besides, of all the islands approaching Charleston Harbor, Morris was the most heavily fortified. Its northern end was a narrow peninsula called Cumming's Point, which faced the channel opposite Fort Moultrie. And Cumming's Point was occupied by Batteries Wagner and Gregg, the former of which was particularly awesome. Yet Gillmore chose Morris Island because its size and shape negated the Confederate numerical advantage. It was only three and three-quarter miles long, and narrow—altogether about four hundred acres. Gillmore had a total of 11,500 men including artillery and engineers, and there simply was not enough room on the island for the Confederates to meet him with an appreciably larger force. On James Island, on the other hand, the much larger Confederate force had room to land reinforcements and outflank the Union troops.[14]

The problem, however, was Battery Wagner. Although General Beauregard later contended that "it never was a 'formidable work,'" the battery was perfectly designed for its purpose, which was entirely defensive. It stretched completely across a narrow neck of Cumming's Point between the high-water mark on the Atlantic side and impassable marshes on the land side. Fashioned with many characteristics similar to Lamb's reconstruction of Fort Fisher, it was built of reinforced sand anchored with turf, with heavy bastions, traverses, and bombproofs that could shelter the entire garrison. General Gillmore later wrote that Battery Wagner was "a work of greater defensive strength than the most exaggerated statements of prisoners and deserters had led us to expect." Another Union officer called it "a towering mass of sand, utterly invulnerable to artillery, and pregnable only by a determined and heroic coup-de-main."

Even the "coup-de-main" was problematic. The approach to Wagner, which included a mile and a half of open beach, was defended by rifle pits, outer works, and a ditch. Aside from its own substantial armament, it was covered by Fort Sumter, batteries on James and Sullivan's Islands, and Battery Gregg, the latter about three-quarters of a mile beyond Wagner at the very end of the point. Mobile artillery was positioned in the sand hills of

Morris Island proper to cover the crossing from the Union position on Folly Island.[15]

Although Dahlgren was an administrator and lacked combat experience, he had made extensive studies of modern coastal bombardment and defense, particularly during the Crimean War. He also understood the theory of combined operations. The general layout of Morris Island and Cumming's Point, as well as the Confederate defenses, disturbed him.[16] The original plan for the army assault on Battery Wagner was based on 1858 Coast Survey maps that showed the island narrowing from two hundred to one hundred yards just short of Wagner. In the intervening six years, however, the Atlantic had cut almost through the island at that point and, during heavy weather, would sweep completely across it. The actual dry land was only twenty-five yards across, forming a bottleneck through which the troops would have to pass; otherwise, at high tide, the right flank would have to advance through the surf. Under these conditions, only the head of the column could be deployed against the enemy until the entire attacking force actually reached the battery. Meanwhile, the soldiers would be exposed to continual Confederate fire. Offshore, treacherous shoals would force the monitors to stand out at least twelve hundred yards, and sand hills on Morris Island would minimize the effect of their supporting fire.[17]

Dahlgren formally assumed command of the naval forces in the Charleston expedition on July 6. Four days later, with his flag in the *Catskill,* he personally led the monitors across the Charleston bar to bombard Morris Island, while Union army batteries opened fire from adjacent Folly Island before crossing over to Morris. At 9:00 A.M. Gillmore's troops started up the beach toward the Confederate fortifications. The monitors, meanwhile, were working up the island, shelling the sand dunes to clear out the Southern mobile batteries and drive them into Wagner. By 9:30 A.M. Dahlgren was abreast of Wagner and exchanged gunfire with the battery until 6:00 P.M. Despite the twelve-hundred-yard limit imposed by shoal waters, he was reasonably satisfied with both the results of the gunfire and the performance of his monitors, some of which had taken a pounding but were still capable of fighting. The ground assault force, meanwhile, had established itself on the south end of Morris Island and pushed within half a mile of Battery Wagner before being repulsed.[18]

Now that he controlled all of Morris Island except for Cumming's

Point, Gillmore scheduled a second attack on July 18. That morning, five wooden gunboats began bombarding Battery Wagner, joined shortly after noon by the *New Ironsides,* five monitors, and the Union batteries down the island. Caught in this cross fire, the Confederates spent much of the day in the shelter of their bombproofs, preparing for the coming assault. Seeing virtually no activity in Wagner, Gillmore mistakenly believed the battery had been smashed to pieces and the garrison was too demoralized to fight.[19]

The ground assault was a classic case of overconfidence bordering on stupidity. Normally, a skirmish line would move in first to cover the main force. These would be followed by pioneer units to cut away obstructions and fill in the ditches. Artillerymen and engineers would accompany the main column, the artillerymen to serve or disable captured guns and the engineers to determine the best means of penetrating the enemy defenses. None of this was done. There were no special instructions for the mission, and no plan was given to the company officers.[20]

About 7:45 P.M., and without advanced preparation, the six-thousand-man assault column started toward Battery Wagner. In the lead the 54th Massachusetts Volunteer Infantry, one of the army's new black units, was expected to storm Battery Wagner with bayonet, closely supported by white units. As the 54th moved up Cumming's Point, the beach became so narrow that the officers of the right-hand companies were wading in water up to their knees. So far, the fleet had maintained "an incessant and accurate fire," and with the rising tide the *Montauk* was able to close within three hundred yards of Wagner's sea face. Now, however, it was too dark to distinguish friend from foe, and Dahlgren was forced to secure his guns. The battery crews from Fort Sumter and Sullivan's Island, on the other hand, had the setting sun behind them, knew the lay of the island, and knew exactly who was who. Finding the range, they began throwing shrapnel into the advancing soldiers.[21]

When the troops were only two hundred yards from Battery Wagner, the Confederate parapet burst into a sheet of flame, the defenders firing point-blank into the Union soldiers. Still they ran forward. "This terrible fire . . . probably caused the greatest number of casualties sustained by the Fifty-fourth in the assault," Capt. Luis F. Emilio, one of the regiment's company commanders, recalled, "for nearer the work the men were somewhat sheltered by the high parapet." Some pushed up the parapet and gained the interior of the battery, where fighting became hand-to-hand. Finally, the blacks and their officers were forced out with heavy losses, joining the white Union regiments that had been pinned down on the beach, unable to move in for support.[22]

Offshore, the Union sailors watched musket flashes from the dark beach, which "continued without intermission until 9:30 P.M., then gradually decreased and died away altogether." Dahlgren resisted any temptation to reopen with supporting fire because he could not see what was happening and feared firing into the Union troops.[23]

The assault cost the United States over eight hundred killed, nearly three hundred from the 54th alone. In that regiment, almost every officer above the rank of first lieutenant was dead or wounded, and command temporarily devolved on Emilio, the most junior of the captains. As the sun rose the next morning, the beach in front of Wagner was so thickly strewn with blue-clad Union dead and wounded that it seemed to one officer in the Union fleet offshore as if the beach itself was blue.[24]

Battery Wagner was never taken by assault, and it held out until the night of September 6–7, when the Confederates evacuated Morris Island. By then it was no longer of any tactical value, because a continuous bombardment by Federal artillery farther down the island and ironclads in the channel had pounded Fort Sumter to rubble. Nor was Sumter essential anymore, because the Confederates had used the time to strengthen their inner defenses and refine the obstructions in the channel beyond the fort.[25]

Nevertheless, Sumter was symbolic to both sides, and as General Gillmore noted, it was "in ruins and destitute of guns." When sunrise revealed that Batteries Wagner and Gregg were empty, Union forces completed the occupation of Morris Island and turned their attention toward Fort Sumter. Throughout September 7, Federal troops mounted heavy guns on Cumming's Point to prevent rearming of the fort and to support future sorties by the monitors. The next morning, Dahlgren sent a truce party to demand the fort's surrender. The Confederates replied "Come and take it," and Dahlgren decided to mount an amphibious assault that night.[26]

The Confederates, however, had anticipated just such a move. Although Dahlgren believed Sumter contained "nothing but a corporal's guard," the small garrison had been relieved three days earlier by a battalion of 320 fresh infantry. The Southerners also had the *Keokuk*'s signal book, and for some time they had been reading the signals between the flagship and Gillmore's headquarters. Shore batteries were trained to cover the approaches, and the ironclad *Chicora* was positioned to sweep Fort Sumter's gorge with grape and canister.

Oblivious to the Confederate preparations, Dahlgren sent in his boats with five hundred sailors and marines in the early-morning darkness of September 9. The effort was doomed. Not only were the Confederates waiting, but the boats became separated and landed piecemeal. Rockets from the fort illuminated the area for the Confederate batteries on James and Sullivan's Islands, while the *Chicora* fired into the gorge. Dahlgren, who was observing the operation from a boat nearby, commented on "the shells breaking around me and screaming in chorus." Trapped, unable to scale the walls, and badly beaten, many of the Union men had no option but surrender. The rest withdrew to their ships as dawn broke over the harbor.[27]

The disastrous summer at Charleston had both a positive and a negative impact on Union thinking. The great slaughter at Battery Wagner frightened many of the army officers who witnessed it, and made them overly cautious. On the other hand, the assault on Fort Sumter—failure though it was—inspired the navy men who took part in it. These two factors combined to form what must be called a "Charleston Effect" that would influence events at Fort Fisher.

5

LOST OPPORTUNITIES AND NEW HEROES

THROUGHOUT THE EFFORT against Charleston, Welles and Fox continued to ponder a Wilmington expedition. As early as March 29, 1863, Admiral Lee advised Fox that pulling the monitors away from the Cape Fear River to use against Charleston removed a distraction from the Confederates, who were using the breathing space to strengthen the defenses along the river. He also insisted the monitors would wear out their guns in a pointless bombardment of the Charleston forts, and worried that replacing them would buy even more time for the Confederates.[1]

The situation was urgent because Fort Fisher was growing at an alarming rate. Not only were the traverses and gun chambers being extended, but there was a new project near the end of Confederate Point that Union naval observers watched with growing apprehension. In March, Lee noted that the Confederates had erected a high, square-frame work tower near the end of the point. Over the next thirty days, they built up the area around the tower with sand and sod, so that by April 17, Lee wrote, "It has now assumed the character of a mound, to construct which they use an inclined railway to the top of the tower. . . . Brush and sods have been used freely at its base to prevent the scattering of the sand by high winds."[2]

This was the Mound Battery, an enormous pile of reinforced sand and sod, sixty feet high, that anchored the southern end of the fort. The project took six months and actually needed two inclined steam-powered railways, the scaffolding for which was scavenged from the wooden lighthouse built twenty-seven years earlier by the U.S. government, and from which Federal Point had originally taken its name. When completed, the Mound was mounted with two heavy guns that Colonel Lamb placed for "a plunging fire on the channel."

Besides serving as a battery, the Mound also provided an elevated signal station for incoming blockade-runners.[3] It was, as one blockade-running captain noted, "an excellent landmark. Joined by a long low isthmus of sand with the higher main land, its regular conical shape enabled the blockade-runners easily to identify it from the offing; and in clear weather, it showed plain and distinct against the sky at night."[4]

From the sea, the fort now looked like a series of sand dunes. From above, it had the shape of an inverted "L," the long arm of which faced the Atlantic was a mile in length, and bristled with twenty-four heavy guns. The base of the "L" blocked the land approach and cut across the point from the beach to the river. In addition to its artillery emplacements, the approach was mined with torpedoes stretching across the peninsula from the river to the beach, placed so they could be exploded independently without one setting off any of the others. These were wired to an electric storage battery in one of the bombproofs. The sea face was equally strong, with the added precaution of a line of marine torpedoes anchored in the water near the channel, also detonated by electricity.[5]

Twenty years later, Adm. David D. Porter, who ultimately led the naval forces that attacked Fort Fisher, recalled these improvements in his naval history of the war: "From a small and unimportant works the huge fortification known as Fort Fisher had gradually arisen. These works bade defiance to any ordinary naval force, unsupported by troops, so that what in the first instance might have been prevented by the persistent attacks of a dozen gun-boats, grew into a series of works so formidable that it was evidently a matter of difficulty to effect their reduction—that is, if the Confederates should make a vigorous defense."[6]

As the man on the spot in that "first instance," Admiral Lee was fully aware that the time had come to take preventive measures. Even without the army, he believed he could take Caswell and garrison it from his ships

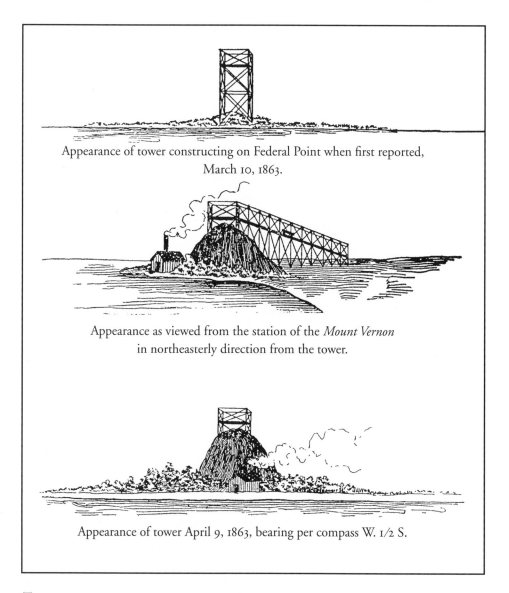

Appearance of tower constructing on Federal Point when first reported,
March 10, 1863.

Appearance as viewed from the station of the *Mount Vernon*
in northeasterly direction from the tower.

Appearance of tower April 9, 1863, bearing per compass W. 1/2 S.

THREE PHASES OF CONSTRUCTION OF THE MOUND BATTERY AS REPORTED BY ADMIRAL LEE
Reprinted from *Official Records of the Union and Confederate Navies in the War of the Rebellion*

for the time being. "Common sense dictates that every floating iron-casemated gun that the Government can spare, shall be used at Wilmington," he told Fox.[7]

It was frustrating for Lee to watch Du Pont and later Dahlgren waste their time against Charleston when the real source of trouble was Wilmington, and he did not hesitate to lobby the Navy Department for support. Welles blamed the War Department, which "has manifested no desire to relieve us and prevent that means of Rebel communication."[8]

As the summer of 1863 progressed, the need to make some sort of move against Wilmington became more apparent, for although Charleston remained in Confederate hands, it was under a more or less constant state of siege by land and sea. Vessels continued to slip into port, but many shipping companies shifted their operations to Wilmington, where the two inlets to the Cape Fear and good railroad connections were more conducive to blockade-running.[9]

Describing the problem, Acting Ensign John W. Grattan, who served as an aide first to Admiral Lee and later to Admiral Porter, noted that the Cape Fear "was the most dangerous and embarrassing to close of any port on the Atlantic coast. The two main entrances New Inlet and Western Bar were forty miles apart by ocean communication, being divided by Frying Pan Shoals which were always dangerous to navigation."[10]

THE MOUND BATTERY
Courtesy of the North Carolina Division of Archives and History

The advantage provided by nature and engineering was made readily evident by Wilmington's commerce. On September 2, 1863, Confederate secretary of state Judah P. Benjamin noted that the city's cotton exports had risen from 526,824 pounds in January to 2,144,887 pounds in July, and speculated that when the August report was received it would show four million pounds. Foreign commerce at Wilmington was estimated at $3,240,000 per annum, compared to $715,488 for the foreign commerce of the entire state of North Carolina in 1858. "Thus," Benjamin wrote, "one blockaded port in 1863 has carried on more than four times the amount of the whole foreign commerce of the State in 1858, and this business is done by ocean steamers running almost with the regularity of packets."[11]

Already decadent because of the wartime boom, Wilmington slid even further toward iniquity now that it was the undisputed center of the blockade trade. From a staid old colonial seaport, it had assumed a character reminiscent of San Francisco at the height of the gold rush. Lt. John Wilkinson, a Confederate naval officer who ran the blockade on government-owned steamers, commented:

> Here resorted the speculators from all parts of the South, to attend the weekly auctions of imported cargoes; and the town was infested with rogues and desperadoes, who made a livelihood by robbery and murder. It was unsafe to venture into the suburbs at night, and even in daylight, there were frequent conflicts in the public streets between the crews of the steamers in port and the soldiers stationed in the town, in which knives and pistols would be freely used; and not unfrequently a dead body would rise to the surface of the water in one of the docks with marks of violence upon it. The civil authorities were powerless to prevent crime. . . . The agents and employes [*sic*] of the different blockade-running companies, lived in magnificent style, paying a king's ransom (in Confederate money) for their household expenses, and nearly monopolizing the supplies in the country market.[12]

Not everyone was mercenary. Among the respectable citizens who remained in town, a ladies aid society was organized by Mrs. William DeRosset. These women met the trains carrying wounded south from Virginia and, during the hour or two of layover, would change the dressings and feed the wounded. Although the best foodstuffs went to the well-heeled blockade-runners and speculators at exorbitant prices, the women

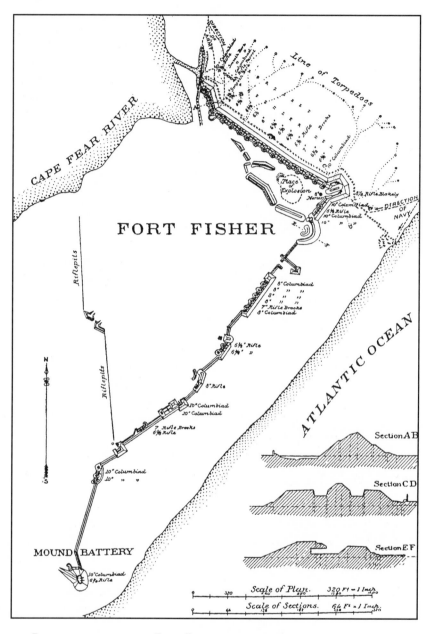

PLAN AND SECTIONS OF FORT FISHER, SHOWING THE DIRECTION OF THE
ARMY AND NAVY ASSAULTS ON JANUARY 15, 1865
Reprinted from Johnson and Buel, *Battles and Leaders of the Civil War*

secured enough contributions from "companies and individuals" so that they could not only feed the wounded but take the leftover food to the young boys serving in the Home Guard at a camp outside town.[13]

The blockade-runners took on their cargoes at wharves constructed on the marshy flats on the west side of the river, where steam cotton presses facilitated loading. As the military situation deteriorated, sentries were posted on the wharves twenty-four hours a day to keep army deserters from slipping aboard and stowing away; as an additional precaution, outbound ships were required to put in at Smithville, where they were fumigated by pumping smoke below decks to drive out anyone who might be hiding. Nevertheless, many managed to remain concealed all the way to Bermuda or Nassau, usually by bribing one or more of the crew.[14]

With Wilmington dominating the blockade business, Northern strategists now committed one of those frequent and glaring errors of omission that did so much to prolong the war. When the evacuation of Battery Wagner left Cumming's Point in Federal hands, the first move should have been to install long-range batteries to neutralize Fort Moultrie and close the entrance to Charleston Harbor. Such an action, together with the ongoing blockade, would have entirely isolated the city from the sea. This, in turn, would have negated Charleston's strategic value while leaving the Confederates with the task of feeding the city's large population from their diminishing resources. The main Union military and naval effort could have shifted northward, attacked the Confederates at the entrances to the Cape Fear, and closed Wilmington.[15] No such action was taken, and the United States remained preoccupied with capturing Charleston while the Confederates continued to strengthen the Cape Fear defenses.

Even if Northern planners missed it, Colonel Lamb and General Whiting still believed an attack on Fort Fisher was the Union's most obvious option and kept themselves in a constant state of alert. It seemed so incredible that the North would allow Wilmington to remain open that they could not bring themselves to believe it. Their sense of alarm was aggravated by Union naval landing parties that had been sporadically raiding the coast since early in the war, generally to gather intelligence or destroy the saltworks that proliferated in the area.

Besides unnerving the Confederates, the raids gave the impression that Federal military power in the area was greater than it actually was, and were partly responsible for Whiting's unrealistic estimate that ten thousand troops were needed to defend his position. At the very least, he wanted a brigade with several batteries of artillery between Wilmington and Weldon to make the Federals think twice before moving against the Cape Fear.[16]

The most notorious forays were conducted by Lt. William Barker Cushing, an audacious young officer from Wisconsin whom an official Navy Department publication described as "unsurpassed for daring and courage."[17] Born on November 24, 1842, Cushing was one day short of his twentieth birthday when he made his first raid, slipping into New River Inlet north of Wilmington in the light steamer *Ellis,* and briefly occupied the town of Jacksonville on the main turnpike from Wilmington to New Bern.[18] He seized the courthouse and twenty-five stand of arms, the post office, a large amount of mail, the slaves belonging to the postmaster (who were later freed), and two schooners, and prompted the Confederates to burn a third schooner loaded with cotton and turpentine to prevent capture.

Steaming back downriver, Cushing came under rifle fire from camps ashore. By the time he reached the mouth of the river it was almost night, and he had to anchor and wait for the morning tide. The next morning, the *Ellis* grounded and could not be freed. After another day of heavy fighting, Cushing abandoned and burned the *Ellis* and escaped in one of the prize schooners.[19]

Three months later, in February 1863, Cushing took a landing party in a small schooner up the Little River, on the line between North and South Carolina, hoping to capture a Cape Fear pilot from the station there. Instead, he surprised and destroyed a military camp. Escaping back downriver to the sea, his ship was caught in a storm that threw it on Frying Pan Shoals. Fortunately for Cushing, the heavy seas lifted the schooner clear before any serious damage was done, and he arrived safely at Beaufort.[20]

Cushing's exploits had a demoralizing effect, and many in the Cape Fear area criticized the Confederate naval detachment at Wilmington for doing nothing. But the navy was preparing to fight back. The *North Carolina,* one of the long-awaited ironclads under construction in Wilmington, was completed, having been delayed first by the yellow fever epidemic of the fall of 1862, then by a strike over wages by yard workers. A formidable-looking ship, she was 150 feet long with a thirty-two-foot beam, mounting four guns. Wilmingtonian and blockade-runner James

LT. WILLIAM B. CUSHING
Courtesy of the North Carolina Division of Archives and History

Sprunt noted, "The timbers of the vessel were heavy pine and hard wood covered with railroad iron, giving the ram, when launched, the appearance of a turtle in the water." Given the U.S. Navy's past experience with such "turtles," the description was far from comical.

The *North Carolina*'s appearance, however, hid many defects. Structurally weak, she was further hampered by the weight of her armor on a twelve-foot draft. She was thus unable to cross the bar except on the most unusually high spring tides, and after crossing she probably could not have gotten back into the river. One of her engines was a worn-out piece of machinery from the captured tugboat *Uncle Ben,* a former Great Laker that had run the gamut of service in both the U.S. and Confederate navies before being scavenged for the new ironclad. Despite the bad engine, the *North Carolina* was commissioned in late 1863 and steamed down the river to Fort Caswell, where Fox noted her presence to Admiral Du Pont.[21]

That was as far as she went. Because of her defective engines and inability to cross the bar, the *North Carolina* was relegated to coastal defense. Aside from an occasional cruise upriver to Wilmington, she spent most of her time anchored in the estuary off Smithville.[22]

Undeterred by the disappointing performance of the *North Carolina,* the Confederates worked through the winter of 1863–64 to complete the second ironclad, *Raleigh,* and were making good progress on a third, the *Wilmington,* which one Confederate officer described as "a fine model 226 feet in length; of such draft of water as will enable her to go in and out of the harbor at all times."[23]

The *Raleigh,* when delivered, was 150 feet long, with a thirty-two-foot beam, and mounting twelve 6-inch rifles. She was commissioned in April 1864 as the flagship of Commodore William F. Lynch's Cape Fear Squadron. Lynch intended to take this awesome-looking ram to sea and break the blockade of New Inlet. He reckoned, however, without the *Raleigh's* greatest defect—like the *North Carolina,* she had a twelve-foot draft and armor too heavy for her frames.[24]

Nevertheless, Lynch was determined to run the *Raleigh* over the bar and engage the fleet. On May 6 he visited Fort Fisher to reconnoiter the blockading squadron and arrange signals with Lamb so that the Confederates would not mistake their departing squadron for Federal warships. At sunset, the blockaders *Tuscarora, Britannia, Nansemond, Howquah, Mount Vernon, Kansas,* and *Niphon* anchored for the night. Lamb sent his most experienced gunners to Fort Fisher's sea face, then went to the ramparts opposite New Inlet bar.[25]

A short time later, the ponderous shape of the *Raleigh* appeared out of the darkness, flashing recognition lights of red above white. Range lights were set on the Mound Battery and, incredibly, the *Raleigh,* commanded by Lt. Pembroke Jones with a marine detachment under 2nd Lt. Henry M. Doak, CSMC, cleared the bar and put to sea, accompanied by the small river steamers *Yadkin* and *Equator.* The Confederate vessels disappeared into the night, and the garrison at Fort Fisher waited. Presently, the soldiers heard gunfire and saw the blue Coston signal lights of the Federal ships.[26]

Upon clearing the bar, the *Raleigh* had steamed directly toward the *Britannia* in an attempt to ram her. The Federal crew opened fire with no apparent effect on the ironclad. Several blockaders moved in, apparently under the impression that a blockade-runner was attempting to escape. The *Raleigh* opened fire at six hundred yards, one shot shattering the *Britannia*'s binnacle light and another passing over her starboard paddlebox. The *Britannia* burned a blue light to signal the other Federal ships, then slipped her cable to get out of the way. As she maneuvered, she came into shallow water and called for assistance.

The *Raleigh* now turned on the *Nansemond*, which steamed away, firing at the ironclad with an aftergun. The Confederate ship returned fire, the shot barely missing the *Nansemond*'s walking beam. Several more shots were exchanged before the *Nansemond* finally got out of range.

At one point in the darkness and the confusion of the fight, Lieutenant Doak, whose marines manned at least part of the battery, was ordered to fire his starboard gun at the next light. He obeyed and sent a shell into Fort Fisher, although apparently with no injuries or damage.

At daylight the *Raleigh* attacked the *Howquah,* putting a shot through her funnel. Now the other Union ships could see what was happening and steamed in to engage the ironclad. Watching from Fort Fisher, Commodore Lynch signaled Jones to bring the flotilla in. The *Raleigh* and her escorts formed in line about five miles out and steamed back toward New Inlet. She passed the Mound and rounded Confederate Point, her flag flying from its staff and drawing a salute from the garrison. But as she came to the bar, her draft was too much for the ebbing tide and she grounded on the bar. Jones gave orders to lighten her, but she broke her back and started coming apart.[27]

After the wreck, Jones asked for a court of inquiry, which determined the *Raleigh* was lost because "her strength seems to have been insufficient to enable her to sustain the weight of her armor long enough to permit every practicable means of lightening her to be exhausted."[28]

Vaguely aware that the *Raleigh* had been damaged, but not realizing that she was a total loss, the Federals worried that she might be repaired for another sortie. Accordingly, Cushing volunteered to go in after her. Although he now commanded the Union blockader *Monticello,* he had continued his hit-and-run raids and was becoming an old hand in the estuaries of southeastern North Carolina.

Ten weeks earlier, on February 22, 1864, Cushing had decided to cele-
brate Washington's birthday by capturing a ship at Smithville and running
her back to the blockade fleet. Slipping past the defenses with forty men
in three boats with muffled oars, he failed to find any ships at anchor, but
reconnoitered the batteries on Smith's Island and decided they could be
taken with a landing party of two hundred men. Denied permission by
the flotilla commander, Capt. Benjamin F. Sands, he swore he would
deliver Sands a Confederate general for breakfast.

The next night, Cushing took a party into Smithville and, although he
missed capturing Brig. Gen. Louis Hebert, commander of artillery for the
Cape Fear District, he did capture Capt. Patrick Kelly of the engineers,
who was taken back to the *Monticello*. The following morning, Cushing
took his prisoner to the flagship for breakfast with an astonished Sands.
He sent an ensign to Fort Caswell under a flag of truce to get clothes for
Kelly and to deliver a note for General Hebert, stating:

My Dear General:
I deeply regret that you were not at home when I called. I enclose my card.
W. B. Cushing.[29]

The *Monticello* was coaling in Beaufort when Cushing learned of the
Raleigh's sortie. Returning to the Cape Fear, he hoped to engage her, but
on finding she had retreated back into the river, he sought permission to
go in and take her by boarding. Mindful of what he felt was Sands's excessive caution, he sent a copy of the request to Admiral Lee. As anticipated,
Sands refused to approve the expedition but was overruled by Lee, who
told him to get whatever men were necessary from the flotilla. Welles and
Fox likewise were enthusiastic.[30]

On the night of June 23, Cushing took two officers and fifteen men
into Old Inlet and up the river. Not finding the *Raleigh*, they continued
on. Passing Fort Anderson, they were spotted by sentries and fired upon.
Cushing turned the boat about and began pulling downriver, then cut to
the opposite shore and turned back up toward Wilmington, leaving the
Confederates at Anderson to launch boats for a wild goose chase downriver. He was within four miles of Wilmington when dawn began to
break, and he landed and hid his boat and crew in the marshes all day.

About nightfall, Cushing captured a party of fishermen in canoes, who
told him the fate of the *Raleigh*. Taking them as guides, he reconnoitered

the city's defenses and managed to capture a hunter and an army mail carrier from Fort Fisher, the latter with over two hundred documents giving "the plan and strength of the defenses and number of men in rebel garrisons."[31] The following day, one of Cushing's officers donned the uniform of the captured courier and procured food for the hungry raiders. Pleased with his luck so far, Cushing decided to wait and capture the next mail carrier. This carrier, however, was more alert and, recognizing Cushing for a Union officer, turned and fled. Cushing cut the telegraph wire to Confederate Point so that Fort Fisher would not be alerted, then took to his boat. Ultimately, he found the wreck of the *Raleigh* and confirmed that she was useless. Setting the captured fishermen adrift in their canoes, Cushing and his men pulled toward New Inlet. Below Fort Anderson they captured a boat with six people, four of them soldiers, who told them troops in boats were blocking the entrance to the river. With this warning, and knowing the river, tides, and bar better than the soldiers, Cushing was able to rush down on the Confederate boats, maneuver past them, and reach open water and the safety of his fleet.[32]

Cushing's exploit made him the darling of the navy and the Northern public. The *New York Herald* called this latest adventure "one of the most daring reconnaissances made during the war."[33] On the Confederate side, General Whiting fumed that without adequate troops, particularly cavalry, Union naval parties could virtually come and go as they pleased.[34]

Although the expedition gave the North a hero, unnerved the Confederates, and gained information on the Cape Fear defenses, one great fact remained—those defenses were still in Confederate hands, and blockade-runners still came and went with frustrating regularity.

6

"THERE SEEMS TO BE SOME DEFECT IN THE BLOCKADE"

IF CUSHING'S EXPLOITS and the Confederate ironclad efforts attracted the most attention during the last half of 1863 and the early part of 1864, the Federal naval command was not idle. As 1863 drew to a close, Admiral Lee made yet another appeal for some sort of action against the Cape Fear. He advised Welles he was "confident that he can land a military force on the open beach to the westward of Fort Caswell, whence the reduction of that important work is easily accomplished by engineers." This would allow the blockading fleet to move into the river, closing Wilmington. Forwarding the recommendation to Secretary of War Edwin Stanton, Welles noted, "As [Wilmington] is the only port by which any supplies whatever reach the rebels, and as the armies are mostly going into winter quarters, it seems a fit opportunity to undertake such an operation."[1] Stanton, of course, did nothing, and General Halleck completely vetoed a move against the Cape Fear, arguing that it would "involve the suspension of other and more important operations."[2]

As 1864 progressed, Fort Fisher assumed its final shape. The land face—the short arm of the "L"—began about one hundred feet from the river. The river end was anchored by Shepperd's Battery, one of the original structures of the old Battery Bolles, but doubled in strength by Lamb. The land face itself was a parapet broken at intervals by fifteen dunelike traverses, each with a hollow, reinforced interior to protect the garrison during bombardment. Between the traverses were open, elevated gun chambers reached by stairs from inside the fort. The traverses themselves were connected by tunnels under the gun chambers. Halfway down the land face, a sally port led to an elevated battery outside the parapet that was served by field artillery.

At the angle of the "L," where the land face joined the sea face, Lamb constructed the massive, forty-three-foot-high Northeast Bastion, covering both faces of the fort. A hundred yards to the south was a crescent-shaped battery curving out toward the beach. Known from its appearance as the Pulpit Battery, it was designed for four casemated guns, but the palmetto internal bracings rapidly deteriorated so that it would not withstand the concussion of gunfire. Consequently, Lamb ordered these protected gun chambers converted into a field hospital for battle and constructed a curtain wall to the rear to protect it from shell explosions in the interior of the fort. Because of the view afforded by the elevated

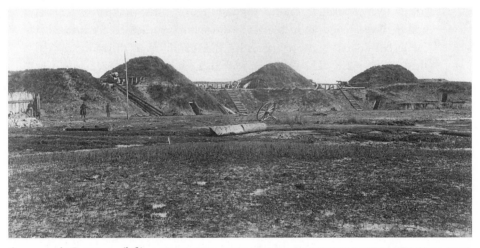

SHEPPERD'S BATTERY *(left)* AND THE LINE OF TRAVERSES EXTENDING ACROSS THE LAND FACE SHOW THE CONSTRUCTION OF THE FORT WITH INTERIOR BUNKERS AND OPEN GUN CHAMBERS. THESE HAVE BEEN RESTORED.
Courtesy of the North Carolina Division of Archives and History

height, the Pulpit Battery also served as combat headquarters. Although each traverse had its own magazine, a heavily reinforced central magazine was built beyond the curtain from the Pulpit.

More traverses extended south along the beach, but these were only about half the size and strength of those on the land face and were built primarily to withstand ricochet fire in case a bombarding fleet tried to bounce shot and shell across the water. Midway down the sea face, however, was the fort's heaviest gun, a monstrous 150-pounder Armstrong rifle. The emplacement, appropriately enough, was called the Armstrong Battery. A telegraph station situated between the Armstrong and Mound Batteries allowed the fort to communicate with Wilmington.[3]

Enclosed in the "L" were whitewashed wooden barracks and other support structures, as well as the administrative headquarters located in the old Federal lighthouse keeper's cottage. A line of rifle pits, angling across the point from just above the telegraph station to the river, covered the rear of the fort.

This, essentially was the layout of the fort when it received its most distinguished visitor, President Davis. Escorted by General Whiting, Davis landed at the end of Confederate Point and rode a horse to the Mound, from which he had a complete view. The sea-face battery was manned and fired a twenty-one-gun salute. Adjourning to Lamb's headquarters, Davis and Whiting forgot their old animosities long enough to get into what Lamb considered "a most interesting discussion" as to the mode of trial they would prefer. The president said he would rather be tried by a jury, while Whiting opted for court-martial.[4]

As intended, the ongoing improvements to Fort Fisher provided security for blockade-runners. Each ship carried a Confederate signalman who communicated by coded lamp flashes with the signal station ashore. After an exchange of signals between ship and shore, range lights were set on the Mound Battery and along the beach. When these lights came into line, the ship's pilot turned into the channel and the lights were immediately extinguished.[5] "The range lights were changed as circumstances required," Lieutenant Wilkinson recalled, "for the New Inlet channel, itself, was . . . constantly changing, being materially affected both in depth of water, and in its course, by a heavy gale of wind or a severe freshet in Cape Fear River."[6]

From time to time, a gunboat would spot one of the incoming blockade-runners and the chase would be on, watched all the while from Fort Fisher.

As soon as the blockade-runner came into range, the fort's guns would open fire, the shells passing over the runner and holding the gunboats at bay until the runner was safely anchored. To increase the effect of his artillery, Lamb adopted a primitive system of saturation fire, using guns at different elevations along the same plane. When all fired at once, an entire stretch of water was covered with shot and shell, giving a reasonable chance of scoring hits.[7]

Technology and nature seemed to favor blockade-running at Wilmington. The British blockade-runner Thomas Taylor later explained, "With due care and pluck the risk was far less than people believed; except in a few cases our losses were caused by ignorance of position in making the port."[8]

During one two-month period in the latter part of 1864, Wilmington and Charleston alone received 8.6 million pounds of meat, 1.5 million pounds of lead, 1.9 million pounds of saltpeter, 546,000 pairs of shoes, 316,000 blankets, 520,000 pounds of coffee, 69,000 rifles, 97 packages of revolvers, 2,639 packages of medicine, 43 cannon, and a large quantity of other articles.

These figures were duly reported in the Richmond *Dispatch*. And because Charleston's blockade trade had been substantially reduced over the past year, anyone reading the paper with the least knowledge of the situation on the coast logically could assume that the bulk of these shipments came through Wilmington. This prompted John B. Jones, clerk of the Confederate War Department, to observe, "Our armies are in no danger of immediately becoming destitute of supplies; but, alas! the publication itself may cause the immediate fall of Wilmington."[9]

The problem in taking Wilmington was the forts, for Commodore Lynch's Cape Fear Squadron was a farcical collection of tugboats and river steamers that posed absolutely no threat to the Union fleet. The *Raleigh* was breaking up and settling into the mud, and the *North Carolina,* lying idle for months in the saline waters of the estuary off Smithville, was exposed to teredoes that attacked her unsheathed hull until, Sprunt commented, it "was like a honeycomb." By August, the *New York Herald* could report, "The two rebel rams at Wilmington are complete failures, and their machinery is being removed." On September 27, the now-gutted *North Carolina* developed a leak and sank at her moorings.[10]

Although the Cape Fear forts remained an obstacle, there was a glimmer of hope in the Navy Department. In March 1864, General Halleck had been replaced by Lt. Gen. U. S. Grant, a man who had given Lincoln desperately needed victories by working with the navy on the western rivers. Yet Halleck out of office did not mean Halleck out of favor, for he still commanded a disproportionate amount of influence in Washington. And Grant, whose recent success and rise to fame had come after a lifetime of mediocrity and failure, did not yet feel confident enough to challenge Halleck's recommendations. Any plans Grant might have for combined operations in the East were shelved as he continued his predecessor's policy of wasteful battles between massed armies, until his troops finally reached the James River below Richmond and settled in for a siege.[11]

Despite the stalemate in Virginia, or perhaps because of it, public opinion in the North appeared to be shifting toward some sort of effort to close the Confederate capital's pipeline through the blockade. No one was more aware of the problem—or more frustrated by it—than Gideon Welles, the man responsible for keeping military supplies from reaching Southern ports. It was no easy task, and he was hindered on land as well as at sea.

By the middle of 1864, the clandestine cotton trade was so well established that a Northern "cotton ring" was operating openly under executive license, sending war matériel to the South by land and by sea in exchange for Confederate cotton that was sold at exorbitant prices on the fiber-starved Northern market. The trade was so widespread that on July 2 of that year, Congress authorized the Treasury Department to regulate it and keep "contraband" from entering or leaving the Confederacy. The *New York Herald*'s correspondent in Beaufort speculated that the new regulations would "restrict hitherto liberal privileges, and greatly limit the amount of business in merchandise of all kinds in the district. It is believed that the design of this new policy is to correct alleged abuses, and to prevent supplies finding their way into the enemy's lines." Yet, with appropriate influence, the regulations were easily circumvented and the trade flourished under the cloak of law until the end of the war, much to Welles's chagrin.[12]

The secretary was further exasperated by Northern newspapers' speculation that the Cape Fear trade continued because of collusion between the blockade-runners and the Federal naval officers assigned to stop them.[13] Although Welles put no stock in such conjecture, he privately

U.S. Secretary of the Navy Gideon Welles
Reprinted from *Diary of Gideon Welles*

commented, "There is a want of effective action. Admiral Lee is true and loyal, careful, and circumspect almost to a fault, but, while vigilant, he has not dash and impetuous daring, and there seems to be some defect in the blockade which makes Wilmington appear an almost open port."[14]

The defect, of course, was not Lee; it was the Cape Fear's geography. The two entrances separated by Frying Pan Shoals split the blockading squadron into two isolated flotillas. The heavy guns of the forts, particularly those of Fort Fisher, forced the divided blockading squadron to keep to a respectful distance at sea, rather than lie anchored in the estuary as they otherwise would have done. To offset the problem, the Federal flotillas covering the two inlets divided themselves into three groups, forming semicircles around the entrances.

A light-draft inshore group, just out of gun range, remained anchored during the day, and patrolled at night. Almost every night, the Confederates in Fisher and other batteries would rake the bar with gunfire to make sure no blockader came too close.[15] "Great care was required not to run ashore and to avoid being disabled by the rebel fire when the moon came out and found us close under a hundred of their cannon," recalled Commander Cushing in the *Monticello*. "I was forced to get all the sleep that I required during the afternoon, never at night."[16]

The inshore group was supported by an offshore cordon of cruisers, "with everything ready to move at a moment's notice," according to Ensign Grattan.[17] Beyond that, detached gunboats prowled to intercept runners on the high seas. Describing the latter, Cushing wrote: "It was the duty of these cruisers to calculate for moon and tide, the time that a steamer would be most likely to escape from the harbor and supposing her to make through the night a certain number of knots speed, place themselves where they would probably sight the black smoke in the morning. The lookout at the mastheads commanded a horizon of some fifteen miles and many a steamer was so seen and captured."[18]

Because such an arrangement required a larger number of ships than often was available, the real danger was not so much the offshore cruisers or detached gunboats but the inshore group steaming along the coast at night. To counter the threat, blockade-runners adopted their own set of tactics. Instead of running directly for the entrance, the favorite method was to come in fifteen or twenty miles north of New Inlet so as to round the northern edge of the inshore squadron, then follow the shore southward in shallow water just outside the line of breakers until reaching the inlet. The batteries and fortifications along the coast helped ensure that there would be little interference from the ships of the inshore group.[19]

"As the sun commenced to light up the ocean the hail could come from aloft, 'Black smoke, sir!' 'Where away?' 'Two points on the port bow, sir!' and the exciting chase would commence," Cushing recalled, adding, "It was exciting. Sometimes a few hours sufficed in which to overhaul the lead colored fugitive, often darkness would terminate an unsuccessful chase and our blue jackets would have to console themselves by saying that 'there are other fish in the sea as ever were caught,' a poor substitute for the half million dollars that had run away from them during the day."[20]

Thus, despite the overall interruption of commerce at Wilmington, enough ships got through to render the blockade ineffective and create an embarrassing diplomatic problem for the United States. Under international convention of the time, a blockade, in order to be recognized by neutrals, had to be strong enough to actually close a port, or at least be so tight that no ship could enter or leave without almost certain capture. And because Cape Fear blockade-runners usually could depend on getting through, the Wilmington blockade simply did not work. Therefore, even as late as the summer of 1864, the neutral powers were under no legal obligation to recognize the blockade or prevent their ships and citizens from attempting to run it. As General Grant later noted in his memoirs, "Foreign governments, particularly the British Government, were constantly threatening that unless ours could maintain the blockade of [the Cape Fear] coast they should cease to recognize any blockade."[21]

In order to close Wilmington, the river itself would have to be completely sealed, and that meant taking the forts. This required a joint army-navy operation, something which, by the end of August, Welles had been urging for two years. The navy's position got a boost on August 29, when information filtered through Confederate lines that Fort Morgan, guarding Mobile Bay, had fallen. Aside from the morale boost to the Union army in Virginia, the news "cheered" Lincoln, and Welles decided the time had come to press the issue of the Cape Fear. With Mobile closed, he pointed out, "Wilmington remained the only important port where blockade running was in the least successful. To close that port, and thus terminate the intercourse of the rebels with the outer world, would be like severing the jugular vein in the human system. Richmond and the whole insurrectionary region, which . . . was in an exhausted and suffering condition, could not, if deprived of foreign aid and succor, long hold out against the Union arms."[22]

Lincoln agreed, and now that Mobile was closed and Grant's forces were settled in for a siege of the Richmond defenses, Secretary of War Stanton and General Halleck appeared amenable. But Stanton doubted Grant would be interested at this point, and both the president and the secretary of war were loath to press him on the matter.[23]

Welles, however, was not willing to let it drop. On August 31, Fox and General Gillmore, whom Stanton wanted as head of a Wilmington expedition, went to the front to discuss the prospect with Grant.[24] Contrary to Stanton's expectations, Grant was prepared to consider the concept, provided it did not borrow too heavily from his troops in front of Richmond. His interest may have been aroused by Admiral Lee, who frequently called on him during the summer. Wilmington appears to have been discussed,

REAR ADM. SAMUEL PHILLIPS LEE WAS A VIRGINIAN WHO RESEMBLED HIS
DISTANT COUSIN, GEN. ROBERT E. LEE. FOR TWO YEARS, ADMIRAL LEE
URGED AN EXPEDITION AGAINST FORT FISHER, ONLY TO HAVE COMMAND OF
THAT EXPEDITION SNATCHED AWAY FOR POLITICAL REASONS.
Courtesy U.S. Naval Historical Center

because Lee, who normally exercised direct command of the James River
Squadron, turned that responsibility over to Capt. Melancton Smith so he
could devote all his own efforts to tightening the Cape Fear blockade.
Now that Grant was agreeable to a move against Wilmington, a tentative
date for the attack was set for October 1, although this soon was postponed until October 15.[25]

A major reason for delay was a command problem facing both army
and navy. Despite Stanton's wishes, Grant was emphatic that Gillmore
should not have charge of the troops; early in the Richmond campaign he

committed a blunder that cost the Union a chance to seize Petersburg while its defenses were still weak, and Grant did not trust him with the Fort Fisher assignment.[26] Although Grant appears to have voiced no opinion on the naval operation, Welles allowed himself to believe that he did not want to work with Admiral Lee either, because Welles had already decided that Lee would have to go. "Farragut," he remarked, "would take [Fort Fisher] three times while Lee was preparing, and hesitating, and looking behind for more aid."[27]

In retrospect, this is patently absurd. There was no indication that Lee would have hesitated, but rather, after two years of being little more than a frustrated observer, that he would move in as soon as he got the chance. But as Lee's biographers, Dudley Cornish and Virginia Laas, point out, the admiral was the victim of a peculiar quirk in the secretary's personality. Welles disliked caution and admired heroes (hence his enthusiasm for Cushing), and he questioned the valor and aggressiveness of any commander until that commander demonstrated otherwise. Despite his administrative brilliance, Welles never completely grasped the realities of a naval assault. He believed a commander who continually asked for more ships and men was timid and needed to be replaced with one who would be more aggressive. And Lee certainly had asked for monitors to use against New Inlet, and for ships and men to assault Fort Caswell.[28]

Another problem was public opinion. The difficulties imposed by Cape Fear geography were aggravated by the development of vessels specifically designed for blockade-running—fast, sleek, light-draft steamers that could outrun any ship in the blockading squadron. The number of successful chases and captures declined at an alarming rate, and the Northern public and press blamed Lee.[29]

Finally, there were purely political reasons to remove Lee. The presidential election would be held in November, and the outcome was by no means certain. To win, Lincoln needed support from Radicals within the Republican Party, who were determined to break the power of Lee's inlaws, the Blairs. Already they had forced one of the admiral's brothers-inlaw, Frank Blair, out of Congress, and were in the process of pushing another, Montgomery Blair, from the postmaster generalship. Lee, often regarded as the "third son" in the Blair household, was a political liability.[30]

Fox wanted to pull Farragut out of Mobile and put him in charge of the North Atlantic Squadron, reasoning that even without the army the crusty old admiral would take some sort of decisive action to close Wilmington. Although the idea appealed to Welles, at first he opposed the transfer, reasoning that with Farragut already in control of Mobile Bay and with Mobile itself about to fall, his removal from Alabama would create adverse public reaction. Besides, Farragut's reputation was such that Welles believed the Confederates would correctly interpret his reassignment and strengthen the Cape Fear defenses accordingly. Nevertheless, the secretary wrote in his diary, "It is important . . . that the port of Wilmington should be closed, and no effort should be spared to secure that object."[31]

The time and distance involved in communications kept Lee ignorant of the events in Washington, discussions with Grant, or Welles's determination to replace him, and this foul-up, which Welles himself admitted was embarrassing, would continue over the remaining six weeks that he commanded the North Atlantic Squadron.[32] Unaware that the decision was already made, Lee wrote Welles as late as September 6 asking for permission to meet with Grant to propose a Cape Fear expedition. He believed that the recent implementation of the draft would provide ample troops, negating any excuses the army might have about manpower shortages.[33]

Welles, meanwhile, was leaning more and more toward Farragut and had already proposed the idea to him. Nevertheless, he also sent Lee a list of fourteen specific questions about the Cape Fear defenses and possible combined operations. Lee responded on September 8, describing possible anchorages and the defenses on Oak Island, Zeek's Island, and Confederate Point. Among other things, he ruled out a landing against Fort Caswell on Oak Island except by surprise attack at night, in part because the island's exposure created support problems. A landing on Smith's Island would bring the Union forces within the long-range guns of Fort Holmes. Describing the channels, he cautioned that the soundings taken by Union officers slipping in at night could not be considered reliable because there was no way to take bearings.[34]

By the time Lee's report was submitted, Welles had decided to order him to change places with Farragut, confident that the latter would accept the North Atlantic command. Accordingly, Farragut was ordered to Port Royal pending reassignment, and on September 17 Lee was advised of the change and told to remain on station until relieved.[35]

The order stunned Lee, who still knew nothing of what had transpired.

Nevertheless, he fully understood the political implications behind his fall from grace. Personally, he attributed much of it to Ben Butler, a darling of the Radicals and Fox's boyhood friend, whose Army of the James was assigned as the ground force for the assault on Fort Fisher. Lee and Butler had continually disputed over regulation of the contraband trade; and Butler had substantial influence in the government.[36]

Lee's suspicions were not altogether groundless, for the *New York Herald* reported from Butler's headquarters that the change of naval command "has brought unqualified joy. . . . Farragut's coming is of itself an earnest [assurance] that the navy is hereafter to enact a conspicuous and honorable part in the reduction of the rebel capital, and that the miserable inefficiency of the fleet in the James [a component of the North Atlantic Squadron] is to give way at once to a manly and comprehensive effort. . . . To Major General Butler personally the accession of Rear Admiral Farragut to the command of the North Atlantic squadron is the source of the greatest possible satisfaction."[37]

On the advice of his father-in-law, Preston Blair, Lee accepted the change in good grace, and prepared a memorandum with supporting documents for Farragut concerning every aspect of the North Atlantic Blockading Squadron and the Wilmington situation. This, at least, would ease the transition.[38]

Now an unanticipated problem arose. Farragut, who was sixty-three years old and had been on almost continuous duty for the past two years, pleaded exhaustion and ill health and asked to be excused from the new assignment. Welles accepted this at face value, believing that Farragut would not have asked to be relieved unless his health were seriously impaired. As time passed, however, he began to realize that the old admiral had outfoxed him. For despite the "ill health" that prevented his assuming command of the North Atlantic Squadron, Farragut practically insisted on staying in Mobile "to finish up the work we have so successfully begun." He even went so far as to enlist the support of Gen. Edward Canby, the Union army commander of the Mobile expedition. Welles grumbled in his diary that Farragut "expressed a decided aversion to taking command at Wilmington," but gave in, nevertheless.[39]

In *Combined Operations in the Civil War,* Rowena Reed suggests two reasons for Farragut's "decided aversion." First, he was loath to replace Admiral Lee, who knew far more about the tactical situation on the Cape

in the South Atlantic chasing the Confederate cruiser *Sumter* when the Union began its offensives on the Carolina coast. He arrived in New York two days after the fall of Port Royal and went to Washington, where he participated in planning the expedition against New Orleans. Although Farragut had overall command, Porter was given a mortar flotilla. After the city fell, he was promoted to acting rear admiral and given command of the Mississippi Squadron for operations against Vicksburg. During this campaign, his gunboats supported the up-and-coming General Grant, and the two developed a good working relationship. His role in the fall of Vicksburg and subsequent operations on the western rivers made his promotion permanent and led Welles to believe he was the best man, after Farragut, to lead the expedition against Fisher.[42]

Porter's rise had not been completely smooth. During the New Orleans campaign, Generals Butler and Godfrey Weitzel both had criticized as inconsequential Porter's mortar bombardment of Forts Jackson and St. Philip near the mouth of the Mississippi. The bombardment caused extensive internal damage to Fort Jackson but had no effect on reducing the works, and the action was a stalemate until Farragut finally decided to run past the forts.[43] As Butler later wrote in his memoirs, "The first day's bombardment set fire to the wooden barracks and officers' quarters, which burned all night. Porter ceased firing while the burning was going on, supposing that the fort would be destroyed. [But the fire] only cleared the fort of obstructions and obstacles."[44]

Although these remarks were essentially accurate, Porter appears to have directed his energies toward resenting Butler and Weitzel rather than learning from the experience, and this would affect his judgment during the first Fort Fisher expedition.

Porter was in Washington when Welles decided to give him the Wilmington assignment. On September 17, the day Lee got notice of his transfer, Porter was preparing to depart for Cairo, Illinois, to resume command of the Mississippi Squadron when he received a summons to meet Welles and Fox that night at Montgomery Blair's house. Welles opened the discussion by saying that after pushing "time and again" for an expedition against the Cape Fear without getting cooperation from the army, it finally appeared troops would be available, and asked Porter's opinion.

When Porter replied that he had never been to the Cape Fear and knew nothing of its defense system, Welles handed him a stack of reports from

Lee, Farragut, and others who had studied the situation. Glancing over the initial estimates of the force required, Porter said he would have to examine them more carefully before giving an opinion. Although he personally preferred keeping command of the Mississippi Squadron, he "had been treated kindly by the Department, and if [Welles] ordered him to go over Niagara Falls in an iron pot he should obey that order." Pleased with that answer, Welles told him to take the material home, study it, and report back with his conclusions.[45]

At home, Porter went over the charts of the Cape Fear area and maps of the forts, noted the Confederate armament, and calculated his own needs for attack. The next morning, he called on Welles and told him that if the navy provided the force he required, "I would promise to take the fort in three days." Heading the list was three hundred guns aboard ship, and all the heaviest frigates.

"Admiral Lee says, in his reports, that the heaviest frigates cannot approach the fort," Welles replied.

"Then these soundings are all wrong," Porter said, referring to those designated on the charts, "for the charts show that we can approach the fort within three-quarters of a mile, and that is near enough."

Satisfied, Welles asked how many men would be required, and Porter said about thirteen thousand with entrenching tools and about fifteen guns. He was willing to command the expedition, but it would be pointless without army cooperation.

"I think we can get the men," Welles replied. "I want you to go down with Mr. Fox to see General Grant."[46]

Fox and Porter went to City Point, where they discussed the operation with Grant, who seemed amicable. On September 22, Porter received orders to relinquish command of the Mississippi Squadron and relieve Admiral Lee as commander of the North Atlantic Blockading Squadron. He brought with him several officers from the Mississippi Squadron, among them Lt. Comdr. K. Randolph Breese, who would serve as chief of staff, and Lt. Comdr. Thomas O. Selfridge, Jr. Armed with Welles's assurance that he could have any ships he wanted, Porter had given the secretary a list for the expedition.[47] On the night of October 11, he arrived in Hampton Roads and presented his letter of appointment to Admiral Lee.

Porter's appearance was yet another blow to Lee, who, once again, was completely in the dark and still expecting Farragut. As Welles anticipated, the new appointment "cut Lee to the quick." As before, however, he accepted the situation, and gave Porter the transition memorandum he had prepared for Farragut. At 12:50 P.M. on October 12, Porter's pennant was hoisted aboard the flagship *Malvern*. Lee, meanwhile, boarded the Washington-bound steamer *Baltimore*. The expedition he had sought for so long was now in the hands of another.[48]

7

THE UNION PREPARES

THE PROJECTED DATE of the Fort Fisher operation, October 15, came and went with the fleet at anchor and the troops dug in around Richmond. Porter needed time to acquaint himself with his new responsibilities, and this, no doubt, was a factor in the postponement. Even without the problem of Wilmington, command of the North Atlantic Blockading Squadron was a large undertaking. The James River was the demarcation between Union forces, with the Army of the Potomac on the north bank and the Army of the James on the south bank, and was the primary means of communication and replenishment for both. Grant's immense supply depot and his troop transports were based at City Point, and the navy was responsible for their protection. Thus Porter's responsibility extended up the James to within a few miles of Richmond, where obstructions had been placed to guard against a sortie by the formidable ironclad squadron that defended the capital.[1]

Porter's own ships and crews presented another problem. After long, monotonous weeks on blockade duty, they used virtually any excuse to leave station and put in at Norfolk, where Porter found the yards "full of blockaders—I am kicking them out as fast as possible—half that came here want but little repairs, and I will promise them they don't get here again in a hurry. They don't do enough of their own repairs, and sigh for the joys of Norfolk as the Peri did for Paradise."[2]

In the sounds of northeastern North Carolina, the ironclad ram *Albemarle* had pushed back the Union blockaders, enabling the Confederates to recapture Plymouth. Now the *Albemarle* was docked at Plymouth, a constant threat, while she awaited completion of another ram to reinforce her. Before Porter could give his full attention to Fort Fisher, the *Albemarle* had to be destroyed and the sounds of North Carolina again secured.[3]

To expedite his many responsibilities, Porter reorganized the unarmored ships into four divisions, with a fifth division composed of the ironclads and monitors. The *Albemarle* problem was resolved on October 27, when the ever-daring Cushing sank the ironclad with a spar torpedo mounted on a steam launch. Four days later, Plymouth once more was in Union hands.[4]

Porter, meanwhile, had not neglected Fort Fisher. On October 15, he again had called on General Grant and told him he could have the fleet assembled in fifteen days, and with twelve thousand soldiers "the place could be taken."

"I cannot send them now," Grant replied, "but when your fleet are assembled I can get them here in 24 hours."[5]

Five days later, on October 20, Porter again inquired about the troops. Grant replied, "Whenever you are ready I can put the men on board the transports in 24 hours."

"Very well," Porter said, "you had better commence now, for I am ready."

The following day, however, Grant called on Porter to say that his position was such that he could not spare the men at that point. Porter said he would be willing to wait, but as time passed with no further action from Grant, he began to grow impatient.[6]

Grant's seeming indifference offended Porter, who felt that their former association during the Vicksburg campaign entitled him to a certain amount of special treatment.[7] He considered Grant entirely too lethargic, and for that he blamed Butler.

"[Grant] is not sufficiently interested in this business," Porter complained to Fox. "Your old Schoolmate *Butler* has charge of him, and he wants to get Richmond (which can not be done) without outside aid. Take the [Cape Fear] forts and Richmond will fall."[8]

Grant the general in chief, however, was in a far different position from Grant the commander of the western theater. His paramount responsibility now was to the Union armies closing in on the Confederacy from two directions, and he was not prepared to divert troops to besiege Fort Fisher.[9] Even if a North Carolina expedition were undertaken, the fort itself did not have a high priority, for as Grant bluntly stated, "The first object of the expedition . . . is to close the enemy port of Wilmington. . . . Should Fort Fisher and the point of land on which it is built fall into the hands of our troops, then it will be worth the attempt to capture Wilmington by a forced march and surprise." In other words, he would be satisfied with simply closing the port, and even that would not be allowed to interfere with the operations of the main armies. The actual capture of Fort Fisher and the city was secondary.[10]

An even greater reason for Grant's hesitation, albeit one interrelated with his concern about the diversion of troops, was the element of surprise. Although Porter pressed for at least twelve thousand troops, Grant intended that the expedition should actually use substantially fewer.[11] This meant they would have to attack the fort and overwhelm the garrison before the Confederates could muster an effective resistance. Initially, the plan seems to have been that the fleet assemble at Port Royal to give the impression of another expedition against Charleston. But for reasons never fully clear, the fleet instead gathered at Hampton Roads, and the massing of ships and naval firepower there was a dead giveaway.[12]

From the very beginning, there had been too much loose talk. As early as September 19, when the expedition was in its earliest stages of planning, Grant advised Fox of rumors from New York "that a formidable expedition was to be sent out from here against Wilmington." As if this Northern hearsay was not bad enough, Grant said, "I receive reports from scouts, showing much more is known about it in the south than is known in the north. Preparations are even being made which will lead to the evacuation of Richmond, if it becomes necessary to save Wilmington."[13] As Grant later commented, "the whole affair was so thoroughly advertised to the enemy and to the country that I kept putting off the expedition."[14]

One of the greatest problems, however, was the least obvious—a dreadful mismatching of commanders. As commander of the Army of the

James, Ben Butler, whom Porter despised, automatically had charge of the organization of ground forces.

Still known in the South as "Beast Butler" for his occupation of New Orleans, and later as one of the architects of Reconstruction, Benjamin Franklin Butler was born in Deerfield, New Hampshire, on what was then the frontier, on November 5, 1818. His father died in the West Indies when Ben was about five months old, and during the next nine years his widowed mother eked out a meager existence in New Hampshire. Finally, she accepted a position as a boardinghouse keeper in the mill town of Lowell, Massachusetts, which Butler henceforth would consider home.

Growing up, Butler was a bright, though often rebellious, student. After completing high school in Lowell, where Fox was one of his classmates, he enrolled in Waterville College. In his second year at Waterville, he applied for an appointment to West Point but was informed that all the appointments from his district already were filled. This left him with a lifelong resentment against West Pointers that may be partly responsible for his often unorthodox behavior as a general in the Union army. He read law and ultimately was admitted to the Massachusetts bar, where he gained notoriety as a sharp though often devious attorney, known to use every legal loophole in the interest of his client. Perhaps because of his own family's struggles, he also attained a reputation as a champion of the underdog.

Butler's scrappy legal style, both in Massachusetts and before the U.S. Supreme Court, kept his name in the papers, and his fame and fortune grew. He also was heavily involved in the reform movement in the Democratic Party. Although he had investments in mills, he fought for a shorter workday and for a secret ballot so that management could not supervise the voting of labor. His controversial career soon attracted the attention of the politicians in Washington, and when Lincoln's troop levy reached Massachusetts he was appointed brigadier general of the volunteers.

Butler's military career ebbed and flowed. After an early defeat at Big Bethel, he redeemed himself by his quick capture of the North Carolina sounds. This led to his appointment as military ruler of New Orleans, where his infamous "Woman Order," stating that any Southern woman who insulted or showed contempt for Union soldiers "shall be regarded and held liable to be treated as a woman of the town plying her avocation," brought a price on his head by the Confederate government, and his likeness was painted in Southern chamberpots.

MAJ. GEN. BENJAMIN F. BUTLER
Courtesy of the North Carolina Division of Archives and History

His business transactions brought accusations from both North and South of plunder and profiteering. One rumor claimed that he had looted family silver in New Orleans, and for the rest of his life he was called "Spoons Butler," among other epithets. True or not, complaints of shady deals brought his removal and reassignment to the Army of the James, where he was defeated in the Second Battle of Drewry's Bluff.[15]

Although Butler was detested in the army, Lincoln needed his political support throughout his first term, and to ensure his reelection to a second.

Admiral Porter later summed Butler up by writing, "The General was then a power in the land. . . . All men seemed afraid of Butler's political power: it was even potential with the President and Secretary of War, although, in justice to Mr. Secretary Welles, we must say, it had much less weight with him."[16]

In appearance, Butler was an almost amusing figure. He was short, fat, balding, and very visibly cross-eyed, and in uniform he looked more like a comic opera general than a bona fide military commander. Beneath the ridiculous exterior, however, he was brilliant, determined, and ruthless.

Porter was not happy over the prospect of coordinating the Fort Fisher operation with Butler because, even after two years, Butler's criticism of the naval bombardment of the New Orleans forts still rankled. He raised the matter with Grant as they strolled one day at City Point and saw Butler approaching.

"Please don't introduce me to Butler," Porter implored. "We had a little difficulty at New Orleans, and although I attach no importance to the matter, perhaps he does."

"Oh!" Grant replied, "You will find Butler quite willing to forget old feuds, and, as the troops who are to accompany you will be taken from his command, it will be necessary for you to communicate with him from time to time."[17]

Porter, of course, was lying, because the "little difficulty" was far more important to him than to Butler. For despite all of Butler's invective against Porter in later years, he seems to have thought very little of it at the time. In fact, as he subsequently told the congressional Joint Committee on the Conduct of the War, he appeared to believe the quarrel was primarily between Porter and Godfrey Weitzel, who also had disparaged the bombardment.[18]

Once the introductions were completed, however, Porter found Butler "very pleasant" and invited him to lunch aboard ship. Before long, they were socializing frequently, getting along reasonably well, and approaching the Fort Fisher project with shared enthusiasm.[19] Yet one cannot escape the impression that the admiral's decision to let bygones be bygones was less influenced by Butler's doubtful charm than by the general's boyhood association and lifelong friendship with Porter's boss, Assistant Secretary Fox. Whatever his public attitude, there is every indication that privately Porter felt nothing but contempt for Butler. Years later, Butler acknowledged this in his memoirs, commenting that while Porter disliked Weitzel, "me he hated as the devil hates holy water."[20]

From the beginning, Grant intended that General Weitzel should lead the actual expedition, and that Butler's involvement would be strictly administrative in his capacity as Weitzel's commanding officer, "a fact," Grant pointed out, "which General Butler understood."[21] His first conversation with Weitzel demonstrated how little Grant knew about the Cape Fear, for he told Weitzel, "This is to be another Mobile affair. The navy will run some of their vessels into Cape Fear river, and I would advise you to land your troops and take a position across the peninsula, and then Fort Fisher and these works will fall exactly as Fort Morgan did."

This was precisely the operation that the navy had already ruled out, because the water was too shallow at the bar. Nevertheless, on Grant's assumption, and equipped with maps, charts, and whatever other information could be acquired, Weitzel left at the end of September to reconnoiter Fort Fisher.[22] He joined the blockading squadron off New Inlet, where he met with Admiral Lee, who had not yet been relieved, and several officers who had been on blockade duty for about two years.

"I also found a number of North Carolinians who were on board our vessels there as pilots, and who said they knew every green pine tree between Wilmington and the mouth of Cape Fear river," Weitzel said. "Through a naval officer I had communication with the president of the Loyal Union League of Wilmington. I got such satisfactory and perfect information of the strength of the enemy's works that I was enabled to return at the end of three days."[23]

Immediately upon his return, the Army of the James was ordered into battle on the north bank of the river, and Weitzel was assigned to replace the wounded Gen. E. O. C. Ord in command of the XVIII Corps. Consequently, it was mid-October before he could report his findings to Grant. On the premise of a Mobile-type operation involving a run past the forts (for Weitzel apparently had learned little about the depth of the bars), he estimated Fort Fisher could be taken with six thousand men. Grant replied that the Confederate newspapers were already speculating on a move against Fort Fisher "and it was known all over the south." For that reason Grant planned to hold off on the expedition, but he told Weitzel to continue his preparations.[24]

About this time, Butler and several of his staff visited Porter on the

Malvern. Over lunch, he said, "Admiral, I have come to propose something to you, to take Fort Caswell." Then he went into detail. Fascinated by technological advances as well as just plain gadgetry, he proposed to send a ship loaded with gunpowder ashore under the sea face of the fort and blow it up. The blast was expected to stun the garrison to such a degree that the Union forces would have no trouble overrunning it.[25]

There were at least two incidents that made the idea seem feasible. In August a Confederate time bomb had blown up a Federal ordnance ship at City Point, setting off nearby ammunition dumps and destroying the surrounding buildings. Two months later, reports arrived from England that two magazines on the banks of the Thames between Erith and the Royal Arsenal in Woolwich had exploded, igniting two powder barges in the river. Although damage was minimal beyond the immediate area of the explosion, Butler was fascinated by the thought and soon extended the idea to Fort Fisher as well as Caswell.[26]

"It was supposed," Butler said a few months later, "that, possibly, by bringing within four hundred or five hundred yards of Fort Fisher a large mass of gunpowder, and exploding it simultaneously—for that was the essence of the affair, to have it all exploded at the same moment—the garrison would at least be so far paralyzed as to enable, by a prompt landing of men, a seizure of the fort."[27]

Porter was interested. In his memoirs, he admitted he "rather liked the notion" and believed it had a chance for success. His chief of staff, Lt. Comdr. Randolph Breese, was less enthusiastic.

"Admiral, you certainly don't believe in that idea of a powder-boat," Breese remarked after Butler and his staff had departed. "It has about as much chance of blowing up the fort as I have of flying!"

Porter replied, "And who knows whether a machine may not soon be perfected to enable us all to fly, as it only requires a forty-horse power in a cubic foot of space, and a propeller that will make such a vacuum that the air will run in and drive the thing along."

As Breese left he muttered, "All bosh!" Porter pretended he had not heard him, and passed the idea along to Fox. He also sent a requisition for powder to Capt. H. A. Wise, the navy's chief of ordnance, who responded, "Why don't you make a requisition for Niagara Falls and Mount Vesuvius? they will do the job for you." Porter was not amused.[28]

Welles was running out of patience. Winter came early to the North

Atlantic, and the storms off the North Carolina coast were particularly vicious. The headland at the end of Smith's Island was known as Cape Fear for very good reason, and if the army delayed much longer the fleet would be in peril when the attack finally came. As October drew to a close, those vessels that could enter the shallow waters of Beaufort Harbor were there, although the largest ships with the heaviest firepower remained in Hampton Roads.[29] Welles wrote Lincoln on October 28, stating once and for all that the depth of the water precluded a run past the Cape Fear forts to Wilmington, otherwise the navy would have repeated its performances of New Orleans, Mobile, and Port Royal. The only way to silence the forts and take the city was through a joint operation.

"I have, as you are aware, often pressed upon the War Department the importance of capturing Wilmington, and urged upon the military authorities the necessity of undertaking a joint operation against the defences of Cape Fear River," Welles wrote. However, he noted, until recently, the War Department had been unable to comply.

> One hundred and fifty vessels-of-war now form the North Atlantic squadron. . . . Every other squadron has been depleted and vessels detached from other duty to strengthen this expedition. The vessels are concentrated at Hampton Roads and Beaufort, where they remain—an immense force lying idle, awaiting the movements of the Army. The detention of so many vessels from blockade and cruising duty is a most serious injury to the public service; and if the expedition cannot go forward for want of troops, I desire to be notified, so that the ships may be relieved and dispersed for other service.

After going over the problems the fleet would face as winter approached, Welles concluded by telling Lincoln: "Of the obstacles which delay or prevent military cooperation at once I cannot judge; but the delay is becoming exceedingly embarrassing to this Department, and the importance of having the military authorities impressed with the necessity of speedy action has prompted this communication to you."[30]

In his 1883 history of the Atlantic Coast operations, Rear Adm. Daniel Ammen (who commanded the USS *Mohican* during the attacks on Fort Fisher) quoted from Welles's letter, adding his own cryptic remark, "The tone . . . indicates potential influences, either to further delay the expedition or cause its abandonment."[31]

Butler, meanwhile, was busy with plans for the powder boat. On November 1, however, he was ordered to New York to command troops maintaining order in the city during the heated presidential election period. During his two-week absence, army and navy ordnance experts examined the project.[32]

The most thorough study was conducted by Gen. Richard Delafield, chief of engineers, who pointed out that a ship drawing ten feet of water could approach Fort Caswell no closer than 450 yards, and even to reach that distance would require a course that would expose her directly to the Confederate batteries. Thus the ship would probably be blown to pieces before it even got into position. Fort Fisher presented an even greater problem, because a ship could not approach those works nearer than 950 yards.

Even if the ship could close in on the works, Delafield contended, it was physically impossible to create enough of a blast to achieve the desired results. Thus, he concluded, "the explosion of a vessel-load of gunpowder at the nearest point it can approach Fort Caswell or Fort Fisher can produce no useful result towards the reduction of those works, and that no such vessels as are proposed to be so loaded can be navigated and placed at the nearest points to these forts, provided the fort is garrisoned and its guns are served with hollow projectiles and hot shot."[33] Delafield's view was shared by Lt. Comdr. W. N. Jeffers, in charge of the Explosive Department at Washington Navy Yard.[34]

A more optimistic opinion was submitted by Maj. J. G. Benton of the Ordnance Department, who was somehow under the preposterous impression that the explosion would occur only a hundred yards from the forts. If two hundred tons of powder were exploded at that distance, he wrote, "I think the work will be seriously damaged by the explosion of its principal magazines, and the traverses and bomb-proofs may be shattered or overturned." He qualified this conclusion, however, by questioning whether the ship could approach that close, and also pointed out that his opinion was entirely theoretical. "Such as it is, you are welcome to it," he remarked.[35]

The army command, however, leaned toward the thorough and skeptical Delafield. General Grant observed: "Whether the report will be sufficient even to wake up the garrison in the fort, if they happen to be asleep at the time of the explosion, I do not know. . . . However, they can use an old boat which is not of much value, and we have plenty of damaged powder which is unserviceable for any other purpose, so that the experiment will not cost much at any rate."[36]

At the Navy Department, Welles likewise expressed "no faith in General Butler's scheme."[37]

To those, Lincoln added, "We might as well explode the notion with powder as with anything else."[38]

But Fox and Porter remained excited about it. So while the army ultimately furnished more than half the powder for the project, it was essentially the navy's creature.[39]

On the night of November 23, Fox convened a meeting of ordnance officers, including Commander Jeffers and Major Benton, at Captain Wise's home. Fox told the group:

> If the explosion would deprive the people of the forts of all power to resist for a period of two to three hours, ample time would thereby be afforded for the fleet to pass. The navy should therefore be ready to move forward immediately, using light-draught vessels to lift torpedoes, &c.
>
> The principal object in view was to silence and destroy or occupy the forts, and thus get command of the mouth of the river, and put an end to all blockade-running. This would place Wilmington in the same condition as Mobile. The possession of Federal Point would give us the key to the whole position.

The ensuing discussion centered less on the pros and cons of the operation than on how it would be carried out. The group unanimously decided to explode three hundred tons of gunpowder "in a vessel as near the earthworks on Federal Point as it might be possible to do." The designation of Federal (or Confederate) Point established that the target was not Fort Caswell but Fort Fisher.[40]

Three days later, Fox, accompanied by Wise and several other ordnance officers from the meeting, went to Hampton Roads to consult with Porter and Butler. Among the papers carried for Porter's study were the reports of Delafield, Benton, and Jeffers and a memorandum of the meeting at Wise's house.[41]

It now remained to select the ship that would be sacrificed, preferably a worn-out vessel of no further value. Ideally, she also would be a former merchant steamer that could pass for a blockade-runner, so that she could be run ashore with her load of powder without attracting attention. The choice was the USS *Louisiana,* a 295-ton, iron-hulled screw steamer that, before the war, had been employed in the Atchafalaya cotton trade. Taken into Federal service a few days after First Manassas, she was commissioned during the summer of 1861.

The *Louisiana* first served as a support ship in the vicinity of Fortress Monroe, after which she was assigned to support land-sea operations in the North Carolina sounds and along the interior rivers.[42] One hundred fifty feet long with a twenty-two-foot beam, and drawing between eight and eight and a half feet of water, she was one of the many ordinary steamers that proved so essential to naval operations during the war. "Insignificant as the 'Louisiana' was in appearance she nevertheless did honor to the service, and her final sacrifice at Fort Fisher was only in keeping with her other good deeds performed during the rebellion," her acting carpenter's mate, Stephen F. Blanding, later wrote.[43]

The *Louisiana* was on patrol duty in the Pamlico River when she was designated as Butler's floating bomb. She proceeded to Baltimore, where her crew was distributed among other steamers. Then she was taken to Norfolk and prepared for her final voyage.[44]

8

"GOODBYE WILMINGTON!"

As Grant anticipated, the Confederates had guessed the Federal plans. As early as October 7, 1864, the *Richmond Dispatch* reported that "the enemy seem to be making preparations to make a determined attack on Wilmington. They appear to be collecting a fleet for that purpose, as a number of vessels have been added to those heretofore lying in and about the port."[1]

Still, the blockade trade continued apace. The Confederate government's efforts to control speculation and give priority to the military were at best half-hearted, and the soldiers received a short shrift when their needs conflicted with the profit margin. On October 28, as the autumn chill began to set in, Jones at the War Department wrote in his diary: "Large amounts of cloth from Europe for the army have recently arrived at Wilmington . . . but the speculators occupy so much space in the [railroad] cars, that transportation cannot be had for it. The poor soldiers are likely to suffer in consequence of this neglect of duty on the part of the government."[2]

A few days later he was more optimistic, noting: "The steamers have brought into Wilmington immense amounts of quartermaster stores, and

perhaps our armies are the best clad in the world. If the spirit of speculation be laid, and all the men and resources of the country be devoted to
defense (as seems now to be the intention), the United States could never
find men and material sufficient for our subjugation. We could maintain
the war for an indefinite period, unless, indeed, fatal dissensions should
spring up among ourselves."³

Jones's fears were well founded. In Washington, all resources that could
be spared from other operations were being diverted to the expedition
against Wilmington, while in the South the dissensions were already coming into play. One of the most serious rifts concerned General Whiting,
who had been feuding almost continuously with civil and naval authorities in Wilmington since his return in 1862. City officials accused him of
playing the dictator, and he was constantly quarreling with the navy over
the management of the blockade trade, which the navy considered its
exclusive domain. In time, he managed to earn the enmity of the powerful Governor Vance.

Anxious to give Whiting a breather as well as a chance for some action,
General Beauregard, who had assumed command of Department of
North Carolina in April 1864, arranged for him to get a field command in
Virginia. There, at Drewry's Bluff in May 1864, his troops became disori-
ented in a heavy fog and failed to attack on schedule, allowing Butler to
withdraw in good order and with little damage. Unfortunately for Whiting, President Davis was visiting the front at the time, witnessed the affair,
and was willing to believe unfounded rumors that the general had been
drunk. Whiting's status was further diminished because he was a protégé
of Beauregard, whom the president despised.⁴

Thus Whiting returned to Wilmington under a cloud and resumed his
old feuds. One point of contention with the navy was the basing of the
commerce raiders *Tallahassee* and *Chickamauga* in Wilmington. Both
were fast screw steamers converted from blockade-runners—the *Chickamauga* formerly being the *Edith,* and the *Tallahassee* transformed from the
Atalanta—and both were successful. The *Tallahassee* in particular had captured thirty-one Union ships, destroying twenty-six and bonding five, in
a single twenty-day cruise between Wilmington and Halifax. Slipping
back into Wilmington on the night of August 25, she was spotted and a
blockader opened fire. After what one Union seaman called "a smart
fight," the *Tallahassee* outran the blockader, only to find the USS *Britan-

nia lying in her path. More shots were exchanged, one hitting the *Britannia* without any serious effect. Finally, the *Tallahassee* broke through and arrived in Wilmington on the twenty-sixth.[5]

Successful and exciting as such cruises were, Whiting saw them as a detriment to the whole purpose of keeping Wilmington open. They burned smokeless anthracite coal that was essential for the blockade-runners, and coal stores taken on by commerce raiders depleted the supply. Gen. Robert E. Lee, whose patience was terribly tried by Whiting's problems, backed him in this instance, pointing out that the blockade-runners were becoming increasingly important for the provisioning of the army. The War and Navy Departments, perhaps carried away with the notion of striking a blow on the high seas, were equally adamant that the raiders were necessary for the war effort.[6]

By late September, Governor Vance had had enough of Whiting and asked General Lee for his removal. Lee sympathized with Vance but considered Whiting the most capable man for the assignment in Wilmington, and President Davis's political position was so precarious that he had no choice but to defer to Lee. Nevertheless, Davis could still humiliate Whiting as well as whip the arrogant Beauregard into line by naming a new commander for the Department of North Carolina. That would be Gen. Braxton Bragg, a man known to the army command as a loser who was detested by his troops. Whiting would continue as commander of the District of the Cape Fear under Bragg.

A native of Warrenton, North Carolina, Braxton Bragg was an 1837 graduate of West Point who had fought the Seminoles in Florida and served with distinction in the Mexican War, where he helped defend Fort Brown during the siege. Despite a generally good record, however, he was ambitious and cantankerous, a perfectionist who insisted on absolute obedience from those who served under him but resented intrusion by his superiors. In some ways a brilliant officer, he was also a chronic worrier, and his naturally frail health was aggravated by severe migraine headaches and hypochondria. Often, when on the edge of success, he was beset by bouts of illness, indecision, and self-doubt, a volatile combination that would cost the Confederacy dearly.[7]

Following the Mexican War, Bragg was posted to the Indian frontier. He detested the duty and spent the better part of two years trying to get another assignment. Despite his efforts, then-Secretary of War Jefferson

Davis was adamant that he remain on the frontier, and on December 31, 1855, Bragg submitted his resignation. The letter was forwarded to Secretary Davis, who accepted it without comment.[8]

Financially secure through his marriage, Bragg became a planter in Louisiana. When that state seceded, he joined the Confederate service as a brigadier general on March 7, 1861. Initially things went well. Named commander of the Army of the Tennessee in 1862, he invaded Kentucky, frustrating Union efforts to stop him. This, however, was the high point of a career which, from then on, was at best erratic and at worst dismal. Eventually forced out of Kentucky, he was defeated at Perryville and retreated back into Tennessee, where he fought a bloody but inconclusive battle at Murfreesboro. On the defensive now, he lost Chattanooga, then won at Chickamauga. But he failed to follow up on that victory and was pushed back into Georgia by Union forces under General Grant, and appears to have suffered a nervous breakdown. Relieved at his own request, Bragg went to Richmond to serve as military adviser to Davis.[9]

With his record, Bragg's position on Davis's staff—indeed his ability to keep any sort of position in the army—has given him the image of a presidential pet. Yet the relationship was more complicated than simple favoritism. Bragg had developed a hatred for Davis during the frontier dispute that prompted his resignation from the U.S. Army. The president, likewise, did not care for Bragg and was fully aware that, however useful he once might have been, he no longer was a competent field officer. The most that could be said was that Bragg was still an excellent administrator and a reasonably good desk tactician who could analyze a problem and make the proper recommendations. Besides, as the Confederate military and political situation deteriorated, Davis found himself opposed and undermined from all sides. He needed someone he could trust implicitly, and for all his faults, Bragg was candid and deferential to Davis's office. He had no business commanding an army, but at this juncture he was the best the beleaguered president could do.[10]

If Bragg was the best Davis could do, it was not good enough for a Confederate public that was rapidly losing confidence in its government. Bragg himself had many enemies in the army, in Congress, and among the Richmond citizenry. With his appointment, many in and out of the army felt Wilmington's fall was more or less assured.[11] Indeed, the *Richmond Examiner*'s editors remarked, probably with more foresight than they realized at the time, "Bragg has been sent to Wilmington. Goodbye Wilmington!"[12]

The Wilmington assignment was expected to be temporary. Bragg retained his responsibilities as Davis's military adviser, and was instructed to leave his staff in charge of his Richmond office. Jones of the War Department believed he was sent to Wilmington as a breather from his enemies because "the combination against him [in Richmond] was too strong."[13]

At Fort Fisher, Colonel Lamb described the news of Bragg's appointment as "a bitter disappointment to my command who felt that no one was so capable of defending the Cape Fear as the brilliant officer [Whiting] who had given so much of his time and ability for its defense."[14] The timing could not have been worse, for the day Bragg assumed command of the Department of North Carolina, October 24, Lamb also noted ominously in his diary, "Information received which leads to the belief that Wilmington is to be attacked by the enemy. Commodore Porter to command the fleet which is said to include the Armored Ships, Ironsides & Dictator [a supermonitor]."[15]

The following day he received a warning that when the attack came, the garrison of Fort Fisher would mutiny, "spike guns, cut telegraph wires & pilot enemy to the city." He entered the information in his diary with the comment, "Don't believe a word of it."[16]

More news arrived from Whiting on October 26, but Lamb did not specify what it contained. Although he never doubted his men, he was uncertain of the future and began preparing himself and his family against any eventualities. He paid his bills and, looking to his financial security, sold a bill of £330 on a Nassau firm for $36,666.50 Confederate, bought some tax-free 6 percent bonds for Daisy, and sent Charleston financiers John Fraser and Co. $8,419.50 Confederate for ten bales of cotton to be run through the blockade from Charleston to Nassau.[17]

Looking to the fort's security as well as his own, Lamb began construction of a nine-foot palisade of sharpened logs, set about fifty feet in front of the land face and behind the minefield. Stretching from river to sea, it was broken only on the river side of Shepperd's Battery, where the Wilmington Road crossed a wooden bridge over a morass and entered the fort. During attack, the gap in the palisade would be closed with sandbags and covered by field artillery. Otherwise, this work was arranged and pierced so that approaching infantrymen would be caught in a cross fire of musketry.

Should enemy troops succeed in breaching the palisade, they would have to take the traverses one by one. Finally, on the night of October 26, he called a meeting of all commissioned officers, for reasons not specified but presumably to discuss the impending attack.[18]

Lamb was also completing the last major construction project at Fort Fisher. Located at the very end of Confederate Point and almost lapped by the waters of New Inlet, it was based on a plan submitted by one of his engineers, Reddin Pittman. Built apart from the fort, yet included in its overall organization, the new work was an ellipse with four heavy guns, two facing the inlet and two covering the land approach. Although Pittman wanted to call it Augusta Battery, after his girlfriend, General Whiting named it Battery Buchanan in honor of Adm. Franklin Buchanan, defender of Mobile. Appropriately, it was to be garrisoned by a naval detachment commanded by Lt. William L. Bradford, who had been executive officer on the CSS *Tennessee,* Buchanan's flagship at Mobile. A wharf for large steamers was located nearby, approximately at the site of the modern ferry landing.

According to Lamb, Battery Buchanan "for its purpose was perfect in design . . . a citadel to which an overpowered garrison might retreat and with proper transportation be carried off at night, and to which reinforcements could be safely sent under cover of darkness."[19] Midshipman

BATTERY BUCHANAN
Courtesy of the North Carolina Division of Archives and History

William R. Mayo, assigned to the battery, agreed, commenting, "It was built somewhat after the fashion of the Mound Battery of Fort Fisher, though a more complete and formidable work."[20]

Fort Fisher now was about as complete as it ever would be. Excluding Battery Buchanan, the land face was 2,046 feet long, and the sea face 5,965 feet. Still, Lamb was not satisfied, for he made numerous notes to himself at the end of his diary concerning the mounting of guns, work on embrasures and traverses, and additions needed to the magazines.[21]

The naval troops took charge of Battery Buchanan on November 5, and almost immediately Lamb had trouble with their commander. Lieutenant Bradford, who was out of his element to begin with, wanted more quarters for his sailors and did not think the battery was capable of fighting. To that, Lamb remarked, "It is stronger & more heavily armed than F. Fisher was when I took command." The quarrel was short-lived, however, for on November 8, Lt. Robert T. Chapman arrived to relieve Bradford. Lamb appeared pleased with Chapman, who had served with Raphael Semmes on the *Sumter*. As Daisy was visiting friends in Cumberland, Lamb invited the young naval officer to spend his first night in The Cottage.[22] His confidence was misplaced, for while Bradford may have been a complainer, Chapman would prove incompetent.

The day after Chapman's arrival, Governor Vance came to inspect the post, accompanied by Generals Bragg and Whiting. There was no mention of the governor's feud with Whiting, and Vance was pleased with Fort Fisher. Lamb escorted the party across the inlets to inspect Forts Caswell, Campbell, and Holmes. Although Fort Holmes, on Smith Island, was strong, Lamb was dubious about Campbell, and remarked in his diary, "Consider Caswell in a bad fix."[23]

Although Lamb's family returned from Cumberland, November was a trying month. He already had lost his daughter, Sallie, to fever, and now one of his sons, Richard, was seriously ill.[24] Aggravating his problems, on November 10 he received a telegram from General Hebert stating, "Fleet off western bar, don't know yet what it means."[25] Three days later, Lamb wrote in his diary: "Genl Hebert says his dispatch of 10th should have read 'Firing in fleet &c' It might have been a serious mistake. Dear little Dick continues very sick."[26]

On November 24 he superintended the execution of deserters Vincent Allen and Dempsey Watts. They were two of three deserters ultimately shot at Fort Fisher, and Lamb considered the executions "among the saddest events which occurred previous to the battles. . . . All three shot at Fort Fisher had been farmers, and were married, and doubtless the condition of their families at home had much to do with their crime. They had not deserted from my command but when captured their companies were stationed at Fort Fisher, and it was my painful duty to see the sentences of the courtmartial enforced."[27] After Allen and Watts were shot, Daisy Lamb gave a gold bracelet to be sold on behalf of their widows. Lamb himself contributed $600 Confederate.[28]

In Virginia, Butler and Porter continued their preparations. For the last two months the armada had been assembling in Hampton Roads, drawing every ship that could be spared from all the squadrons on the Atlantic and the Gulf. "The great ironclad *New Ironsides,* the monitors, the frigates and the sloops-of-war, and many gunboats, strangers hitherto to those waters, were in the roadstead," Acting Master Francis Sands of the *Gettysburg* wrote. The warships were taking on ordnance for the impending operation. Nearby were anchored the transports designated to carry the troops.[29]

Secrecy was impossible. Acting Master's Mate William Read of the frigate *Wabash* wrote his parents, "We will probably go to Wilmington in the fight which will come off soon I hope."[30] On the USS *Powhatan,* a side-wheel frigate and division flagship, eighteen-year-old Ensign Robley Evans, a native Virginian, received a letter from his brother, a Confederate captain on General Lee's staff. Brought through the lines under a flag of truce, it stated, "We will give you a warm reception at Fort Fisher when you get there!" Evans showed the letter to his commanding officer, Commodore James Schenck, who immediately sent him to Porter. The admiral, Evans noted, "was very indignant when he had read it."[31]

Yet there were leaks even on Porter's staff. His aide, Ensign Grattan, wrote to his parents on December 1:

> I will give you a peice [*sic*] of information, which is *confidential* and [must] not go out of our family on any account whatever.
>
> General Grant is ready with his men and we will attack *Wilmington* in 5 days from now. Everything is ready and working smoothly. The attack will be a surprise. . . .
>
> Keep your eyes open for newspaper accounts, and I wish you would keep every paper. Get Frank Leslies [*Illustrated News*] and Harpers Weekly

every week and keep them home. I will pay for them. I am anxious to keep full accounts of this fight, which will be the grandest naval fight of the world either in ancient or modern history. If I come out all right I shall feel proud to say I participated in the splendid engagement. if [*sic*] I fall, it may be all for the best.[32]

In late November, as Porter waited for the army to complete its preparations, he took the *Malvern* up the James to Dutch Gap to leave orders with the ships that would remain behind in his absence. Dutch Gap was an unofficial demilitarized zone where the belligerents exchanged prisoners and conducted various transactions—legitimate and otherwise. "I never saw so many hang-dog-looking rascals congregated together in one place," Porter noted. "The Confederates doubtless had spies there all the time among the adventurers who always follow in the wake of a great army."[33]

While Porter was in Dutch Gap, Butler arrived in the *Greyhound,* his government-chartered yacht, to advise him that Fox was in Hampton Roads, waiting to see him "without delay." Because the *Greyhound* was faster than the *Malvern,* Butler offered to carry him back. Among the passengers was Maj. Gen. Robert C. Schenk of the House Committee on Military Affairs, with whom Butler was discussing what he considered to be necessary reorganizations in the army. There were also the *Greyhound's* captain, pilot, engineer, firemen, stokers, deckhands, cook, and steward.

Porter was alarmed to find that, except for Butler's personal sword, there were no weapons on board, even though the *Greyhound* was traveling near a war zone with two generals and an admiral. He was especially uneasy after he wandered into the main saloon and "found half a dozen of those cut-throat-looking fellows, such as haunted Dutch Gap, scattered through the apartment."

"What are you doing here?" he demanded. "Does the *Greyhound* carry first class passengers?"

"We are just lookin' round to see how you fellers live," one of the men answered. "We ain't a doin' no harm."

Accepting the reply nonchalantly, Porter loitered for a few minutes, then wandered out and went straight to Butler.

"General," he began, "I don't particularly care to be captured just now, as I have important business on hand, and I don't suppose you do either; but you have a cargo of the worst-looking wretches on board this vessel that I ever laid eyes on; hadn't you better look after them before they do any harm?"

Butler agreed and put in at Bermuda Hundred, where the suspects were placed under guard and removed from the yacht. After a thorough search for stowaways, the *Greyhound* continued downriver.

Six miles below Bermuda Hundred, however, the yacht was rocked by an explosion and smoke poured out of the engine room. The steam pipes shrieked as the engineer stopped the yacht and opened the safety valve.

"What's that?" Butler demanded.

"Torpedo!" Porter replied. "I know the sound."

The entire midship section of the *Greyhound* was now in flames, and the crew jumped overboard. Porter and the steward managed to launch the general's gig, and some of the crew swam over to man it. Porter and the generals climbed in, followed by Butler's aide, who had stayed behind to rescue the general's papers and suffered burns on one hand.

The *Greyhound* was sinking fast. The captain worked his way aft, lowered the colors, and climbed out onto the rudder stock, where he was rescued by the gig. As the yacht sank, they heard the screams of Butler's horses burning in their stalls below decks. An army transport pulled alongside and offered to take them off, but Porter, having had enough of army transport for one day, opted instead for a navy tug.

Although the cause of the explosion was never determined, Porter theorized that one of the rough characters in the saloon had managed to plant a small incendiary bomb in the coal scuttles before being put off at Bermuda Hundred. Later, an unsuspecting stoker probably heaved the bomb with a shovelful of coal into the firebox, where it exploded.[34] He may have been right, for the explosion blew open the firebox door, scattering burning coals throughout the fireroom.[35] Butler later received at least two letters from friends in Massachusetts who had learned that a plan to sabotage the *Greyhound* had been rumored in Halifax and Liverpool for weeks. Whatever the cause, Porter "resolved to keep clear of army steamers in the future."[36]

Shaken but undeterred, Butler continued to plan. But he became more cautious—delaying, he said, to reduce cost in men and equipment. Now, however, it was General Grant who was running out of patience. The military situation had changed to favor a move against Wilmington. The reason was that Bragg had stripped the garrison at Fort Fisher of ten companies that were sent south to oppose Gen. William T. Sherman's march through Georgia. Correctly surmising that upon reaching Savannah Sherman would turn north through the heart of the Confederate seaboard, reserves from five Southern states were moving to meet the Union juggernaut. In the meantime, Fisher was substantially weakened.[37]

Grant's worries were twofold. First, Southern newspapers reported that Bragg had eight thousand troops to meet Sherman. If Savannah fell before the Cape Fear was closed, further Confederate resistance in Georgia would be pointless and large numbers of troops would be released to defend Fort Fisher.[38] Second, winter was approaching, and like Welles, he worried about the weather. Accordingly, on November 30 he notified Butler to get his troops under way before either the weather or returning Confederates could interfere.[39]

As the sixty-five hundred Union soldiers sailed down the James for their rendezvous with the navy at Hampton Roads, Butler stopped off at City Point. There he informed General Grant that as commander of the Army of the James, and therefore Weitzel's superior, he intended to accompany the expedition. Among his reasons was the bad blood between Porter and Weitzel over the New Orleans forts. Also, while he considered Weitzel "a very able general," he was only twenty-nine and needed the supervision of an older person, specifically himself. "I am anxious to see this powder experiment go on and succeed for it is a very grave one," he told Grant, "and I think I had better go with the expedition to take responsibility off General Weitzel."[40]

Butler's decision surprised Grant, who had never contemplated that he might accompany the expedition. Normally, a commanding general stayed with the main body of troops under his command, and the Fort Fisher expeditionary force was but a small fraction of the Army of the James. Aside from that, Grant had very little confidence in Butler's military abilities. Nevertheless, Butler had a right to accompany his troops, and the only option was to entirely relieve him from command. Therefore Grant assented, presuming that Weitzel would still lead the landing force. Perhaps with a thought of keeping an eye on Butler, he ordered his own aide-de-camp, Col. Cyrus B. Comstock, to go as well.[41]

The soldiers were now prepared to depart for Fort Fisher. Still, Butler dragged his heels, determined not to sail until his powder boat was ready.[42] Finally, on December 4, an exasperated Grant notified him, "I feel great anxiety to see the Wilmington expedition off, both on account of the present fine weather, which we can expect no great continuance of, and because Sherman may now be expected to strike the sea coast any day, leaving Bragg free to return. I think it advisable for you to notify Admiral Porter and get off without any delay with or without your powder boat."[43]

That same day, however, the *Louisiana* was ready. Her appearance was substantially altered. Her guns and masts had been removed, and a false deckhouse was constructed from her funnel almost to the bow. Her sides were built up with painted canvas over frame, and a false funnel, forward of the real one, had been fabricated from hoops and canvas. Finally, the entire ship was painted white. "Thus," one near-contemporary account stated, "when turned over by the navy-yard authorities to the ordnance officers, she was as fair an imitation of a blockade-runner as could be desired, and one not easily detected at night."[44]

Once the conversion was completed, she had been taken to the ordnance depot at Craney Island, where Maj. Thomas J. Rodman and Commander Jeffers supervised loading the tons of powder that would transform the ship into a floating bomb. Because the purpose was to produce a lateral blast against the earthworks of the fort, it was decided to keep as much of the powder as possible above the waterline. This would make her top-heavy, so it was decided to load 185 tons at Craney Island and wait until she reached Beaufort before loading the balance; ultimately she would be packed with 215 tons of explosives. In the initial loading, 100 tons was placed on the berth deck and 85 tons against the bulkhead of the deckhouse. To guard against failure of the ignition system, two separate systems were installed, one consisting of three clockwork detonators and the other of six slow matches. Both systems connected to Gomez fuse trains that were supposed to be laid in a serpentine pattern throughout the ship.[45]

The crew of the *Louisiana* was selected from a group that responded to a private circular from Admiral Porter, calling for volunteers "for a most hazardous enterprise which offers the alternatives of death, capture, glory, and promotion."[46] The commanding officer was Comdr. Alexander C. Rhind of the *Agawam,* who was offered the position because his own ship was laid up for repairs and not expected to be ready in time for the battle.

Although not as famous as Cushing, Rhind was equally bold. Already he had received the formal thanks of the Navy Department for a daring

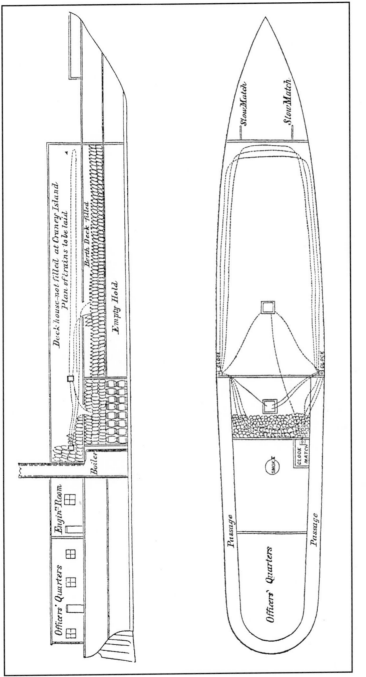

DIAGRAMS OF THE USS *LOUISIANA*, SHOWING POWDER STORAGE AND FUSE TRAIN

Reprinted from *Report of the Joint Committee on the Conduct of the War*

landing at Dawho, South Carolina, where his men drove the Confederates from the defenses and disabled the guns. He had also commanded the ill-fated ironclad *Keokuk* in her fatal fight off Charleston, where she had been struck at the rate of three times a minute by the concentrated fire of Forts Sumter and Moultrie. Nevertheless, Rhind bluntly told Porter that he had "a very poor opinion of the plan" but accepted it because the Navy Department considered the powder boat necessary for the attack.[47]

Rhind himself selected the remainder of the ship's company. Second in command was Flag Lt. Samuel W. Preston, one of Admiral Porter's aides, who had previously served Admirals Du Pont and Dahlgren in a similar capacity. A Canadian by birth, Preston grew up in Illinois and was appointed to Annapolis, where he graduated first in his class. Du Pont called him "the most precocious intellect I have yet met with in life—it made him almost a miracle at his age."[48] Preston no doubt felt a personal sense of mission against Fort Fisher, for he had been among those captured in the abortive attempt to seize Fort Sumter on September 8, 1863. He spent a year in a prison camp in South Carolina before being exchanged.[49]

In filling out the *Louisiana's* officers, Rhind selected Second Assistant Engineer Anthony T. E. Mullin of *Agawam*. The petty officers and ratings were all volunteers from the *Agawam*. Visiting the powder boat as she was being readied for sea, Porter was pleased with the crew's enthusiasm.[50] The admiral's ego was riding high; he was convinced the mission would succeed.

9

THE LAST VOYAGE OF
THE LOUISIANA

BY SATURDAY, DECEMBER 3, the weather had closed in. The air was almost continuously cold and damp, and a haze hung over the drab, gray Atlantic. Colonel Lamb conducted target practice with the Armstrong rifle against wrecks along the shore. The 150-pound steel shells were propelled by thirty pounds of powder. The first struck the rear funnel of the abandoned blockade-runner *Condor,* and the second, her forward funnel. A third shell struck the wreck of a blockader.

That night the blockade-runner *Emma Henry* started out but turned back when she ran into several Union ships on the bar. "We shelled the bar furiously for a short time but did not effect anything as far as we could see," Lamb wrote.[1]

The next morning Lamb came down with chills, and by the end of the day he was in bed with a high fever. Though well enough to briefly visit the fort the next day, he spent most of the time at home listening to Daisy read to him.

Early on the morning of December 7, the inbound blockade-runner *Stormy Petrel* grounded, and at about 7 A.M. the Union ships opened fire, overshooting the *Stormy Petrel* and sending several shells into Fort Fisher.

Lamb hurried back and took charge, and within two hours the big guns of the fort had forced the blockaders to cease fire and put back to sea. Attempts to salvage the cargo were thwarted by a gale, and the ship broke up, a complete loss. The effort sent Lamb back to bed with a relapse. He was unable to resume command until December 12.[2]

Admiral Porter, however, was optimistic. The day the *Louisiana* was ready, a member of his staff visited General Weitzel's camp and reported that the troops for the Fort Fisher expedition were being told off and that the transports were assembling at Dutch Gap. The soldiers believed the explosion of the *Louisiana* would flatten the fort, allowing them to occupy the point and close New Inlet with little trouble.

"Breese," Porter told his chief of staff, "I hope you now believe in the powder-boat. Issue an order for all the vessels to be ready to sail at noon to-morrow, and have two steamers on hand to tow the powder-boat."[3]

The ships did not sail at noon the following day, nor in the days immediately after, although the transports began loading. The troops were on their ships the night of December 8, when the weather turned bitterly cold. The soldiers in steerage were packed close enough to keep warm, but those above suffered. The cold continued into the next day. Chaplain Henry M. Turner of the First United States Colored Regiment, one of the few black officers in the army, noted that his ship was unheated. "Everybody complains," he wrote in his journal. "Some of the soldiers are frostbitten. We have all suffered severely today." The transports were so crowded "we can hardly find room to turn around." By December 11, morale among the troops was low. "I never felt more like resigning," Turner commented.[4]

Finally, on December 13, the expedition was ready. The transports departed before daylight, moving up Chesapeake Bay and into the Potomac. Butler knew that Confederate scouts at the mouth of the Potomac kept an eye on troopships, and he wanted them to believe they were bound toward Washington.[5]

At daybreak the *Malvern* fired a gun and hoisted the signal, "Prepare to get under way." Then, at 8 A.M., the ironclads and twenty-five of the smaller warships started for the Atlantic. The *New Ironsides* and the twin-turret supermonitor *Monadnock* steamed out under their own power. The smaller, single-turret monitors left harbor under steam, but nearing Cape Henry they were taken in tow. The frigates and sloops of war sailed two

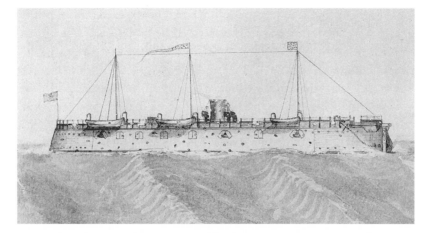

THE USS *NEW IRONSIDES* WAS SKETCHED AS SHE APPEARED OFF CHARLESTON, SOUTH CAROLINA, AFTER SEVERAL ENGAGEMENTS IN 1863. THIS VIEW SHOWS DETAILS OF THE SUPER-IRONCLAD, WHICH APPEARS REMARKABLY MODERN FOR HER ERA.
Courtesy U.S. Naval Historical Center

hours after the ironclads. By noon the entire fleet was under way except the *Malvern*. At 5 P.M., Porter ordered the flagship to sea. His wife, who had been staying on board with him, was transferred to a Washington-bound steamer, and as the *Malvern* moved out she waved goodbye with her handkerchief.[6]

The organization of the fleet was: commander in chief, Rear Adm. David D. Porter in *Malvern;* First Division, Commodore Henry K. Thatcher in *Colorado;* Second Division, Commodore Joseph Lanman in *Minnesota;* Third Division, Commodore James Findlay Schenck in *Powhatan;* Fourth Division, Commodore S. W. Gordon in *Susquehanna;* and Ironclad Division, Commodore William Radford in *New Ironsides.* In addition to responsibilities for his respective division, each commodore also served as commanding officer of his own flagship.

Altogether the squadron, at the time of the first attack on Fort Fisher, mounted 619 guns, ranging from ten giant 15-inchers to dozens of 12-pounders and howitzers. Total broadside weight of starboard and port was over twenty-two tons.[7]

The officers and crews, however, left much to be desired. Most of the officers were volunteers, and while some were very competent, others had secured their commissions through political influence and were, in the words of one career officer, "inferior in every way to many of the men over whom they were supposed to exercise command." Some of the crewmen were substitutes hired by people who could afford to duck the draft, while others were "bounty jumpers" who would enlist and then desert after they had received their enlistment bonus. Still others, realizing the war was drawing to a close, joined up to qualify for a pension.[8]

The departure of the huge armada made Hampton Roads look almost barren. After weeks at anchor, the fleet had become almost part of the scenery and people had grown accustomed to it. Now the ships were gone, no doubt bringing comment from ferry passengers traveling to and from Norfolk.[9]

Despite all the leaks and rumors, the talk among the troops, and the newspaper speculation during the preceding months, in the end secrecy was maintained. While people originally might have believed that the target was Wilmington, it was deemed too late in the year for landings on the Cape Fear. Gossip among Norfolk's Unionists and secessionists now had it that the warships and transports were bound for Georgia to support Sherman's advance.[10]

As the warships headed south, the troopships continued up the Potomac, coming within sight of Washington. Unsure of Butler's intentions, the soldiers were speculating about the possibility of visiting the capital when the lead transport *Baltic* signaled a 180-degree turn and started back downriver. They reached Chesapeake Bay after dark and ran without lights until they anchored off Cape Charles. The next day, the transports got under way again and followed the fleet toward North Carolina. The ruse worked. Confederate observers saw the ships going up the Potomac, but did not see them return.[11]

On board his yacht, the *Ben De Ford*, chartered by the government to replace the sunken *Greyhound*, Butler carried a set of orders from Grant. They were intended for General Weitzel, but military courtesy required they go through Butler as Weitzel's commanding officer. The orders were brief and to the point. The object was to close Wilmington, with a secondary objective of capturing the city itself. The most important section stated: "The object of the expedition will be gained by effecting a landing on the mainland between Cape Fear River and the Atlantic north of the north entrance of the river [i.e., New Inlet]. Should such landing be effected whilst the enemy still hold Fort Fisher and the batteries guarding the entrance to the river, then the troops should entrench themselves, and by co-operating with the navy effect the reduction and capture of those places. These in our hands, the navy could enter the harbor and the port of Wilmington would be sealed." If an attempted landing failed—but only then—the troops would return "to the army operating against Richmond without delay."[12] Weitzel never saw the orders and, in fact, did not learn until much later that they even existed.[13]

Fortune favored the expedition. The sea was calm and the weather mild. Unaware that Butler had sent the transports up the Potomac, Porter stopped in Beaufort on December 15 to wait for them, as well as to take on a full supply of coal and ammunition. The fleet anchored in and around the harbor was the largest number of vessels ever to serve in one place under the U.S. flag. Among them was the *Louisiana,* which arrived under tow behind the double-ender *Sassacus* and "took an out-of-the-way place for anchorage." Here she received the final 30 tons of powder, to bring her total load to 215 tons. She had become nothing more than a floating bomb.[14]

Commander Rhind was even less happy with the project than before. As he had prepared for sea at Craney Island, he noticed the ship was out of trim, and the fuses had not even been laid before the powder was stowed. He spent much of the morning of December 13 restowing and securing the powder in the upper works. It was not feasible to unload all the powder in the hold, so he and Preston laid the fuse train as best they could, although he was not satisfied with it. The clocks to the detonators "were common deck time-pieces, altogether unfit for an experiment of that magnitude"; in Beaufort he had them altered to compensate for the motion of the ship, after which he and Preston tested them.[15]

After three days, Porter grew tired of waiting and ordered his ships to sea. As the fleet steamed the last ninety miles toward the Cape Fear, some took time to reflect on the battle, which, if everything went according to plan, would be in the next day or so. On the *Wabash,* Acting Master's Mate Read wrote to his parents that the fight "will be one of the bigest [sic] ever gotten up since the Rebellion [began]. . . . You know that this is the first time that I ever had to be under fire and taking command of a

[gun] division to myself is the greatest thing I look at. That is a great honor I can tell you and on the USS Frigate Wabash too. I hope that I may succeed in all my endeavors and get my name up as they say."[16]

Before leaving Beaufort, Porter had dispatched Lt. Comdr. P. G. Watmough in the USS *Kansas* ahead to New Inlet to advise the local commander what was expected, as well as to designate a tender to follow the *Louisiana* in toward Fort Fisher and take off her crew once the fuses had been set. The *Nansemond* initially was selected, but she was off the Western Bar by Old Inlet. Porter intended to blow up the *Louisiana* upon arrival on the night of December 18, and the *Nansemond* could not round Frying Pan Shoals in time. The armed tug *Wilderness* was designated instead.[17]

Rhind and his crew made the trip on the *Sassacus*. They would not board the *Louisiana* until she arrived at New Inlet, so they would be rested and fresh for the task ahead. Meanwhile, the ship was being handled by a temporary delivery crew. As he watched the *Louisiana* wallow under tow, Rhind decided she would make better time if her propeller was used to keep her bow straight, so he called for the delivery crew to get up steam. The crew fired up the engine, but after several hours he saw steam escaping from her steam pipe and no improvement in her headway. He demanded to know why her engine was not engaged.

"We have no engineer on board, sir!" one of the crewmen called. An engineer was quickly dispatched and the engine was started.[18]

Porter was certain that the blast from the *Louisiana* would flatten the Mound and cave in Fort Fisher's bombproofs, as well as knock down houses as far away as Wilmington. Believing the shock might burst his boilers, he ordered the ships off both inlets to withdraw at least twelve miles out to sea and let their steam go down. One captain suggested sending down topgallant masts and yards and bracing the lower yards sharp up, but Porter refused. There was always the possibility that "a gun or two" in Fort Fisher might survive the blast and send a shot through a boiler when the fleet moved in. In that case, the damaged ship would need its sails.

Not completely trusting the fuses and timing mechanisms, he advised Rhind to pile up half a cord of pine knots in the after cabin. These would be set on fire by the last man to abandon the *Louisiana*. "There may be something yet unthought of that will affect the clocks and fuzes," Porter explained, "but there will be no mistake in a fire."[19]

The transports, meanwhile, had steamed past the fleet and arrived off Masonboro Inlet eighteen miles north of Fort Fisher on the night of December 15, only hours after Porter anchored in Beaufort. The timing was carefully arranged to arrive after dark and heave to about twenty miles off-shore, to avoid being spotted by shore observers or by blockade-runners and fishing boats. Unaware that Porter was in Beaufort, Butler took the *Ben De Ford* as far as New Inlet in search of the admiral. Returning to the transports, he sent his son-in-law, Gen. Adelbert Ames, back in a tug, together with General Weitzel and Colonel Comstock, to reconnoiter the fort. The weather was growing warm. The sea was glassy, and Butler exercised by rowing out in his gig while the troops remained packed on their ships. For the next two days, they waited. Fresh water was growing scarce, and the diet had become monotonous. Every soldier who could procure a hook and line fished.[20]

"We still float in the same place," Chaplain Turner wrote in his diary. "Every body wonders why we lie here; but no one, with the exception of General Butler and Admiral Porter knows."

Turner conducted a service for the officers but was displeased with their conduct, which he called "very ungrateful to God," so he cut it short and left without giving a benediction. He then held services for the black troops of his regiment, and "we had a glorious meeting."[21]

Lamb also attended church that day. When the service ended, he received news that the fleet had sailed from Hampton Roads bound for Wilmington. His command had been extended to the defenses on the Sugar Loaf, a rise overlooking the Cape Fear some six miles north of Fort Fisher, and he inspected the battery there and at Battery Gatlin, which faced the Atlantic across the peninsula from the Sugar Loaf. Slave laborers were drafted from nearby plantations and farms to strengthen the defenses at Fisher.[22]

As Sunday progressed, the weather intervened on the side of the Confederates. Although the barometer was high, there was a strong northeasterly wind, and old sailors were predicting a storm. Porter did not like the look of things when he reached the rendezvous that evening. Nevertheless, he intended to follow his original plan and send the *Louisiana* on her mission that night. He earlier had sent a dispatch to that effect to Butler, and as the warships steamed past Masonboro toward their positions out from New Inlet, Butler fell in, trying to catch up with the admiral.[23]

At 7:45 P.M. the *Louisiana* drew up alongside the *Kansas*. The *Sassacus* transferred Rhind and his crew aboard the powder boat, then took up station north-northeast. All nonessential personnel were taken off the *Wilderness*, leaving just enough to handle the tug with the *Louisiana* in tow. Getting bearings from the range light on the Mound, the *Kansas* flashed hooded white and green lights, and the *Sassacus* responded with two white lights. At 9:30 P.M. the *Wilderness* started towing the *Louisiana* toward Fort Fisher, triangulating her position by the lights from the two Union ships and the Mound. The sea was now heavy, and although the powder boat was under steam, she wallowed and rolled badly.[24]

Back on the *Malvern*, Ensign Grattan noted the departure of the *Louisiana* in his journal and wrote: "This is the night before the battle, as I sit here my thoughts wander to home, and to the fair girl who I have promised to make my wife. If I should be killed in this engagement my last breath will be to echo her name, and to bid my father & mother, sisters & brothers good bye."[25]

Meanwhile, Porter sent Breese to the *Ben De Ford* to advise Butler that the *Louisiana* was already under way. Butler held a quick conference with Weitzel and Comstock. Based on their reconnaissance, they believed the explosion would serve no purpose unless troops were already in place to assault the fort or whatever was left of it. Likewise, if the *Louisiana* was blown up now, the Confederates would have at least eight hours to recover before daylight, when troop landings could begin. Butler sent Weitzel to the *Malvern* with a request that the mission be postponed for several days until a late moon so that the *Louisiana* could move into position later in the night. Porter dispatched the captured blockade-runner *A.D. Vance* (also known as *Advance*) to overhaul the powder boat and send it back.[26]

Porter was glad he decided to cancel the mission, for the sea was breaking heavily at two fathoms and the Confederates had extinguished the Mound light. Rhind decided it was impractical to continue, and was already returning to the fleet when he met the *A.D. Vance*. Meanwhile, a team from the Coast Survey went in to reconnoiter, and found the surf so bad that its boat was nearly capsized. "No boat of any kind could have gone on the beach without being destroyed by the breakers," Porter later observed, and he instructed Rhind to wait until "there is little or no surf, so that they army can land on the beach without difficulty."[27]

The weather grew worse, and Chaplain Turner wrote in his diary, "I fear for the monitors tonight. The waters are very rough."[28] The monitors came through Sunday night, but the storm continued throughout Monday. There being no way the soldiers could land, and with the troopships running low on food, coal, and water, Butler ordered them to Beaufort to replenish.[29] As his transport labored through tempest, Chaplain Turner noticed that "even the crew looked and spoke apprehensively."

> Finally, an awful sea came and broke in our wheel-house. Still the raging waters and howling winds grew worse.
>
> At last many of us gave up all hope. I lay down and bade my mother, wife, and children farewell, and after asking God to protect them and bring us together in heaven to be separated no more, I begged the Lord to put me to sleep, and that if it was His will that the ship should be dashed to pieces, I should remain asleep and be spared the heart-rending spectacle of nearly fifteen hundred men launched into eternity in one moment.[30]

Despite the fears, all arrived safely in Beaufort.

Porter, unaware of Butler's plan, presumed the general had sent the transports farther out to sea. On Monday he exercised his ships and was pleased at how well they maneuvered given the size of the fleet, the rough sea, and the distance over which the vessels were scattered. At sunset he ordered them to anchor twelve miles out, beyond sight of land. The storm grew worse as the wind shifted and the sea grew heavy, and the little monitors swung on their cables, sometimes disappearing from view as waves broke over them. Several ships dragged their anchors.[31]

A *New York Times* correspondent on board the *Santiago de Cuba* wrote, "The steamer commenced rolling and tossing about in the most violent manner, heavy gusts of wind went shrieking and howling through the rigging, and huge waves leaped up to the deck in a manner unwelcome and frightful."[32]

As the storm grew worse, the monitor *Mahopac* began to leak around the turret. An hour later, she signaled the *Santiago de Cuba* that her pumps had failed and the men were bailing. Watching from the larger ship, the *Times* correspondent wrote, "It seemed as if each heavy sea that swept over her, and completely buried her from our sight, would be the one to send her to the bottom." Finally, the storm abated and the monitor's exhausted crew got the flooding under control.[33]

The supermonitor *Monadnock,* operating under her own steam, had been rushed to completion, and many of her innovations kept breaking down. At the height of the gale, the steering gear parted and she went into a trough. Aware of the poor seakeeping reputation of monitors, her commanding officer, Comdr. Enoch G. Parrott, feared she might capsize. But the twin-screw *Monadnock* proved to be a stable ship, and by using the lee propeller Parrott was able to keep her head into the sea while the damage was repaired.[34]

The heavily laden *Louisiana,* tied to the *Wilderness* and standing apart from the rest of the fleet, was particularly exposed. "She wallowed and rolled, and dragged the Wilderness almost down to the fleet," one account recorded. Finally, she was cast off and taken in tow by the heavier *Nansemond,* now arrived from Old Inlet, until the weather cleared.[35]

On Tuesday, December 20, Lamb was awakened with the long-awaited news that the enemy fleet had arrived within sight of the fort. Going out, he saw five blockaders at their anchorages, and twenty-five warships "including several frigates" almost all hull down on the horizon. Expecting them to come in at high tide about noon, he sent Daisy and the children to Orton, discharged the slave laborers, and had the fort cleared for action. Time passed and Lamb realized the storm would keep the ships away at least for awhile. General Whiting and Flag Officer Robert F. Pinkney came out and inspected the fort. Whiting promised reinforcements, but the grim-faced Pinkney told Lamb that the broadsides from the Union frigates would drive his men from the sea-face guns. Lamb "respectfully disagreed with him."[36]

Despite his optimism, Lamb's situation was serious. With five companies of the 36th North Carolina detached from Fort Fisher to oppose Sherman in the south, the garrison was about half-strength, or a total of 667 men. Another 800 reservists were at the Sugar Loaf. General Lee had dispatched Maj. Gen. Robert F. Hoke's division of about 6,000 men to Wilmington, but it was still en route from Virginia. Battery Buchanan had a naval garrison of 19 officers and warrant officers, 136 enlisted men, and a marine guard under Lt. J. Campbell Murdoch consisting of 2 sergeants, 3 corporals and 20 enlisted men.[37]

The bad weather continued, keeping the Union fleet offshore. Nevertheless, "great excitement prevailed" in Wilmington, according to one Confederate navy officer. There was a surplus of naval personnel in the city these days. The *Tallahassee* had been decommissioned, returned to service as the blockade-runner *Chameleon,* and loaded with cotton for an outward run. The *Chickamauga,* meanwhile, lay idle in port, and the possibility of an attack on Fort Fisher prompted naval authorities to keep her there. Consequently, a large number of officers and crewmen from these ships were free for other duty, and all available officers, seamen, and marines were ordered to Battery Buchanan. Two midshipmen and twenty-nine sailors under Lt. Francis M. Roby, and additional marines commanded by Capt. Alfred C. van Benthuysen, boarded the *Yadkin* for the trip downriver. Upon arrival, Roby was told to use sailors and marines to serve the 7-inch Brooke guns in Fort Fisher. The ratings found quarters in the fort, but lack of accommodation for the officers forced Roby and the midshipmen to move into a hut up the beach from the fort.[38]

Looking out over the water, Midshipman Clarence Cary recalled, "The advance vessels of the fleet were already hovering on the coast, a little way to the northward, and it was 'in the air' than the attack might begin at any moment."[39]

On Thursday, December 22, General Hebert visited the fort. "He is very blue," Lamb noted in his diary. Like Fort Fisher, the garrisons of other forts along the Cape Fear had been reduced to send men against Sherman, and there was nothing Hebert could do to help. After almost four years of war, the Confederate forces were simply spread too thin, and there was little manpower to be had.[40]

Some relief did come the following day, when a battalion of the 10th North Carolina Regiment arrived under the command of Maj. James Reilly. Ironically, this was the same Reilly who, as a U.S. Army ordnance sergeant, had demanded a receipt when secessionists seized Fort Johnston in the spring of 1861. Along with the 110 men in Reilly's battalion, reinforcements included 115 men of the 13th North Carolina Battery and 140 boys of the 7th Battery of Junior Reserves. Slowly, bit by bit, Fort Fisher's garrison had grown to about 900.[41]

Lamb worried about the reserves, none of whom was over eighteen. Yet he had to admire them. "The brave little boys torn from their firesides by the cruel necessities of the struggle were as bright and manly as if anticipating a parade. They should never have been called out for service at that point, it was robbing the cradle. . . . Self-sacrificing courage seems indigenous to North Carolina . . . even the boys of this sturdy Commonwealth have been ever ready to rally to her defense."[42]

The weather on December 23 was clear but bitterly cold. Late in the day a few of Butler's transports could be seen in the distance, although most were still coaling and watering in Beaufort. The general's aide-de-camp, Capt. Haswell C. Clarke, arrived and advised Porter that Butler expected to reach New Inlet with his troops the following night; the attack could begin on Christmas Day. Porter, however, said he intended to blow up the *Louisiana* that night. Clarke replied that it would be impossible for Butler to be have the troops there in time, but said he would inform the general. At 1 P.M., Clarke departed for Beaufort. Porter, meanwhile, notified Commander Rhind to prepare the *Louisiana,* and ordered Lieutenant Commander Watmough in the *Kansas* to support Rhind as before. Porter intended to attack Fort Fisher December 24—with or without the army.[43]

There were several reasons for Porter's decision. He was tired of waiting, and his colossal ego was taking hold. He had concluded that the powder boat would work, and believed his seamen could storm the fort and take it without sharing the victory with the army. But there was more than simple vanity. The gale had already proven the instability of the Cape Fear winter. Porter now had a clear night, and there was no way of knowing when there might be another one. As he saw it, he simply had to use this hole in the weather while it lasted.[44]

There was a hitch. Even before the fleet left Hampton Roads, there had been rumors that a "fire-ship" was being fitted out for an unknown destination. By the time the *Louisiana* arrived in Beaufort, her mission was common knowledge. The news had even reached New Bern, where communications through the lines was maintained with Wilmington, and Rhind now feared that the Confederates might be ready and waiting. It would be a simple matter to board and take the unarmed and thinly crewed *Louisiana.*[45] In that event the *Wilderness* would open fire with grapeshot and canister. If fire from the fort disabled the *Wilderness* and capture appeared imminent, Rhind would rap on the deck, signaling Lieutenant Preston in the *Louisiana's* lower powder room to blow up the ship. Porter vetoed the idea of self-destruction but, on learning that the officers and crew had unanimously voted on it, reluctantly agreed.[46]

That night, the *Kansas* once again took up her position as range ship, and at about 10:30 P.M. the *Wilderness* started in toward Fort Fisher with the *Louisiana* in tow. The approach was supervised by Lt. R. H. Lamson, sent over from the *Gettysburg,* J. S. Bradford of the Coast Survey, and a bar pilot named Bowen. An hour later, with the dark parapets of Fort Fisher plainly visible against the night sky, the powder boat cast off. She was on her own now, and the *Wilderness* anchored to wait for her. The tug's commander, Acting Master Henry Arey, had her guns cleared and ready for action.

As the *Louisiana* steamed in, she was overtaken and passed by the blockade-runner *Little Hattie,* whose captain apparently mistook her for a comrade. Taking advantage of the situation, Rhind steered his ship into the *Little Hattie's* wake to follow her in. It seemed to those on the *Wilderness* that she was practically on the beach. Suddenly a light flared up from the powder boat, completely illuminating her. Many of the people on the *Wilderness* thought the fire was out of control and braced themselves for a massive explosion.

"They are only hauling fires, and the light shines through the canvas of the false smoke-stack!" Lamson remarked.

Ashore, the Confederate sentries apparently saw her and mistook her for a Union blockader that had grounded on the shoals and was set on fire to avoid capture. It had happened before. The flare soon died out. The crew finished drawing the *Louisiana's* fires, and she was anchored bow and stern. They could hear the calls of the sentries as they made their rounds on the beach. Rhind estimated he was about three hundred yards from the beach. But the darkness, the range of sound across water, and the sheer mass of Fort Fisher were deceiving. Actually he was at least six hundred yards away. Nevertheless, he believed he had done his job, and after putting most of the men over the side in a boat, he, Preston, and Assistant Engineer Mullin set the timers and lit the match fuses and the fire in the deckhouse. The timers were set to detonate at 1:20 A.M.; if they failed, the match fuses would go off at 1:35 A.M.—assuming, of course, that the deck-house fire had not destroyed the ship first.

Rhind, Preston, and Mullin climbed into the boat, and the crew rowed out to the *Wilderness.* As soon as they were on board, the tug headed for sea, firing rockets to notify the admiral that the powder boat was in place. An hour later, the *Wilderness* was in her assigned position twelve miles out to sea, where Arey hove to and let her steam go down. The after section of the *Louisiana* was now engulfed in flames from the deckhouse fire.[47]

The Federals waited anxiously for the explosion, but nothing happened at the scheduled times. Finally, at 1:40 A.M., "a glare on the horizon and a dull report were the indications that the floating mine had been sprung," recalled Lieutenant Commander Selfridge, who commanded the USS *Huron.*[48]

Ensign Grattan recorded: "A stream of fire ascended from the burning vessel and reaching a great height in the air, spread out in one brilliant sheet of flames which illuminated the whole horizon. After a little space of time a deep booming roar accompanied with a loud report told us that the powder boat had executed its mission and nothing now remains for the fleet to do but fight."[49]

The Federals got a much better show than the Confederates inside Fort Fisher. Many slept right through the explosion. Those on duty presumed that a blockade-runner had blown a boiler, or that a magazine had exploded on one of the Federal ships. Colonel Lamb hardly thought it worth noting, writing in his diary only that "a blockader got aground near fort, set fire to herself & blew up."[50]

Lieutenant Roby and the midshipmen, asleep on the floor of the hut up the beach, were probably closest to the explosion. They "half heard a muffled report, such as might come from a distant, heavy gun." Instantly they were awake, believing it was an alarm gun from the fort and expecting it to be followed by a drum roll calling the men to their batteries. As time passed and nothing happened, they rolled back up in their blankets and went back to sleep.[51]

Twelve miles out on the *Wilderness,* Rhind could have guessed as much. He had never trusted the layout of the fuses, and believed they had failed. The noise and shock of the blast were minimal. As the column of flame from the *Louisiana* flickered out and darkness returned, he remarked "There's a fizzle!" and went below.[52]

10

"ENGAGE THE ENEMY"

AT 2:15 A.M., PORTER SIGNALED the fleet to prepare for action. The ships got under way at daylight and began moving into position by divisions in line of battle, with the heavy, protected ironclads closest to shore. The formation was, at best, haphazard. The wind, blowing from shore, gained strength, and the ships lost steerageway in the heavy sea. Looking back on it almost fifty years later, Adm. George Dewey, who as a young lieutenant was executive officer of the *Colorado* at Fort Fisher, remarked that an officer of the modern navy could "hardly realize the difficulties of securing anything like precision with the utterly inharmonious elements that Porter had under his command." At 10:00 A.M. the ships anchored to wait for a shift in the wind.[1]

Weather notwithstanding, both sides were preparing for battle. On the *Minnesota,* Commodore Lanman visited all his gun crews, telling them to aim carefully and to observe the effect of each shot before firing again.[2] Inside the fort, the Confederates waited, the navy and marine gun crews manning the Brooke Battery at the lower end, and army artillerymen north along the sea face and across the land face to the marshes by the river. "One could see the motionless groups of gray-uniformed gunners standing silently at the barbette guns, no movement showing anywhere, except in the flags which still fluttered gaily in the wind," Midshipman Cary remembered.[3]

Commander Rhind and the officers and crew of the *Louisiana* boarded the *Malvern* at 10:15 A.M. The effect of the explosion had not been accurately ascertained, but by now most had surmised that the damage to Fort Fisher was negligible. "There it was," Lieutenant Commander Selfridge remarked, "as grim as ever, apparently uninjured, with its flag floating as defiantly as before."[4] Another Union officer commented that the explosion "was simply a fine piece of pyrotechnics with no good results following."[5]

The wind shifted, and at 11:30 A.M. the *Malvern* signaled "Engage the enemy." The fleet was under way within fifteen minutes. Paymaster Henry Rogers watched on board the *Gettysburg*. His station was the *Wilderness*, but he had been reassigned with the nonessential personnel while she was on her mission with the *Louisiana*.

THE USS *MALVERN*, PORTER'S FLAGSHIP, WAS A CAPTURED BLOCKADE-RUNNER.
IN HER, THE ADMIRAL COULD MOVE ABOUT THE ANCHORED FLEET, OBSERVING
THE BOMBARDMENT AND COMMUNICATING WITH HIS SHIPS.
Reprinted from *Official Records of the Union and Confederate Navies
in the War of the Rebellion*

"It was a sight worth living for," he wrote his parents, "to see this immense fleet get under way, drawn up in line, and steaming in towards the Rebel works, not a sound to be heard, not a drumbeat even, but on every ship the crews could be seen at quarters, the guns run out, and all preparations for immediate action."[6]

While still beyond the range of the fort, the wooden ships slowed and the ironclads steamed ahead. The *New Ironsides* led a column of monitors as near to the beach as their drafts permitted. They came into line and anchored in broadside at an angle about a mile above the Northeast Bastion. The wooden warships then took position, dropping bow and stern anchors broadside to the Confederate defenses, each vessel becoming virtually a floating battery. The fleet formed a staggered line more than a mile long. The *New Ironsides* opened fire with one of her starboard guns. An 11-inch shell screamed over the heads of the Confederate defenders and exploded harmlessly near the flagstaff. It was 12:53 P.M.

Lamb had been training one of his 10-inch guns along the course of the *Susquehanna,* and now he gave the command to open fire. The gunner jerked the lanyard to the friction fuse, and the gun roared. The shot skipped across the water and ricocheted through the frigate's funnel. The battle had begun.[7]

The *New Ironsides'*s first shot started a chain of broadside down the length of the divisions until it seemed to one officer "as if a line of fire ran down the whole face of the fleet."[8] When the *Wabash* and the frigates *Minnesota* and *Colorado* opened up, Selfridge wrote: "The enemy replied briskly, but when these frigates found the range and commenced firing rapidly nothing could withstand their broadsides of twenty-five 9-inch guns. It was a magnificent sight to see these frigates fairly engaged, and one never to be forgotten. Their sides seemed a sheet of flame, and the roar of their guns like a mighty thunderbolt."[9]

Anchored behind the ironclads, the wooden ships were firing over them and into the fort, making the deck of a monitor dangerous. Not only was a person exposed to Confederate fire, but he risked injury or death from poor aim or a premature shell explosion from one of the wooden ships.

Comdr. Enoch G. Parrott, taking his chances on the *Monadnock*'s deck, heard the increasingly loud whistle of a Confederate shell and knew it was coming toward him. "It burst pretty near," he wrote his wife, "and the pieces went sizzling and humming by me."[10]

Meanwhile the ironclads, firing from close in, kept the Confederate gunners down. "We could plainly see their guns and men and would drive their men away when they would attempt to load a gun, so that they would sometimes try some four or five times before succeeding," Parrott wrote.[11]

At Fort Fisher's Brooke Battery, Midshipman Cary agreed. "Firing was too hot to get the men at their guns," he noted in his diary. The sailors and marines serving the battery were particularly exposed because the traverses protecting them were incomplete.[12] The Confederates took shelter in their bunkers and returned fire only sporadically.

The generally feeble Confederate return fire convinced many Federal navy officers that Fort Fisher's guns had been silenced. One officer even speculated that the batteries on the Northeast Bastion might even be "Quakers"—dummy guns made of tree trunks shaped and painted black that Confederates often used to make fortifications appear more formidable. Most accounts also noted "a cloud of thick black smoke and flames," as well as explosions within the fort and presumed massive damage. On the *Minnesota* and the *Wabash*, the crews gave three cheers at the explosions and fires, believing they were the ones who had done it. Hits on the Mound and the traverses threw great clouds of sand into the air.[13]

In fact, Colonel Lamb was concerned about his ammunition supply and had given orders that each gun was to fire only every half hour unless the fort was actually assaulted. He was afraid Porter would use the standard American naval tactic of running across the bar, past the fort, and into the river. If that happened, the battle was lost because Fort Fisher's defense system was directed seaward. Consequently, he reserved the bulk of his ammunition against a possible run toward the bar. Altogether, the forty-four guns of Fort Fisher fired only 672 shots that day.[14]

Meanwhile, the Union fire rained into the fort with everything from 15-inch shells to 3-inch rifle bolts. "The noise of the guns and the bursting shell was deafening," Cary wrote. Because so much of the fire was concentrated on the flagstaff, most of the bolts fell harmlessly onto the parade ground, while many of the shells and solid shot passed completely over the fort and fell into the river. Still, there were some casualties. A courier dashed across the open plain trying to get shelter behind the Brooke Battery. Before he reached it, a 15-inch shell scored an almost direct hit on him, exploding and blowing into so many pieces that the Confederate sailors could hardly find enough to bury in the shallow grave they scraped out of the sand.[15]

Despite their restrictions, some of the fort's gunners made their shots tell. "I can tell you . . . to hear those Whitworth shells whistling over head is what makes a man feel small," Acting Master's Mate Read wrote to his parents.[16]

It seemed to monitor commanders that the Confederates were ignoring the ironclads and concentrating on the wooden warships. The sailors and marines in the Brooke Battery watched as hits from their heavy rifles sent splinters flying from the ships abreast of their position.[17]

A 150-pound rifle shell, undoubtedly from the Armstrong Battery, struck the double-ended gunboat *Mackinaw* at the waterline, tearing through a coal bunker and smashing into the port boiler. The engine room was flooded and filled with live steam, nearly extinguishing the fires and scalding eight men.[18]

On board the *Powhatan,* a Confederate round carried off the spanker gaff with the colors, which were promptly hoisted to the mizzen. A large-caliber bolt then cut the mizzen ratlines about four feet below Ensign Evans, who was standing in the rigging just beneath the crosstrees scouting the guns of the fort. Evans, who was clutching a piece of breakfast hardtack between his teeth, swung back and slammed into the mast. Shaken but otherwise unhurt, he noticed the hardtack was missing and believed he must have swallowed it whole.[19]

The crew of the *Powhatan* now occupied itself with throwing shots from the pivot rifle at the flagstaff on the Mound Battery, which was knocked down after some twenty-five minutes. The commanding officer, Commodore Schenck, subsequently reported in perfect seriousness, "Not a shell was wasted from the XI-inch and rifles."[20]

"All day the fury of the bombardment was on," Acting Master Francis Sands of the *Gettysburg* later recalled, "and as a spectacle it was simply grand." From where he stood, it seemed that the Confederates were maintaining a steady return fire, throwing "shot and shell over and into the line of vessels."[21]

The *Malvern* steamed among the anchored warships, giving Porter a close-up view of the fighting and allowing him to communicate more conveniently. Shot splashed and shells burst all around her. One hit within a foot of the bow, sending a geyser of water onto her deck.

At 3:40 P.M., Porter ran up a general signal for the ships to "move in closer and engage the enemy with deliberation." About that moment, a shell burst overhead, sending a large fragment into the flagship's wheel-house and barely missing the admiral. Less than half an hour later, a Whitworth shell came screaming down into the water and struck the *Malvern* below the waterline. It was almost spent, though, and damage was minimal.[22]

Even as the flagship was ducking Confederate shells, other ships in the squadron began experiencing a series of near catastrophes from their own guns. The USS *Yantic* was anchored some two thousand yards northeast of Fort Fisher and, according to Lt. Comdr. T. C. Harris, her command-ing officer, was "doing good execution" when the 100-pounder Parrott rifle burst. The commander of the gun division, Acting Ensign Edward Winnemore, was cut down by the flying metal, his right leg blown off at the knee. He died later in the day, as did Boatswain's Mate James Horton, the gun captain. One member of the gun crew suffered contusions, and two were burned.

Harris was not certain what had happened. He only knew that his ship was badly damaged and that what was supposed to be his most effective gun was lost. The *Yantic* pulled out of line and sought additional medical assistance from the hospital ship *Fort Jackson*. Ninety minutes after the explosion, Harris took her back into line and began firing into the fort with his two remaining effective guns, a 30-pounder and a 9-incher. A sur-vey of the ship later showed that the *Yantic's* damage was substantially worse than Harris originally believed. Had the 100-pounder been firing at a slightly higher elevation, it would have smashed downward through the deck, tearing through the port boiler and out the side of the ship.[23]

On the screw sloop *Juniata*, Capt. William Rogers Taylor noted that once the range was obtained, "the firing appeared to me like target practice." Then his Parrott gun exploded, turning the deck into a charnel house. Two lieutenants, D. D. Wemple of the navy and Jones Pile of the marines, were maimed to death. Pile's body was knocked overboard by flying pieces of gun and carriage, then recovered as it floated by the *Malvern*. Two sailors were eviscerated and died of hemorrhage and shock, and a ship's boy died shortly after amputation of his leg. Seven others suffered fractures, contusions, and burns, and one was deafened.[24] Yet another Parrott burst, this time aboard the screw sloop *Ticonderoga,* killing eight and wounding twelve. Coxswain William Shipman, captain of a nearby gun, told his crew, "Go ahead, boys; this is only a fortune of war!" Other gun leaders picked up the refrain, encouraging their men as they worked the guns.[25]

Damage was less severe on the *Quaker City,* which was exchanging fire with the Mound when the barrel of her Parrott blew off about four feet behind the muzzle. A large piece landed on deck, slightly wounding one man.[26]

A 10-inch shot from the Mound struck the *Osceola* three feet below the waterline, tearing through the sandbags placed around the boiler and through the boiler itself, finally coming to rest in the furnace. Six men were scalded, and the engine room began to flood. Nevertheless, the *Osceola* continued to hammer away at the fort until the water was almost up to the fires. Comdr. J. M. B. Clitz ordered the ship out of line and signaled "Disabled." As the *Osceola* began to settle and the fires went out, Clitz changed the signal to "Sinking." The *A.D. Vance* and *Tacony* moved out to assist, while a boat crew from the *Osceola* managed to partially block the hole in her side. The *Vance* took the injured ship under tow to a safe anchorage where temporary repairs were made, allowing her to return to the line the next day.[27]

Not all the damage was from Confederate fire or defective Parrott guns. The double-ender *Pawtuxet* dropped out of line in response to a signal from the *Malvern* and was steaming toward the flagship when she collided with the hapless *Ticonderoga.* The starboard bulwarks were stove in, and a cutter already battered by a Confederate shell was carried away.[28]

In the Brooke Battery, the Confederate sailors and marines were calm but tired, having worked their guns all day without relief. Because of their exposed position and the tendency of the Brooke rifles to overheat, they had been restricted to firing at fifteen-minute intervals. Between rounds, they crouched behind the traverses and watched the shells flying overhead and landing and exploding in the fort. The shells were fired with a wooden or lead plug called a sabot at their bases, which expanded into the rifling of the barrel and gave them a truer trajectory. Occasionally a shell would land behind the battery intact, then explode, and the sailors scrambled to dodge the flying pieces of sabot. Once, as the grog ration was being issued, a shell exploded and fragments of the sabot smashed the bottle and injured the man getting his drink.[29]

Late in the afternoon, as the firing tapered off, a shell exploded over the battery, mortally wounding one gunner, tearing the leg off another, and slightly wounding Midshipman Cary in the left knee. Lt. T. L. Dornin took over the gun while Cary went to the hospital to get his knee patched up.[30] He found the surgeons working in their bombproof under the Pulpit. Just outside the entrance, by the curtain wall that separated the hospital from the main magazine, was a pile of arms and legs that had been tossed out after amputation.[31]

Despite the optimistic reports of the Union commanders, damage to the fort was negligible. "Never since the invention of gun powder was there so much harmlessly expended, as in the first day's attack on Fort Fisher," Lamb commented. Much of the fire and smoke seen by the Union sailors came from the wooden barracks behind the flagstaff. About half the quarters were lost, and tar and pitch stored nearby added to the conflagration. Three gun carriages were disabled and the earthworks were furrowed, but the most important components of the fort—the bombproofs, magazines, and gun chambers—were intact. More serious was the loss of overcoats and blankets when the barracks burned. The day was unseasonably warm and balmy, and most of the men had left them in their bunks. Now they were lost in the fire, leaving no protection from the cold days that were sure to follow.[32]

Porter has been accused of deliberately sabotaging the bombardment because of his old quarrel with Butler.[33] Despite the admiral's many faults, this does not appear to be the case. The navy's failure to knock out the guns of Fort Fisher seems to be due to lack of coordination and poor gunnery rather than any actual attempt to sabotage the expedition (and by extension Butler's prestige).

Although the Union ship commanders almost universally congratulated themselves on excellent gunfire on December 24 and 25, they are contradicted not only by Lamb's damage reports but by circumstances.[34] Blockade duty actually involved very little precision gunfire. Blockaders were armed; blockade-runners were not. When a blockade-runner was at bay, a shot across the bow often was enough to convince a nervous captain to surrender. As early as mid-October, when Porter drilled his crews at target firing, he noted, "The firing is generally very poor—no wonder, when they have scarcely ever fired a gun."[35]

The Confederates held little if any advantage because most of their gunnery over the last three years had been warning shots at blockaders that ventured too close. Although Lamb occasionally held target practice, regular exercises were limited—as was the fire during the battle itself—by the chronic ammunition shortage. Yet as the battle progressed, there was a marked improvement in gunnery on both sides. Union and Confederate alike were firing at stationary targets—the Confederates at the anchored warships, the Union at a massive, static fort. Battle is the best of all drills, and simple repetition meant that ultimately the gunners would find the range and go into effective fire. Had there been better gun discipline aboard ship, it may reasonably be assumed that damage to the fort would have been much more severe.

As it was, while the Federal fleet was laying in the heaviest bombardment of the war (an estimated ten thousand heavy shells in five hours), the navy gunners fired at targets of opportunity all along the lines of parapets, rather than concentrating on the land face where it was most needed. When the barracks and stables caught fire, throwing a pall of smoke and

INTERIOR VIEW OF THE FORT FISHER SEA FACE AFTER THE SECOND BATTLE, SHOWING UNEXPLODED SHELLS LITTERING THE PARADE. MUCH OF THE SEA FACE STILL EXISTED AS LATE AS 1957, BUT IT HAS SINCE WASHED AWAY.
Courtesy of the North Carolina Division of Archives and History

flame over the fort, many of the ships shifted their fire in that direction because it was a visible target. In the burning stables, the terrified horses broke loose and escaped, running up and down the plain inside the fort until, one by one, they were killed.[36]

While the navy bombarded Fort Fisher, Butler was hurrying his transports back from Beaufort. Captain Clarke had arrived in Beaufort with Porter's decision only that morning, reporting that he had been delayed outside the harbor by rough seas. Most of the transports had finished coaling and watering, and Butler, realizing that the powder boat had already been blown up, immediately ordered them to New Inlet. Those still taking on coal and water were told to follow as soon as they finished.

Butler arrived shortly before 5 P.M., in time for the finale of the naval bombardment. He waited until the warships ceased fire, and moved out. When the *Malvern* dropped anchor about four or five miles offshore, he anchored the *Ben De Ford* alongside and sent word that Weitzel and Comstock would call on the admiral to finalize plans for the assault.[37]

Butler later insisted that he sent Weitzel rather than going himself because Weitzel would command the troops ashore and he wanted to be certain that everything was perfectly coordinated between those troops and the fleet; Comstock was detailed as a member of General Grant's staff. Very likely, however, Butler was furious at having been excluded from the explosion of the *Louisiana,* the failure of which he blamed on the navy. Already, he and Porter were barely on speaking terms because of the admiral's delay in arriving at New Inlet. Porter likewise appears to have been less than eager to deal with Butler, because he at first begged off a meeting, claiming fatigue. Eventually, though, he did receive Weitzel and Comstock very briefly, just long enough to assure them that his ships had thoroughly battered Fort Fisher and it would be "an easy capture."[38]

Across the water, in Fort Fisher, there was a more cordial meeting, for General Whiting had arrived. He had no intention of taking command from Lamb, in whom he had total confidence. He merely intended to share the hazards of battle and offer such advice as Lamb might need or want.[39]

11

THE GHOST OF BATTERY WAGNER

SUNDAY WAS CHRISTMAS DAY, and there was no question that this would be the day of reckoning. At 6:30 A.M., Weitzel called on Admiral Porter to complete the arrangements for the landings. Although some were uneasy about fighting on a day celebrating the Prince of Peace, the needs of war superseded all others. "All the transports have arrived an[d] it is intended to land them to day," Grattan noted in his journal. His pessimism of the previous week was gone. A short time earlier he had commented, "It is more than probable that we shall enjoy two holidays in one (Christmas and victory over the enemy)."[1]

With most of the ships involved with Fort Fisher, blockade-runners took advantage of the light patrols to the west and ran out from Old Inlet. During the predawn hours, the USS *Eolus* had spotted two slipping over the Western Bar and chased one eighty-five miles before losing her in the darkness.[2]

Off Confederate Point, the *Santiago de Cuba* commenced the day's bombardment at 10:06 A.M. when she opened fire on Battery Gatlin, or Half Moon Battery, which covered the proposed troop landing zone.

Some forty minutes later the *New Ironsides* and the monitors began blasting away at the fort proper.[3]

The *Britannia* had been blockading off Old Inlet when the attack started and, having to put out to sea to clear Frying Pan Shoals, did not arrive until Saturday night. Now she was formed in a line of reserve ships headed by the *Santiago de Cuba,* pounding away at Battery Gatlin and a second beach defense, Battery Anderson, which Northern troops called Flag Pond Battery.

"Such Heavy cannonading I never before heard," *Britannia* crewman Joseph Fernald wrote to his wife, "5 monitors and 70 ships besides Army Transports of very large size with 1500 Troops. . . . [I]t was a grand but awful Sight[.] Such Broad-sides it was deaff[en]ing."[4]

About noon, Porter began to consider running into New Inlet past the forts, and sent several double-enders under Comdr. John Guest to reconnoiter the channel. Pounding away at the Mound and Battery Buchanan to keep the Confederate gunners down, the double-enders scouted the entrance and found that the large number of wrecked blockade-runners had completely changed the formation of the channel and the bar from prewar maps. There was also a real danger from underwater torpedoes. The channel would have to be sounded and buoyed from small boats, so Lieutenant Cushing was told to take ten boats and do the job while the double-enders dragged for torpedoes.[5]

About 2:30 P.M., Lieutenant Chapman, commanding the Confederate naval detachment at Battery Buchanan, noticed Cushing's boats heading toward the channel from the fleet. Chapman opened fire with one of the battery's guns, and the fourth shot cut the *Tacony's* cutter in two, tearing off the legs of Seaman Henry Sands and mortally wounding him. Splinters struck Quartermaster Joseph Riley in the left buttock, inflicting two wounds that, while no doubt painful, were not serious. The *Tacony's* cutter sank, but the men continued at their work.[6]

The Brooke Battery was also firing on the boats when one of its guns burst at the breach. The tube was split and the top half of the breach went flying over the heads of a group of officers behind it, while the bottom half smashed through the carriage into the ground. The entire crew was knocked down. Miraculously, no one was killed, although Lieutenant Dornin and several men were wounded by the heavy iron reinforcing bands. About ninety minutes later, the second Brooke gun burst. Again, no one was killed.[7]

Solid shot, shells, and shrapnel splashed around the boats, but the Union sailors kept easing along the channel. So much grape and canister peppered them that it reminded Seaman Asa Betham of the *Pontoosuc* of a hailstorm. The artillery splashes threw enough water into the boats that from time to time the sailors had to bail to keep from sinking.[8]

As the day grew late and the troops were slow in coming ashore, Porter eventually recalled Cushing's boats and sent them to assist the landing. Had Cushing been allowed to complete the task, Porter believed he might have succeeded in buoying the channel. Cushing, however, was equally happy to get out without being blown out of the water.[9]

The troops were already coming ashore by the time Cushing returned to the fleet. The first wave went in at about 2 P.M. The *Santiago de Cuba's* commanding officer, Capt. O. S. Glisson, who was responsible for the landings, organized the reserves into two divisions with the transports anchored between. After ordering boats away to pick up and land the troops, he went over to the *Ben De Ford,* where Butler said he planned to send only five hundred soldiers. Glisson replied that he had better land as many as possible because the good weather might not last another day. Butler pondered this, remarking that it might be better not to land any at all, but finally gave orders to proceed. Forty-one boats started ashore with five hundred men, touching the beach about five miles up the point from Fort Fisher. This group, under the command of Bvt. Brig. Gen. Martin Curtis, a twenty-nine-year-old New Yorker, was charged with establishing a beachhead while the boats returned to the transports for more troops.[10]

A cheer went up from the soldiers on the transports as the troops landed. When the first boats touched the beach, Curtis sent skirmishers into the woods on the far side of the point to cover the rest as they disembarked. Meanwhile, a white flag went up over Battery Anderson, about three-quarters of a mile down the beach. Seeing the flag, Acting Lt. Samuel Huse of the *Britannia* ordered Acting Ensign W. H. Bryant to take a boat and receive the surrender. Boats also started out from the *Tristram Shandy, Howquah,* and *Santiago de Cuba,* each eager to take the battery. The troops were running just as hard, trying to get there before the navy.

The *Britannia's* crew arrived first, and Bryant planted the U.S. flag on the battery. "Mid the cheers of thousands," Joseph Fernald wrote, "the first Flag that has been hoisted since the war." Prisoners included the battery's commander, Capt. Jacob Koonts, a lieutenant, and sixty-four privates. They had been badly battered during the bombardment, and Koonts, realizing they were hopelessly outnumbered, had no intention of sacrificing them needlessly. The Confederates were taken on boats and transferred to the *Santiago de Cuba*.[11]

As the troops were landing, the *Malvern* came alongside the *Ben De Ford* and Porter hailed Butler with his speaking trumpet, the first direct communication between the two since they left Hampton Roads.

"How do you do, General?" the admiral called.

"Very well, I thank you," Butler replied.

"How many troops are you going to land?"

"All I can."

"There is not a rebel within five miles of the fort," Porter said. "You have nothing to do but to land and take possession of it."

As the *Malvern* steamed on, Butler remarked to his staff, "I think there is a man on shore, by the name of Weitzel, who will find that out, if it is so."[12]

General Weitzel, who had accompanied the first wave of troops, told Curtis to push down the beach as far as he could go toward Fort Fisher. Throwing out flankers, Curtis came within a mile and a half of the fort. Here, he sent a detachment across the point to the river side to cut the telegraph wires and block the road into Wilmington. His rear protected, he continued onward. Observing the troops safely ashore and moving unopposed against Fort Fisher, Butler sent in the rest of Curtis's First Brigade, along with the Second Brigade under twenty-year-old Col. Galusha Pennypacker, and Col. Louis Bell's Third Brigade.[13]

At about eight hundred yards, Weitzel was able to get a good view of the fort. "I counted seventeen guns in position bearing up the beach, and between each pair of guns there was a traverse so thick and so high above the parapet that I have no doubt they were all bomb-proofs," he later wrote. "I saw plainly that the work had not been materially injured by the heavy and very accurate shell fire of the navy." The parallels between Fort Fisher and Battery Wagner were all too evident and frightening, and Weitzel returned to the boats. He planned to tell General Butler "that it would be butchery to order an assault."[14] Long since abandoned, Battery Wagner was still working its terrible spell on the Union command.

Weitzel also may have been influenced by the capture of some 250

Junior Reserves, the teenage boys who had come to help defend the fort. Already one had been killed and several wounded during the bombardment, and there was no room for them in Fort Fisher's bombproofs. Frightened and disillusioned, they had been ordered out of the fort and up the road to keep them out of the way, and there they encountered Curtis's flankers. Their commander, Maj. John M. Reece, apparently was looking for Union troops to accept their surrender so that no more of the boys would be harmed. But the large number of Confederates outside the fort was unnerving for their captors. One Union officer wrote that their capture "seems to prove that there must have been a garrison large enough to man the parapet of the fort without drawing upon these reserves. This . . . clearly shows that there was a well-disciplined garrison within the walls always ready to man the parapet and palisade as soon as the bombardment should end."[15]

Had the Union commanders known the true situation inside Fort Fisher, they might have been more confident. The ouster of the Junior Reserves from the fort was no indication of Confederate strength; it merely meant that Lamb was loath to commit frightened children to battle. In fact, the weakness of the garrison and demoralization from the constant bombardment were serious. Reinforcements were summoned from Battery Buchanan, and Chapman sent two-thirds of his sailors and marines.[16] Although not part of that group, Midshipman Cary had wandered over to headquarters on the Pulpit to see if he could make himself useful now that the Brooke Battery was out of action.

"I carried a few dispatches for General Whiting and Colonel Lamb," he wrote, "but I was mostly employed in getting the militiamen out of the bombproofs, where they were huddled together like so many sheep." Eventually, a colonel from Whiting's staff managed to get them up on the parapets "by much threatening and persuasion." After the way his sailors had borne up, both from the Union pounding and their own exploding guns, Cary considered the behavior of these troops "most disgraceful."[17]

The defective 100-pounder Parrott rifles that dogged the Union navy during Christmas Eve continued to burst on Christmas Day. The *Mackinaw* had begun firing on the Mound Battery at 12:40 P.M. Just over an hour later her Parrott gun burst, killing the division captain and seriously wounding the gun captain.[18]

At 3:30 P.M., Confederate gunners found the range of the *Powhatan*. In rapid succession, the ship was hit by three rounds. The first, an 8-inch solid shot, hit three feet above the waterline and landed on a mattress in a storeroom. The second and third hit twenty inches below the waterline. One lodged in the ship's side, while the other smashed through and hit a beam on the orlop deck, causing her to leak badly. Two shells exploded near the waterline on either side of the starboard paddle wheel, tearing off some of the copper sheathing of the hull, and several more caused negligible damage to the stern and running rigging. Nevertheless, the *Powhatan* remained in action until her ammunition was almost exhausted and she was ordered to move out.[19]

The *Powhatan* was not alone. On the *Wabash*, Capt. Melancton Smith found his ship under heavy fire and increased his gunnery until the entire starboard battery was in action. The Union gun captains watched the spaces between the fort's traverses, and when the Confederates fired they trained their own guns on the muzzle blast. Shells began bursting directly over the gun chambers, hampering the Confederate gunners so that their fire "became less rapid and accurate." When all of his shells were expended, Smith pulled out of the line and moved to assist the troop landings.[20]

While Weitzel worried that Fort Fisher might become another Wagner, boatloads of troops were coming in. The sea was growing heavier, and the surf was beginning to pound against the beach. Boats overturned, either coming ashore or starting back out toward the transports. "None of the men after three o'clock reached the shore without getting a thorough drenching," Union captain Henry C. Lockwood remembered.[21]

Curtis's immediate superior was General Ames, Butler's son-in-law, who commanded the division. While Curtis moved down the point against the fort, Ames took a detail in the opposite direction and captured Battery Gatlin. From Major Reece and other prisoners, Butler learned that some of the Confederates did not even belong to Fort Fisher. They were part of Kirkland's Brigade, the vanguard of Hoke's Division, which, together with Hagood's Brigade, had begun arriving in Wilmington on December 22 and was deploying around the Sugar Loaf. This added sixteen hundred men to the equation, and Hoke himself was expected with the main force at any time. Butler remembered the costly Union repulses at Port Hudson and Battery Wagner, and neither of those assaulting forces had fresh enemy troops massed at its rear. He already had concluded that Fort Fisher was stronger than either Port Hudson or Wagner, and Porter shortly before had advised him that the fleet was running low on ammunition and soon would need to return to Beaufort and replenish. Weighing these factors together with the reinforcement, he canceled the assault. Then, in violation of General Grant's orders to entrench and lay siege, he ordered his own soldiers reembarked on the transports.[22]

Had Butler been blessed with more nerve and more accurate information he might have acted differently, for the Confederates to his rear were not nearly so strong as he believed. Kirkland's and Hagood's men were exhausted from their forced marches, and a furious General Hoke was spending Christmas in Greensboro, halfway across North Carolina from Wilmington. Stranded because of squabbles between rival railroad companies, and painfully aware of the urgency of his mission, he telegraphed General Lee, advising military control of the railroads. Otherwise, he said, operations in both North Carolina and Virginia would be seriously jeopardized. "My troops are now wanted in Wilmington, where they should have been two days ago," he fumed.[23]

By now over twenty-three hundred Union soldiers had landed on Confederate Point, and it was growing dark. Curtis was within fifty yards of Fort Fisher. One of his officers, Lt. William Walling, had even managed to slip through the palisade and retrieve a Confederate banner knocked down by navy gunfire, a feat for which he received the Medal of Honor. Curtis sent word back that he was in a position to assault the fort, and Ames, unaware that Butler had decided to cancel the expedition, gave his approval.[24]

The navy, likewise, was unaware of Butler's decision, and as the troops neared the fort, the ships ceased fire to avoid hitting them. Lamb had been waiting for this moment. Gunners swarmed from the bombproofs and opened up with grape and canister from the land-face guns. The startled Union troops momentarily fell back. Still wanting to be useful, Midshipman Cary acquired a rifle and fired eight shots at a Federal soldier hunkered down in a rifle pit, but believed he missed in the growing darkness.[25] To Joseph Fernald on the *Britannia,* the musket fire on the beach "sounded like the snapcrackers of a fourth [of] July."[26]

In Wilmington, windows shook from the bombardment, and people prayed for their troops at Fort Fisher and for their city. With the telegraph wire cut, communication with the fort was haphazard at best. Toward nightfall wild rumors reached the city that the enemy was on the parapet at Fort Fisher. At 9 P.M., General Bragg put his wife on a special train out of the city. Word of her departure stirred panic among the citizens, and by the next morning a mass exodus was under way. The general himself remained in Wilmington, but two hours after he sent his wife away, one of his officers noticed that he was "quite unnerved" and his hand trembled.[27]

Meanwhile, off Confederate Point, those on the ships noticed that Union troops were stalled. On the USS *Seneca,* Lt. Comdr. Montgomery Sicard could not understand what was happening. He had watched as Curtis's skirmish line advanced "within pistol shot" of the fort before he lost sight of it. He had tapered off his fire because he wanted to conserve shrapnel to cover the main assault. Eventually, he saw two Union soldiers heading up the beach with one of Fort Fisher's flags. It was inconceivable that the Confederates would be able to withstand a general attack, yet no one was attacking. Instead, it appeared that the troops were being withdrawn.[28]

Butler's orders had finally been passed down to General Curtis. Cursing Butler aloud, his men withdrew under heavy fire and in an orderly fashion, arriving at the boats without losses. The sailors worked on taking troops aboard until about 10 P.M., when the heavy surf forced them to suspend operations. About seven hundred men were left ashore. Believing themselves about to be abandoned, some soldiers from this group attempted to rush the boats as they pulled away.[29]

During the recovery operations the large frigates kept the Confederate gunners in their bunkers, and return fire was only sporadic. Then Porter signaled cease fire, and all the ships began drawing out of range except the *Colorado* and *Minnesota,* which had not received, or at least had not seen, a signal to withdraw. The withdrawal of the fleet brought the Confederates back to their guns, and they concentrated everything on the two frigates.

On the *Colorado* the capstan was shot away, two guns were damaged, and the ship was hulled in several places. One man was killed and five wounded. Commodore Thatcher briefly considered slipping his cables and moving out, but realized his ship would be pounded to pieces as she retreated. He signaled the *Minnesota* to resume firing, and signaled *Malvern,* "Commenced firing because the enemy were hulling us."

On the gun deck, Lieutenant Dewey "found the men chafing in their inaction or astounded and apprehensive over the damage that was being wrought."

"Fire! Fire as fast as you can!" he shouted. "That is the way to stop their fire!"

The frigates blazed away, forcing the Confederates back into their bombproofs. Meanwhile, the *Malvern* signaled the two ships to retire, and as soon as the fire from the fort tapered off, they withdrew.[30]

The skies opened up, and it was raining hard as the soldiers who had managed to get off the beach reached the ships. They were cold, wet, and tired, and they were angry. They believed a great victory had been snatched from them just as it was within their grasp. A company captain taken aboard the *Britannia* complained to Fernald that if his brigade had been supported, it would have taken the fort.[31]

In Battery Buchanan, Chapman kept his naval gunners at quarters, expecting an attack from the Union boats. The Confederates were exhausted after two days of fighting, and the hard, blowing rain added to their misery. The soldiers in the fort proper "were much exposed as they were under arms all night," according to General Whiting, who likewise expected renewal of the attack. Shortly after midnight, he sent a message to General Bragg asking for "500 veteran infantry," but the Union soldiers up the beach were in no position to make trouble. Now clearly outnumbered, they had been left ashore with no blankets or entrenching tools, and their rations and water were inadequate.[32]

The fires inside the fort raged long into Christmas night, clearly visible to the warships at sea. At 3 A.M. boats were reported to be coming in, and the nervous Confederates opened fire with grape and shell. Monday was spent repairing damage and cleaning up. "The inside of the fort is covered with pieces and whole shell," Midshipman Cary wrote in his diary. The Confederates watched as the Union soldiers resumed embarking. Their commander was already gone, for Butler had departed for Hampton Roads that morning, adding to the feeling of abandonment.[33]

It took another day to get all the Union soldiers back to their ships, and Curtis was livid. As his men were being loaded on boats from the USS *Nereus* on December 27, he told anyone who would listen that "if he had been reinforced when he requested, he could have captured Fort Fisher." Most of the army officers coming from shore expressed the same opinion. One told Acting Master's Mate Francis H. Poole of the USS *Governor Buckingham* that "ten of his men lay under the embrasures all night, and that it could have been carried very easily."[34]

The soldiers' undisguised contempt for Butler quickly spread to the sailors, who felt nothing but sympathy for their army counterparts. Rumors of bravery on the beach and imbelicity at the top made rounds among the ships. One story had it that "the Generl [*sic*] in command [presumably Curtis] all most got down on His [k]nees to let Him take the Fort[.] He was on the ramparts of it and said that the rebs wer[e] all in the bomb proof casemates[.] they did not even fire muskettry at our troops, and He knew that we could take it."[35]

Commenting on the soldier who captured the flag, Lt. James Parker of the *Minnesota* remarked, "If this could be done, the uneducated mind, not so profoundly versed in the military science as was General Butler, may be pardoned a belief that more soldiers might have followed that one into the fort."[36]

The condemnation appeared almost universal. In a letter to his mentor, Admiral Du Pont, Preston called Butler a "shrewd political trickster and military imbecile who had the address to force himself into the command of the military part of the expedition against Wilmington."[37]

"What did he go there for?" Parrott wondered to his wife. "To take possession after we had conquered? We could do that ourselves."[38] Ensign Grattan went further, writing his parents, "We all believe Butler to be a rank traitor and a coward and everything but a gentleman."[39]

Meanwhile, on the Confederate side, Hoke's main force finally arrived at the Sugar Loaf. After two stormy days and nights on the parapets, Lamb's cold, wet, exhausted troops could stand down. As he continued his repairs, Lamb wrote a memorandum to himself to request heavy timbers. No doubt expecting a new attack in the not-too-distant future, he also noted, "Ask for men accustomed to mortar firing."[40]

Tuesday evening, Lieutenant Roby's sailors and marines, a "small squad, all that were left of 24 used-up men," returned to Battery Buchanan, where Chapman turned out the garrison to give them three cheers. The following day, they boarded a ship back for Wilmington.[41]

with him, more tourists to distract the colonel from the work at hand. Lamb got some relief from his military and social obligations that night, when Daisy and the children returned from Orton.[20]

Two days later, however, work was again interrupted when General Bragg and "quite a number of citizens" accompanied the Ladies Soldier's Aid Society. Their representatives addressed the garrison, and Lamb had to respond. He did so, assuring "the noble women of Wilmington . . . that their homes would be protected by my garrison."

Despite these interruptions, work continued. New guns were mounted, and a new face was laid out on Battery Buchanan. To avoid a disruption of the telegraph, as had occurred when Curtis's troops cut the wire, a new, protected line was laid in a trench from Fort Fisher to the river, and underwater across the river to Battery Lamb, where it connected with the line from Fort Caswell into Wilmington. Finally, there was the ever-present reminder of why Fort Fisher existed in the first place, as blockade-runners came and went—on December 28, *Banshee* and *Wild Rover* arrived from Nassau and *Little Hattie* departed for Nassau; *Night Hawk* departed on January 3; and four Union blockaders nosed around off the point on January 8.[21]

Welles, meanwhile, was worried about the vast number of ships "locked up" with Porter. The admiral was determined to take Wilmington, but Welles wondered when. Charleston was no longer a serious consideration because General Sherman, who did not suffer from the Union obsession with the city, proposed to bypass it and march straight through the Carolinas to Wilmington. That, however, would take four or five weeks, and Welles could not have the ships tied down for so long; they were needed elsewhere. He was encouraged because, unbeknownst to Sherman, General Grant had made up his mind to take Wilmington, and had sent Bvt. Brig. Gen. Alfred H. Terry with orders to cooperate with the fleet. But Terry was a civilian volunteer who, like Butler, was from the Army of the James, and Welles was not certain he would succeed "unless attended by a well-trained and experienced artillery or engineer officer."[22]

Porter was even more critical of the choice. As far as he was concerned, Terry was another incompetent New England citizen-soldier of the Butler mold, one who would hesitate and worry and "will likely white-wash Butler by doing just as he did," he wrote Fox from Beaufort, adding, "Don't be surprised if I send him home with a flea in his ear, I will as sure as a gun

BRIG. GEN. ALFRED H. TERRY WAS ASSIGNED THE TASK OF TAKING FORT
FISHER AFTER BUTLER FAILED. QUIET, DIPLOMATIC, AND TENACIOUS, HE
ACCOMPLISHED THE TASK AND KEPT THE IRASCIBLE PORTER'S GOODWILL.
Courtesy Little Bighorn Battlefield National Monument

if he comes here with any of his 'ifs and buts,' and stops to consider as to
taking the forts."[23]

Not everyone agreed. Preston was encouraged by the choice, for he
wrote Admiral Du Pont: "In addition to being an honest man with fair
military ability, [Terry] is capable of looking to the good of the country
without first considering his own personal aggrandizement, or the gratifi-
cation of personal vindictiveness."[24]

Preston proved a much better judge of character than Porter or Welles,
for Grant had chosen wisely. Alfred Howe Terry is best remembered as the
general who discovered the bodies of Lt. Col. George Armstrong Custer's

battalion on the Little Bighorn River two days after the disastrous Indian fight of June 25, 1876. Yet he had a solid reputation as a soldier. A wealthy, educated Connecticut bachelor, Terry was an attorney and former clerk of the New Haven County Superior Court. When the war broke out, he entered the army as a ninety-day volunteer but remained when his term expired. He proved a competent soldier and within a year had risen to brigadier general. His easygoing disposition made him almost universally loved among his men, although junior officers occasionally took advantage of it and became insubordinate (eleven years later, this insubordination to Terry would cost Custer his life). His handling of his troops in previous campaigns had impressed Grant and was among the reasons he considered the New Englander the best man for the job.[25]

Because he believed loose talk had greatly contributed to the previous failure, Grant became obsessed with secrecy. Even General Terry was not to know the target until absolutely necessary. When Terry reported to City Point on January 2, Grant told him he would learn the destination at the time of departure. Troops would include 3,300 men from General Ames's Second Division, XXIV Corps; a like number from Brig. Gen. Charles J. Paine's Third Division, XXV Corps, and 1,400 men from the Second Brigade, First Division, XXIV Corps, under Col. J. C. Abbott. As the troops assembled at Bermuda Hundred, Grant circulated a rumor that they would join Sherman in Savannah.[26]

At Beaufort the fleet was coaling and replenishing ammunition and stores. The lighter-draft ships were in the shelter of the harbor, while the larger ones had to anchor in the open sea. Winter weather made the seas rough, and winds sometimes reached gale force. The anchored ships pitched and rolled in the Atlantic. Lifelines were rigged to keep the men on deck from being swept overboard, and often the ships had to slip their anchors and put to sea to ride out the weather away from the dangerous coast.[27]

Despite the change of command, Porter felt the army was out of place in what should have been an entirely naval affair. "I have my doubts about Grant's sending troops here," he wrote, "I don't believe in any body but my own good officers and men." Anxious that the navy have the lion's share of the glory, he intended to land an assault force of sailors and marines that would charge up the beach, storm the works, "and show the soldiers how to do it." A call went out for volunteers, and the response was so great that finally each ship was ordered to assign a detail.[28] "I can do anything with them," the admiral boasted to Fox, "and you need not be surprised to hear that the webfooters have gone into the forts."[29]

To some, the idea of charging across an open beach and assaulting and "boarding" a heavily protected fort was absurd. Nevertheless, on January 4, Porter issued General Order No. 81, stating:

> Before going into action, the Commander of each vessel will detail as many of his men as he can spare from the guns as a landing party.
>
> That we may have a share in the assault when it takes place, the boats will be kept ready, lowered near the water on the OFF side of the vessels. The sailors will be armed with cutlasses, well sharpened, and with revolvers. When the signal is made to man the boats, the men will get in but not show themselves. When the signal is made to assault, the boats will pull around the stern of the monitors land right abreast of them, and board the fort on the run in a seamanlike way.
>
> The marines will form in the rear and cover the sailors. While the soldiers are going over the parapets in front, the sailors will take the sea-face of Fort Fisher.
>
> We can land two thousand men from the fleet and not feel it. Two thousand active men from the fleet will carry the day.[30]

Lieutenant Dewey on the *Colorado* commented that the weapons "evidently were chosen with the idea that storming the face of the strongest work in the Civil War was the same sort of operation as boarding a frigate in 1812."[31]

Terry's troops began boarding their transports at sunset on January 4 and continued until noon the following day. As each vessel completed loading, it headed downriver to Hampton Roads. By 9 P.M. on the fifth, the entire fleet was assembled. "It was not until this time that I was informed that Fort Fisher was the point against which we were to operate," Terry wrote. Even now, however, he was the only one that knew. The transports departed under sealed orders at 4 A.M. on the sixth, and the captains were not allowed to open them until off Cape Henry.[32]

A severe gale set in, scattering the troopships. The trip to Beaufort took two days, and when Terry arrived at the rendezvous point Colonel Abbott's flagship was still taking on a siege train and had not even left Hampton Roads. Terry left General Paine to wait for Abbott and assemble the other ships while he steamed into Beaufort. "Here we found the greater portion of Porter's magnificent fleet and the grim Admiral himself," Capt. Adrian Terry, the general's brother and adjutant, wrote in a letter to his wife.[33]

General Grant's instructions to Terry regarding the irascible Porter were very clear: "It is exceedingly desirable that the most complete understanding should exist between yourself and the naval commander. I suggest, therefore, that you consult with Admiral Porter freely, and get from him the part to be performed by each branch of the public service, so that there may be unity of action. . . . I would, therefore, defer to him as much as is consistent with your own responsibilities."[34]

The initial meeting was formal. As Butler's subordinate, Terry had heard only one side of the Christmas Day failure and was as suspicious of Porter as the admiral was of him. He nevertheless intended to cooperate with the navy, and Porter received him cordially. The second meeting went much better, and the two commanders soon won each other's confidence.[35]

If Terry could establish a solid beachhead on Confederate Point, Grant had written, "the siege of Fort Fisher will not be abandoned until its reduction is accomplished or another plan of campaign is ordered from these headquarters."[36] These orders reflected Terry's own attitude, which he stated to Porter. There would be no withdrawal and no abandoned troops. Upon landing, he intended to hold the beach until Fort Fisher was taken. There was no doubt in Porter's mind that he meant it.[37]

The two commanders set about working out the details of the operation. Three brigades of Ames's Division, under Curtis, Pennypacker, and Bell, would lead the assault, as had been intended during Butler's expedition. Paine's and Abbott's Divisions would form the reserve. To ensure communication between ships and shore, Terry assigned 2nd Lt. W. W. Clements of the U.S. Army Signal Corps to serve as signal officer on Porter's staff. Clements taught the army code to at least one officer on board each ship.[38]

The navy men were confident. As the *Wilderness* finished coaling in Beaufort and prepared to join the fleet as it sailed for New Inlet on January 12, Henry Rogers wrote his parents in Boston, "I would not be anywhere else for all the money in Boston and all the pleasure that could be crammed into an unlimited leave of absence."[39]

13

"THEY'LL HAVE TO SWIM FOR IT"

IN THE CONFEDERACY, General Lee began suspecting something was afoot and advised Lamb that he could not continue the war without supplies from Wilmington. Lee's problem was a critical shortage of food. By December 1864 the situation had become so desperate that the Confederate commissary general paid British blockade-runner Thomas E. Taylor a profit of 350 percent to bring in supplies before the army completely exhausted its rations. By January the food from that run was nearly gone, and Lee told Taylor that if Wilmington fell, he "could not save Richmond."[1]

In retrospect, it seems incredible that Lee even tried to continue the war, given his situation. With the Northern scythe cutting the South into increasingly smaller fragments, the Confederate government's effective control now was limited to portions of Virginia and the two Carolinas, with the remainder of the country either occupied or isolated.

But while the Confederacy could no longer hope to win a decisive victory on the battlefield, the policy, as stated by President Davis, was to prolong the war to such a degree that the United States would exhaust itself in the effort and accept a negotiated peace. Addressing Congress, Davis had said that neither the fall of Atlanta nor a potential loss of Wilmington,

Charleston, or even Richmond would defeat the Confederate cause.[2] Privately, the president was realistic enough to understand that a strategic disaster like the fall of Fort Fisher and the occupation of Wilmington would seriously undermine the Southern bargaining position.[3]

Lamb and Whiting were far from complacent. On January 1, Whiting wrote Secretary Seddon, "It can scarcely be possible that after such extraordinary preparations the enemy has altogether abandoned, or even long postponed his designs upon this port on account of the repulse of the 24th and 25th of December." He pointed out that while Fort Fisher was designed to repel sea assault, it was highly vulnerable from the land side. Unaware that Porter had virtually ruled out running the channel, he believed the Union navy could run past the bar and into the river, taking the fort from behind. The two ironclads, *Raleigh* and *North Carolina,* "would have answered all the purposes of obstructions," one covering each inlet, but they had proven worthless. Consequently, he said more obstructions were needed in the inlets.

The other thing that worried Whiting was that the Union again would do exactly as Weitzel had done—land troops "to occupy the neck above Confederate Point . . . and attempt either to carry Fort Fisher or to establish themselves." Weitzel's effort was unsuccessful "solely owing to the manifest favor of Providence." Because of the fort's vulnerability in that quarter, he said it should be garrisoned by at least twelve hundred to two thousand men, with a substantial supporting force in reserve.[4]

Seddon forwarded the letter to Davis, who saw the logic and suggested it be referred to General Bragg for action. From there the letter made its way through Confederate military bureaucracy until January 20, when the final endorsement stated laconically, "No further disposition required, Fort Fisher having fallen."[5]

Meanwhile, life in Bragg's headquarters in Wilmington had become even more divorced from reality. Although Lamb knew that the fleet was assembling at Beaufort and guessed he was its objective, the reserve units had been withdrawn. This left him with only eight hundred men, one hundred of whom were unfit for duty. Bragg withdrew Hoke's Division from the Sugar Loaf and ordered it into camp north of Wilmington, where, in Lamb's words, the general "had a grand review." The colonel's application for marine torpedoes to lay where the Union ironclads anchored was ignored, as were his requests for additional ammunition, grenades, and other antipersonnel equipment to repel assault.[6]

Oddly enough, Bragg appeared very interested in the completion of a "gun-boat" (presumably the *Wilmington*) then under construction, because he assured Secretary of the Navy Stephen Mallory, "Every assistance in my power will be rendered. The vessel will be of vast importance. Her want was most seriously felt in our late engagement."[7] Actually, what was most seriously wanted in the late engagement was Hoke's Division, which probably could have rounded up Weitzel and his men as prisoners of war in short order.

On January 12, pickets advised Lamb that the returning fleet had been spotted in the distance. At 10 P.M., Col. T. J. Lipscomb, commanding the defenses at Masonboro some thirty miles up the coast, notified Whiting's headquarters that he had seen the lights of some "thirty and more vessels in view moving toward Fisher."[8]

Lamb himself saw lights flashing U.S. Navy signals off the coast. Later, standing on the parapet, he saw the dark forms of the ships come over the horizon and ordered his guns cleared for action. Daisy and the children were sent back across the river to safety.[9]

The appearance of the Union fleet off Fisher finally stirred General Bragg from his lethargy. He ordered Hoke to send a brigade back to the Sugar Loaf to throw up a line of works on the beach between the head of Masonboro Sound and Fort Fisher. Furloughs of the Senior Reserves in Wilmington were suspended, and they were ordered to stand ready to move to the Sugar Loaf as soon as the steamers had finished delivering Hoke's men. One company of 2nd South Carolina Cavalry was ordered to remain at Masonboro while the rest likewise reported to the Sugar Loaf. Bragg also asked Governor Vance for state troops, explaining, "The enemy would not return without the means and the will for a desperate effort." General Hebert, in Smithville, was instructed to inform his commanders that the Cape Fear defenses were to be held "at every hazard and to the last extremity."[10]

The Union ironclads began the bombardment at 7:30 A.M. on January 13. They were much closer than in December—between seven hundred and a thousand yards—and their fire was far more effective. According to Lamb, the shot and shell slamming into the fort, woods, and beach caused "the very earth and sea to tremble." He ordered his men to return fire. This was a mistake. The muzzle flashes gave Union gunners the precise location of his artillery. Ignoring the fortifications, they got the range on the Confederate gun emplacements and began knocking them out with concentrated fire.[11]

While the ironclads pounded the fort, the reserve gunboat division was firing into the woods to clear it of Confederate troops who might oppose Terry's landing. At 8 A.M. the Union soldiers began moving ashore. This time the Confederates stayed by their guns, and a line from the reserve gunboats moved in to give covering fire. These little ships took a pounding until the heavier ships arrived and used their broadsides to force the Confederates to seek shelter. Still, enough men stayed on the parapets to make the landing dangerous.[12]

Shells splashed around the boats carrying the first wave of troops as they pulled toward shore. Nearing the beach, they encountered rifle fire. Despite the efforts of the boat crews to land them in shallow water, most of the troops got caught up in swells and literally were washed ashore. Cold and soaking wet, they picked themselves up and spread out in a skirmish line. One group of Union soldiers moved toward the woods, where they ran across some cattle. By the time the second wave came in, they had killed several of the animals and were skinning them, oblivious to the shooting between the skirmish lines only a few hundred yards away. On the *Malvern,* Ensign Grattan saw the cooking fires and noted with satisfaction, "It was very evident that the troops had come to stay this time."[13]

Watching them, Lamb was desperate for reinforcements. A detachment of sailors arrived from Battery Buchanan and took over three of the fort's guns, but Hoke's Division, held under the thumb of General Bragg, was sprawled aimlessly between Wilmington and the Sugar Loaf. Reilly's battalion had returned to its station after the first battle, only to be ordered by General Whiting back to Fort Fisher to assist the beleaguered Lamb.[14] Reilly, however, was still en route somewhere. Frustrated, Lamb sent an urgent message to Whiting's aide, Maj. James Hill: "Where is Hoke? The Yankees are landing a heavy force. I should have a regiment of veterans before sundown. I have plenty of shelter, and the firing is slow. They [reinforcements] can come in. I have fewer men than on the 24th. When will Reilly arrive? Answer."[15]

During the day, General Whiting arrived with his staff at Battery Buchanan and hiked across the mile or so of exposed plain to Fort Fisher.

Lamb was so busy directing the defense that he was not aware of the general's presence until Whiting walked up alongside on the parapet.

"Lamb, my boy," Whiting said, "I have come to share your fate. You and your garrison are to be sacrificed."

"Don't say so, General," Lamb replied. "We shall certainly whip the enemy again."

Whiting told him that when he left Wilmington, General Bragg was already preparing to abandon the city. Lamb then offered command of the fort to Whiting as senior officer, but the general refused, saying he would be available for advice.[16] This did not prevent him from taking up Lamb's cause, however hopeless it might seem, for he notified Bragg: "The enemy have landed in large force. Garrison too weak to resist assault and prevent their advance. You must attack them at once."[17] But, as Whiting pointed out, Bragg had sunk back into his usual indecision. In fact, the commanding general was so confused about what was happening that, in the midst of the bombardment, he ordered Lamb to report to departmental headquarters in Wilmington. Lamb ignored the message.[18]

Up the beach, the last of the eight thousand Union troops had landed with entrenching tools and provisions for twelve days. It was now 2 P.M. The landings had taken six hours.[19] Admiral Porter remarked, "Now if those soldiers want to get back to their ships they'll have to swim for it, for I'll be damned if I'll let them have any boats to come off in."[20]

The soldiers, however, showed no intention of wanting to get back to their ships. They immediately began entrenching, and within six hours had erected a solid breastwork across the point to protect their rear. "From this time," General Terry reported, "our foothold on the peninsula was secured."

The next morning, the artillery was landed. While it was being placed, Curtis's brigade accompanied Terry and Comstock down Confederate Point. As they marched, the *Chickamauga,* lying in the river, threw a shell that seriously wounded four men. The newly placed Federal batteries opened up, forcing the gunboat a respectful distance upriver. Curtis's men formed a skirmish line while he, Terry, and Comstock reconnoitered. Sheltered among the dunes within six hundred yards of Fort Fisher, they discussed the pros and cons, and Terry decided to assault the fort the following day, assuming naval gunfire could knock enough gaps in the palisade to let the troops through.[21]

Meanwhile, reinforcements were slowly trickling into Fort Fisher. One Confederate naval gunner recalled: "The Yankees had been firing on the fort all day [January 13] with 3 monitors and the iron sides [*New Ironsides*] but at 4 PM they brought the whole fleet to bear and kept up a terrific fire until dark. . . . We were all nearly buried in sand several times. This was caused by shell bursting in the sand. Whenever one would strike near us in the sand it would throw the sand all over us by the cart load."[22] Artist Frank Vizetelly sketched all the scenes of battle—exploding shells, dying men, and shattered gun mounts, the latter becoming more and more common as the highly concentrated Union fire smashed into the gun chambers.[23]

A 15-inch shell from one of the monitors penetrated through more than thirteen feet of dirt and sand on the land face and dropped, completely spent, into a bombproof containing several tons of powder. A Union navy officer who later saw it where it fell estimated that had the shell exploded, the blast "would have blown up every Rebel within rods of it and would have probably made a breach in the Fort large enough to drive two or three wagons abreast through at the same time." Had that happened, he believed the troops could have forced their way in at considerably less risk.[24]

"All day and all night on the 13th and 14th of January the fleet kept up a ceaseless and terrific bombardment," Lamb remembered. "It was impossible for us to repair damage on the land-face at night, for the ironsides and monitors bowled eleven and fifteen-inch shells along the parapet, scattering shrapnel in the darkness. No meals could be prepared for the exhausted garrison; we could scarcely bury our dead without fresh casualties. . . . Not more than three or four of my land guns were serviceable."[25]

During those two days he received seven hundred additional men, including sailors and marines, raising the garrison to fifteen hundred. But this was offset by more than two hundred casualties from the bombardment. As the sun went down on January 14, Fort Fisher was a shattered ruin.[26]

Watching the scene on board the USS *Susquehanna,* Lt. John Bartlett wrote: "The sun set directly behind the fort. I think I never saw a more beautiful one. The smoke of bursting shell against the bright red sky and half the fort in full blaze made it the most magnificent picture ever seen."[27]

Ashore, the soldiers had finished placing the artillery, most of which was along the river. That would be Terry's weakest point during an attack from the rear, because here the Confederates would be most sheltered from the navy guns. Terry himself went out to the *Malvern* to consult with Porter. He told the admiral his troops had recovered from confinement onboard ship and from the drenching as they came ashore, and were ready to fight. They agreed that the warships would move in early the next morning and bombard continuously, with one line of gunboats firing on the palisade. The ships would fire until 3 P.M. Then the assault would begin.[28]

The wooden warships were ordered out to sea for the night, while the ironclads continued firing. A pall of smoke hung over the ocean, obscuring Fort Fisher until a breeze came up and blew it away. The men on the ships could now see it clearly, lit by the bursts of the Union shells.[29]

Among the sailors and marines who had volunteered to assault the fort, the reality of their task was beginning to sink in. On board the *Powhatan,* a sailor named James Flannigan came to Ensign Evans's cabin with a small box.

"Mr. Evans," he began, "will you be kind enough to take charge of this box for me—it has some little trinkets in it—and give it to my sister in Philadelphia?"

When Evans asked why, Flannigan replied, "I am going ashore with you tomorrow and will be killed."

Evans tried to dissuade him, citing the odds against it, but Flannigan was adamant. What struck Evans most was that Flannigan did not appear nervous or frightened, simply resigned to death. Finally he agreed and took the box, making a note for the disposition.[30]

On the *Colorado,* George Dewey was frustrated. As executive officer, he felt he should lead the detail from his ship, but Commodore Thatcher had flatly refused to allow him ashore. As senior officer after Porter, he would assume command of the fleet should anything happen to the admiral. In that case, Dewey would command the *Colorado.*[31]

On Sunday, January 15, the sun rose on a flat, calm sea. The fleet steamed back into position and resumed pounding the fort. Selfridge recalled that "such a storm of shell . . . poured into Fort Fisher, that forenoon, as I believe had never been seen before in any naval engagement."[32]

With practice, the navy's accuracy had steadily improved, and by noon every heavy gun on the land face had been smashed except for one that was protected by the angle of the Northeast Bastion, and three Napoleon fieldpieces in front of the parapet. Two were at the sally port and one at the Riverside Gate to sweep the palisade. Although the Union forces did not realize it at the time, their greatest danger would be from sea-face guns turned toward the beach, concentrated musket fire from the parapets, and the three Napoleons.[33]

Late in the morning, the *Malvern* signaled "Land naval brigade," and sailors and marines from thirty-five of the sixty ships in the fleet began pulling ashore. They came in line abreast, each ship sending as many men as could be spared. The large first-raters provided almost 200 per ship, while as few as twenty came from the little gunboats. Nevertheless, every man was determined to do honor to his ship.[34]

Lt. James Parker was struck by the beauty of the scene. The sun was shining, the sea flat and calm. The ships were "gaily dressed with flags at each masthead and peak and bowsprit, enveloped by the smoke from three hundred guns, whose roar deafened the ear; more than a hundred boats of every size, each carrying the flag of the Union, and loaded to the gunwale with men eager to do [their jobs] and dare to plant the flag in victory upon the fort."[35]

Evans, who led the party from the *Powhatan,* carried half a dozen silk handkerchiefs in his pocket to stop the blood in case he was wounded.[36] Lieutenant Preston, who was going ashore with the group from the *Malvern,* had a premonition he would be killed. Even so, or perhaps because of it, he wore a new blue uniform replete with gold braid. Carrying the admiral's flag during the assault would be Lt. Benjamin Porter, who, although only nineteen, had already risen to succeed Cushing as commanding officer of the *Malvern.* Despite his youth, he had been in the navy for five years, had been cited for bravery, and was a professional who had strengthened discipline on the flagship's crew.

Porter and Preston were friends; Admiral Du Pont called them "two of the brightest young men . . . in the Navy." Captured together at Fort Sumter, they shared imprisonment and were exchanged together. Like Preston, Porter wore a new blue and gold uniform.[37]

As the boats came in and the men debarked on the beach, the fleet kept up a steady fire on the defenses. "Such a hell of a noise I never expect to hear again," Lieutenant Cushing observed as he went ashore with forty men from the *Monticello.* "Hundreds of shell[s] were in the air at once, varying from the five hundred-pounders of the iron-clad to those of a half

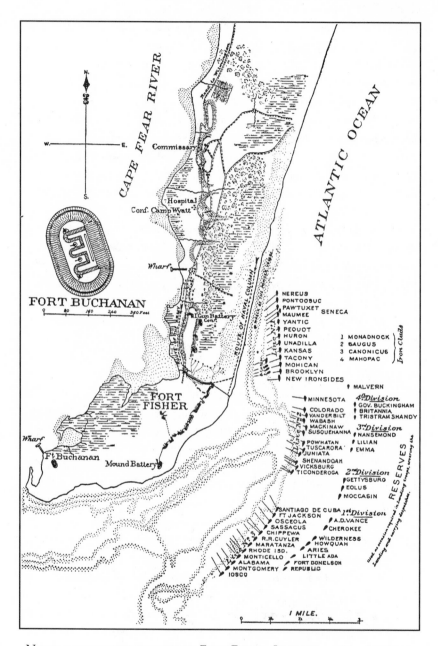

NAVAL AND MILITARY ATTACKS ON FORT FISHER, JANUARY 15, 1865, SHOWING
DIRECTION OF FIRE OF UNION VESSELS
Reprinted from Johnson and Buel, *Battles and Leaders of the Civil War*

and fourth of that weight, but all shrieking in a grand martial chorus that was a fitting accompaniment to the death dance of the hundreds about to fall."[38]

Lieutenant Preston was first ashore, with about ten firemen from each ship. Dodging grape and musket fire, the firemen toted their coal shovels to within 600 yards of the fort and threw up a breastwork. From there, they began edging closer and digging rifle pits. As each series of entrenchments was completed, marines moved in, advancing 400 yards at first; after waiting awhile, they moved another 400 yards. Finally, twenty-five skirmishers advanced 150 yards and dug in.

Although Porter's order had stated the marines were to provide covering fire from the rear, their commander, Capt. L. L. Dawson, USMC, understood his men were to make a final push that would bring them within 200 yards of the fort and complete their cover; as they moved ahead, the sailors would come up behind. When the assault began, the marines would open fire and pin down the defenders on the parapets while the sailors rushed the fort. Once they had gained the parapet, the marines would bring up the rear. "Thus," Dawson noted, "in the event of a repulse, we would have cover to fall back to."[39]

Inside the fort, Lamb did not intend to stand idly by and let the Union men push forward. Despite the risk from marine sharpshooters, he ordered the Napoleons loaded with grape and canister and had his single remaining land-face gun brought to bear. The two guns on the Mound Battery were likewise ordered to shift their fire from the sailors in the boats to the landing party ashore, but despite their height, the range was too great to provide effective antipersonnel fire.

At this juncture, and in Bragg's tardy response to Whiting's pleas, a steamer carrying Hagood's Brigade of South Carolinians approached Battery Buchanan. As it approached the docks, the gunners on the Union warships spotted it and concentrated their fire on it. Only two regiments were landed before the steamer was forced to cast off and head upriver to safety with the remaining troops still on board. The two regiments—or sections of regiments, for the total numbered only 350—ran the mile of open plain from Battery Buchanan to the fort, arriving at the Mound breathless and disorganized. Lamb sent them to one of the bombproofs to rest and catch their breath before deciding what to do with them.[40]

All the while, the boats kept bringing more Union sailors ashore. The

LT. COMDR. K. RANDOLPH BREESE
Reprinted from Johnson and Buel, *Battles and Leaders of the Civil War*

parade between fleet and beach seemed interminable. Altogether there were 1,600 sailors and 350 marines, and it took several hours to land them all. Lieutenant Cushing recalled "the officers all in uniform, bright with gold lace and every man dressed as for inspection." The sand was ankle deep and would slow the advance, and it seemed to him that the blue uniforms contrasting against the sunlit white beach made the sailors perfect targets.[41]

No one knew what he was supposed to do. Each ship's party came ashore under the command of its own officers, many of whom did not know to whom they were supposed to report or who was in charge of the assault. Porter's flag captain, Lieutenant Commander Breese, was at army headquarters to discuss communications between the two forces with General Terry, and nothing would be settled until he returned.[42]

Parker, however, came ashore believing himself in command. When Porter had called for volunteers, he offered his services to lead the column, and Commodore Lanman agreed because he had received no word from the admiral of any other arrangements. Reaching the beach, he landed his 240 *Minnesota* men, who huddled together as fire from the fort passed around them. Soon the Confederates began to find the range, and Parker decided that if the Naval Brigade expected to accomplish anything, it had to assemble and get moving. He went among the commanders of each detachment, ordering them to report to the senior lieutenant commanders of their respective squadrons of the fleet and form into line of battle.[43]

At that moment, Breese arrived and produced orders from Porter naming himself to lead the assault. It was, as Commodore Lanman commented, "a humiliating position" for Parker, who was the senior officer, but upon reading the admiral's orders, he immediately accepted the situation and set about organizing his own men from the *Minnesota*.[44]

In an era when seniority could (and often did) outweigh the desires of a commanding officer, it was to Parker's credit that he did not dispute the choice, for Breese had many worries besides professional jealously. Whatever their combat experience at sea, the navy men knew nothing about land assault. It would be difficult enough just to assemble them, much less coordinate their advance with the army. Breese had the additional headache of keeping an eye on Carlisle Porter, the admiral's son, whom he put to work as a courier, perhaps trying to keep him out of the way.[45]

After some consultation with the senior officers, Breese continued Parker's effort to form the group into three divisions, based on each of the squadrons, as well as the marines. The marines in the lead would be followed by the First Division under Lt. Comdr. Charles H. Cushman, the Second Division under Lieutenant Commander Parker, and the Third Division under Lieutenant Commander Selfridge. The three divisions of sailors were about equal strength, which is to say just over five hundred men each. In theory, it seemed practical. In reality, it was haphazard at best. Unlike soldiers, who are trained in mass maneuver with members of other units, ships' crews are isolated and not accustomed to working in unison with other crews; coordination is a command-level function in the navy. The landing party was composed of small, individual squads from different ships, suddenly thrown together. As the officers tightened the formation, the confused sailors became separated and lost contact with their own officers, crews, and divisions.[46]

General Curtis saw the potential for heavy casualties. Conferring with Ben Porter, he said:

Your men are too compactly formed—your front is too narrow for the
depth of your column. To go into action as your men are now formed
places you under a great disadvantage. You should hold back your main
body until your advanced line gets a foothold on the fort. If you go forward as you are you will be fearfully punished, and the only good your column will do us will be to receive the fire which otherwise would come to
our lines. I fully understand the great advantage the troops will derive from
this movement of the navy, but hesitate to commend it in making it in the
formation you have adopted.

Porter, who resented the advice, coldly informed Curtis "that the Navy
would do its part and merit approval whether the Army gave it or not."
The sailors, after all, had volunteered to help the army on its own ground.
The fact that the army understood ground better than the navy apparently
did not occur to anyone in the navy command.[47]

As the divisions assembled, Parker ran into Acting Volunteer Lt.
Comdr. Joseph D. Danels, executive officer of the *Vanderbilt*, who was
dying of tuberculosis but had left his bunk to lead the party from his ship.
For him, this was more than just a fight; it was a way to restore lost honor.

In 1861 Danels was a regular officer assigned to a ship stationed in his
hometown of Baltimore. With secessionist sentiment rampant, he was
afraid his ship might be ordered to fire on the city. In that case he could
not have obeyed, and felt honor-bound to resign. Eventually, loyalty to
the Union overrode his feelings for Baltimore, but when he tried to withdraw his resignation, the ever-suspicious Gideon Welles refused and
ordered him dismissed along with the secessionist officers. Leaving the
secretary's office, he had encountered Parker, who, unaware of what had
happened, had vented his rage about the officers who had resigned on the
eve of a national crisis.

Danels subsequently secured a commission in the Volunteer Navy.
Now, four years later, he stumbled ashore at Confederate Point, determined to prove himself. Parker was astonished when he saw him.

"Joe, why did you come here?" he demanded. "You are too weak for the
work of to-day."

"Parker, do you remember what you said to me in the Navy Department four years ago?"

"Perfectly, Joe," Parker replied.

"You didn't know how your words stung me, though you didn't mean

LT. COMDR. THOMAS O. SELFRIDGE
Reprinted from Johnson and Buel, *Battles and Leaders of the Civil War*

them for me," Danels said. "This is the first chance I have had since then to redeem that fatal mistake and demonstrate my love for the Union. Do you think I could let it go by?"

"No, Joe; you're right," Parker agreed. "Go on with your men."[48]

The terrain in front of Fort Fisher was an open plain. As it neared the shoreline, however, it sloped sharply downward before the last gentle incline to the water's edge. The slope provided some cover for the advance. So, while the sailors milled about, Ben Porter sought out Captain Dawson and gave him an order from Breese to pull his marines back below the slope while Porter brought up the sailors. Although taken aback by the order, Dawson complied. He did not indicate he was given a reason, but possibly Breese believed, as Lieutenant Commander Selfridge later noted, that it was impossible to dig trenches or rifle pits close enough to the fort "to do much good under broad daylight."[49]

Whatever the motive, the withdrawal of the marines only added to the confusion below the slope as the Naval Brigade moved toward the fort. Dawson contended that once the initial plans for their deployment had been scrapped, he received "*no orders whatever*" for his marines, who ended up abreast Cushman's division.[50]

Partway down the beach, the sick Joe Danels collapsed. "My strength is gone, and with it my last hope," he told Parker, and began crying in frustration.

Parker ordered him carried to the shelter of one of the trenches thrown up by Preston's party. "Turn round, Joe," he said, "keep your face to the foe, and if I come out of this alive I'll see that justice is done you."[51]

True to his word, Parker later reported to Admiral Porter, "It was no fault of his that he was not found in the front of the advance when the order to charge came."[52]

Watching the beach from the parapet of Fort Fisher, Private Arthur Muldoon spotted the advancing bluejackets and called to Lamb, "Colonel, the enemy are about to charge."

Lamb asked Whiting to telegraph Bragg at the Sugar Loaf for assistance. Whiting's message reflected his own frustration: "The enemy are about to assault; they outnumber us heavily. We are just manning our parapets. Fleet have extended down the sea-front outside and are firing very heavily. Enemy on the beach in front of us in very heavy force, not more than seven hundred yards from us. Nearly all land guns disabled. Attack! Attack! It is all I can say and all you can do."[53]

Despite the heavy bombardment, Lamb entered the land face and went through the galleries connecting the traverses, turning out his men. He knew that with the coming assault, the fleet would have to cease fire soon, or risk hitting the Union forces on the beach. He sent sharpshooters up to the gun chambers with instructions to pick off the officers leading the columns. Battery commanders were ordered to form their detachments and, as soon as the bombardment stopped, rush to their guns and drive the assaulting columns back. Making his way back to the Pulpit, he stopped and spoke to the squads assembling under the traverses, going over their assignments one last time. As he was nearing the Pulpit, the fleet fell silent.[54]

14

DISASTER AND TRIUMPH: THE FALL OF FORT FISHER

THE NAVAL BOMBARDMENT ceased at 3 P.M., and the air grew still. As the Confederates watched the sailors and marines working toward them, the quiet was suddenly shattered by dozens of steam whistles from the ships throughout the fleet. It was the signal for the assault, and even Lamb had to admit, "It was a soul-stirring signal both to besiegers and besieged."[1]

The cheering Union men broke into a run down the beach toward one of Fort Fisher's strongest points, the towering Northeast Bastion. Believing this was the main assault force, Lamb placed about 300 men on the bastion and adjoining parapets, with another 200 in adjacent batteries. On the opposite end of the land face, at Shepperd's Battery and the Riverside Gate, were about 200 under Major Reilly, whose detachment had arrived back at the fort in time for the fight. Lamb sent about 350 men from the 21st and 25th South Carolina to reinforce Reilly, believing that these troops with the Napoleon fieldpieces, along with the minefield in front of the land face, would be enough to defend the weak riverfront. He planned to wait until the attackers reached the berm by the palisade before firing the torpedoes. The explosion would cut off the first line of the column, allowing them to be killed or captured, and the supporting lines would be destroyed or thrown back in confusion.[2]

At about eight hundred yards, the Confederates opened fire. "The Rebs let fly with Grape, Canister, and Shots from Small arms, and wee had to face it all with nothing in our hands but a Saber and Revolver," Seaman William T. Cobb wrote to his father.[3]

One of the first to fall was Seaman James Flannigan, the man with the box on the *Powhatan*. Seeing him spin to one side and drop, Evans hurried over and asked if he was badly hurt. Flannigan smiled and slumped over dead.[4]

With the marines caught up next to Cushman's division and the entire line scattered into a single confused column some three hundred yards from front to rear, there was no covering fire, and the Confederates played havoc. Some marines and sailors armed with Sharps rifles managed to get to the front, but their fire was too feeble to do any good.

The plain in front of the fort was absolutely flat, and high on the bastion the Confederate riflemen had no trouble finding a target. "I have been in a grate number of Battles," Seaman Cobb wrote, "But for the Space of time I never Saw men fall so fast in my life. I cannot Describe it with pen and paper." Many sailors now were simply trying to get to the only cover they could see—the fort's palisade.[5]

NORTHEAST BASTION WITH THE STOCKADE AS IT APPEARED TO THE NAVAL BRIGADE. EVEN IN THIS PHOTO, TAKEN AFTER FORT FISHER WAS CAPTURED, THE STRENGTH OF DEFENSES THAT FRUSTRATED THE SAILORS AND MARINES IS EVIDENT.
Courtesy of the North Carolina Division of Archives and History

Evans, who was almost up to the palisade, saw a Confederate officer who he later maintained was Colonel Lamb, standing up on the parapet and calling for his men to fire. The officer was a clear target against the sky, and Evans took aim with his revolver. As he fired, a Confederate bullet ripped through his coat and scraped across his chest. The impact spun the young ensign completely around. Looking down, he saw blood coming out of the hole in his coat. Caught up in the rush of seamen, he continued on.[6]

Several sailors saw a Confederate who may have been the same officer, waving his saber and shouting orders as he directed the defense. The man was about forty yards away, and the shots from their revolvers fell short. Finally, one sailor took a musket from a dead marine and fired. The first shot missed, but the second appeared to have wounded the officer.[7]

As they reached the palisade, a Confederate sharpshooter hit Evans a second time, three inches below the left knee. The force of the shot at close range knocked his legs out from under him, and he landed face down in the sand. He took out one of the handkerchiefs, and with the help of Hoban Sands, a classmate from Annapolis, he tied off the flow of blood and managed to get to his feet. His leg seemed asleep, but he was determined to lead his men through a gap he had spotted in the palisade.[8]

Shells from the bombardment had churned up the sand in front of the palisade, exposing the wires to the minefield. The sailors tripped over them and, realizing what they were, began cutting them. The line of upright logs, however, proved to be an almost insurmountable barrier. Most of the palisade was intact, and the sailors did not have equipment to cut it down.

In the excitement of the charge, many of the officers had moved far to the head of the column, and now they were bunched together with some sailors and a few marines between the palisade and the surf where the Confederates had a clear field of fire. Bullets tore into the gold-braided mass, "and almost every shot from the enemy carried its message of wound or death to some one of our number," Parker reported.

Lieutenant Preston, who had had the premonition of death, was almost to the palisade when a bullet hit him in the left thigh, severing the femoral artery. A sailor who turned to help him was shot and fell on top of him. Someone pulled the sailor off and turned Preston over, but he bled to death from the gushing artery. His friend Lieutenant Porter was mortally wounded only a few yards away. Almost thirty years later, Parker said he could still "see Porter's quivering body stretching out in the last composing agonies of death as I passed it lying on the white sand."

Lt. R. H. Lamson of the *Gettysburg* managed to get twenty paces beyond Porter and Preston before he was shot in the left arm and shoulder. Picking himself up, he kept on toward the fort until he collapsed from loss of blood.

Separated from their leaders, blocked by the palisade, and with grape and canister tearing into their ranks, the divisions disintegrated into a disorganized mass. Most of the marine riflemen were still in the rear, unable to find a position where they could open fire and clear the parapets.[9]

Spotting a gap in the palisade, Evans managed to lead seven men through. The wall was before them, and he began to realize how steep the climb would be. Just then "my sharpshooter friend" got off another round, this one going through his right knee. He tried to stand back up, but his legs would no longer hold him and he was bleeding profusely. The others who had gone in with Evans were also shot down; the company color-bearer managed to get halfway up the parapet before he was killed.[10]

Watching the assault from the *Colorado,* Dewey recalled that "the falling figures of the killed and wounded and the desperate rallies of the living were as clear as a stage pantomime to their shipmates on board the fleet, who witnessed a piece of splendid folly of the same order as the charge of the Light Brigade."[11] The whole thing, he concluded, was "sheer, murderous madness. But the seamen had been told to go and they went."[12]

Evans's men were among only a handful of sailors that managed to get around the palisade or through the gap before they were either killed or thrown back by the withering Confederate fire. Captain Dawson of the marines, less than sixty yards from the palisade, saw only a few get through, and they fell back almost immediately. Seeing them hurry back to the protection of the palisade, someone yelled "They are retreating!" The officers were almost all at the head of the column, and with no one to steady the men in the rear, the tail of the column began to come apart as the men fell back. It all happened so fast that Dawson later insisted no one reached the parapet.[13]

Parker managed to reach an angle where the palisade swung back to parallel the beach around the corner of the Northeast Bastion. Looking up, he saw some Confederates on the parapet who appeared to be un-

SAILORS AND MARINES RUSH THE PALISADE BY THE NORTHEAST BASTION
Reprinted from Johnson and Buel, *Battles and Leaders of the Civil War*

armed and waving their hats at him. Shouting "Forward," he led a group of officers, sailors, and marines toward the gap in the palisade, assuming that the rest of the brigade would follow. But on looking back, he saw most of the men running up the beach away from the fort. Officers were trying to rally them, and some of the sailors and marines shouted after them that they were cowards, but it was no use.[14]

Parker now had about sixty men, and the cheering Confederates concentrated all their fire on them. Four officers—Lieutenant Commander Cushman, Acting Ensign Frederick A. O'Connor, and Acting Master's Mates Joseph Simms and Arthur F. Aldrich—went down immediately. Realizing any further effort would be suicidal, Parker ordered the men to fall back to the angle of the palisade. Nevertheless, the wounded Aldrich, Acting Ensign George T. Davis, Seaman Louis C. Shepard, an unknown petty officer from the *Tacony*, and marine private Henry Thompson actually got inside the palisade before being driven back. Parker's men huddled behind the angle until dark, with the Confederates taking potshots at anyone who showed himself. The petty officer was killed and Aldrich was wounded again, this time severely.[15]

The collapse of the rear threw the entire Naval Brigade into confusion. Most fled directly up the beach, though some had the good sense to take cover where the beach sloped down toward the surf and the angle of the palisade blocked fire from the bastion. Dawson later complained that had the example been followed "by the whole of the First Division . . . we would have gained shelter with a considerable force about 100 yards from the main bastion . . . and lost fewer men than we did."[16]

Some officers tried to get control, but their shouts, threats, and curses were lost in the chaos. Even the exhausted, tubercular Joe Danels, still lying in the trench where Parker had left him, got to his feet and staggered up to the column, trying to rally the men. Breese rushed toward the rear, hoping to assemble those with rifles and get them under cover so they could pin down the Confederates on the parapet. By now, though, the line was too far back, and he gave up and went back up to what remained of the head of the column.[17]

Another officer, Lt. John Bartlett, shouted and waved his sword in frustration. He was determined to hold his ground and go into the fort, but it was no use. "I could have cried when the blue-jackets retreated," he wrote his sisters, "but it was high time for me to look out for myself." He dove behind the angle of the palisade and began burrowing into the sand. It was soft and dry, and with very little trouble, he managed to throw up enough of a breastwork to shield himself from the fire. Still he kept digging, and inadvertently gave the Confederate riflemen a target; every time he threw up another handful of sand, bullets whined over his head, knocking the sand down on top of him.[18]

Back at the palisade, Evans pulled out another handkerchief and tried to stop the blood. By now he had lost so much that he was weak, and it took considerable effort. "In the meantime," he recalled, "my sharpshooter friend, about thirty-five yards away, continued to shoot at me, at the same time addressing me in a very forcible but uncomplimentary language."

The sharpshooter scored another hit, and Evans felt a sharp pain in his ankle. At first he thought it had hit him there, but then he realized the ankle was simply twisted from the bullet striking the toe of his shoe. It knocked off the end of one of his toes and tore off the sole of the shoe.

Now Evans had had enough of the man. He rolled over to face him and, raising his revolver, "addressed a few brief remarks" to the Southerner. Just as the Confederate was handed a freshly loaded rifle, Evans

ENSIGN ROBLEY D. EVANS WAS PHOTOGRAPHED ON CRUTCHES AFTER BEING
SEVERELY WOUNDED IN BOTH LEGS DURING THE ASSAULT ON FORT FISHER.
EVANS, WHO REFUSED A DISABILITY DISCHARGE, BECAME KNOWN AS
"FIGHTING BOB" AND RETIRED A REAR ADMIRAL AND NATIONAL HERO.
Reprinted from Evans, *A Sailor's Log*

fired, striking the man in the throat. He staggered for a moment, then fell off the parapet and rolled down the embankment. Evans could see his feet sticking up over a pile of sand and knew the man was dead.[19]

As the column fell back, a marine named Wasmouth from the *Powhatan* dashed through the palisade, grabbed Evans under one arm, and pulled him back behind cover. At that moment the fleet opened a covering fire; with shells from the ironclads exploding dangerously close, Wasmouth pulled him back another fifty yards and put him in a shell hole where he had cover.

Evans, now groggy from the loss of blood, managed to tell Wasmouth to take cover, but the marine replied, "The bullet has not been made that will kill me." Evans was roused back to consciousness by the sound of a bullet striking something very close. He looked up and saw Wasmouth clutching his neck, with jets of blood shooting from a severed jugular. He staggered to the edge of the surf, fell over, and bled to death. Evans passed out.[20]

Although some of the marines were caught up in the mass confusion of the retreating sailors, Dawson still had most of them under control. He ordered them to take cover behind the slope of the beach and return fire. This gave them protection and distracted the Confederates, forcing them to seek cover. As fire from the fort slackened, he ordered them to retreat up the beach in squads, keeping one group on the slope about fifty yards from the end of the palisade.[21]

Inside the fort, the cheering Confederates believed they had thrown back the main assault. Lamb, who had not been wounded in the fighting thus far, wrote, "The heroic bravery of [the Union] officers . . . could not restrain the men from panic and retreat, and with small loss to ourselves, we witnessed what had never been seen before, a disorderly rout of American sailors and marines."

But when he glanced toward the Riverside Gate, he was amazed to see Federal battle flags on the traverses. The navy assault had not been the main attack after all; it had merely drawn attention from the soldiers, who had taken advantage of the confusion on the Northeast Bastion and rushed the gate and Shepperd's Battery. Now they were actually inside the fort.[22]

The soldiers had worked down the river side under the cover of the woods, even as the sailors and marines were coming down the beach. Curtis's brigade was in the lead, with Colonels Pennypacker and Bell follow-ing. As the ships' whistles blasted, Curtis ordered them forward. The Union soldiers rushed out of the trees and slogged through the morass until they reached the palisade. Except for the rattle of their equipment, they were silent; Curtis had forbidden cheering to conserve their wind. Despite the bombardment, much of the palisade was intact, and Union sharpshooters with Spencer repeating rifles opened a covering fire while pioneers hacked away at the upright logs with their axes.[23]

Despite heavy fire from the fort, forty or fifty got through the palisade, scaled the parapet, and overran the one columbiad still serviceable in Shepperd's Battery. The flag of the 117th New York was raised on the tra-verse, then Curtis's men captured the Napoleon at the Riverside Gate. Pennypacker's men rushed into the fort, some through the gate and others over the parapets.[24]

While Whiting led a counterattack against the Federals on the third traverse, Lamb rushed through the sally port to get a better view of the Union hold. From outside, he could see a furious hand-to-hand fight for the fourth gun chamber as Whiting's men reinforced Reilly. "They had recovered one gun chamber with great slaughter, and on the parapet and on the long traverse of the next gun chamber the contestants were savagely firing into each others faces, and in some cases clubbing their guns, being too close to load and fire," Lamb remembered. The Confederates were exposed not only to fire from the front but from the captured works cov-ering the Riverside Gate. Union troops were pouring through the gate unopposed.[25]

Going back into the fort, Lamb found that General Whiting had been wounded and taken to the hospital. He was not alone, for the carnage was heavy among officers on both sides. Young Pennypacker was shot com-pletely through; although he survived, he would remain partially disabled. Colonel Bell was mortally wounded on the bridge over the morass as he rushed toward the Riverside Gate. "Our killed and wounded on the para-pet impeded our advance to the fourth traverse so that we were scarcely able to go forward without treading on them," Curtis later wrote.[26]

The remnants of the hard-fighting Confederates in the first two gun chambers were now being herded out of the way as prisoners. Many of the South Carolinians sent to support them when the assault began were cow-ering in the bombproofs. The fort's electrician could not detonate the mines because of the torn-up wires. Lamb telegraphed Bragg for help.[27]

At Battery Buchanan, Chapman saw the Federal flags on Fort Fisher's traverses and concluded the situation was hopeless. All hands were mustered for roll call. According to Seaman Robert Watson, Chapman "informed us that the fort was lost and it was useless for him to keep us here to be taken prisoners or slaughter, that we could fight the battery for some time and probably do the enemy some damage but that we could not hold it for any length of time."

Chapman ordered them into the boats to cross to the opposite shore, but as the sailors boarded, waist deep in the frigid Cape Fear, he changed his mind and sent them back to their posts. Two of Battery Buchanan's four guns would not bear on Fort Fisher, but the others, an 11-inch and a 10-incher, opened fire. The shells screamed into the fort, exploding among friend and foe alike.[28]

The shelling from Buchanan temporarily halted the Union advance. Pressing the advantage, Lamb ordered the guns on the Mound and the two remaining sea-face columbiads to fire into the Federal ranks inside the fort. With the other sea-face guns knocked out, most of those troops no longer had anything to do, and about a hundred returned with Lamb to reinforce the land face. He went among the South Carolinians urging them to flank the Federals, and had the Napoleons brought in from the sally port. "I went along the galleries and begged the sick and slightly wounded to come out and make one supreme effort to dislodge the enemy," he wrote. "As I passed through portions of the work, the scene was indescribably horrible. Great cannon broken in two, their carriages wrecked and among their ruins the mutilated bodies of my dead and dying comrades. . . . I passed quickly down the rear of the line and asked officers and men if they would follow me; they all responded that they would."

Ordering "charge bayonets," Lamb led his troops up onto the parapet, waving his saber and shouting, "Forward, double quick, march!" Then he fell to his knees, blood gushing from a bullet wound in his hip. The same Federal volley forced his men back behind the breastwork. The brief counterattack failed, and Lamb was carried to the hospital and placed on a stretcher next to General Whiting.[29]

Meanwhile, Pennypacker's men forced their way toward Fort Fisher's sally port and opened it from behind. About a quarter of the land face was in Federal hands, and they were pushing their way down the parapet. As the Union men scaled a traverse from one side, the Confederates scaled it from the other, and vicious fighting broke out on the narrow summit.[30]

Water pouring into his shell hole brought Evans back to consciousness. Weak and confused, he began to realize that the tide was coming in and the hole was filling with water. Offshore, he saw a monitor firing on the fort, and thought if he could just get a piece of driftwood he could swim out to her. As he grew more aware, however, he knew that if he did not get out of the hole, he would drown. "Dead and wounded men were lying about in ghastly piles, but no one to lend me a helping hand," he remembered. His legs useless, he tried to pull himself out with his hands, but the sand gave way and he fell back in. Finally, with one last effort, he managed to roll himself up the side and out onto the beach.

A short distance away, Evans saw a marine behind a pile of sand firing into the fort. Evans called to come pull him behind cover, but the marine refused, saying the Confederate fire was too heavy. Evans pulled his revolver and repeated the order, and the marine rushed over and pulled him back behind his sandpile.

He felt some movement under him, and realized he was lying across a second marine, so frightened that he had completely buried himself in the land. A shell exploded over his head, and the buried marine pulled his knees up under his chin. The motion sent pain shooting through Evans's broken legs.

"Hello!" Evans said. "Are you wounded?"

"No, sir," the marine whimpered. "I am afraid to move."

"All right, then. Keep quiet, and don't hurt my legs again!"

But every time a shell came over, the buried marine jerked. Finally, Evans "tapped him between the eyes" with the butt of his revolver. After that, "the poor creature . . . would lie still and cry as the shells flew over us."[31]

From their shelter in the angle of the palisade, the trapped sailors and marines could hear the sounds of the fight inside the fort. They quickly learned to distinguish the cheering of the Union troops from the ear-piercing yell of the Confederates, and knew when their troops had taken another traverse.[32]

Bragg, meanwhile, had momentarily stirred and sent two of Hoke's brigades toward Fort Fisher. They overran the Federal picket line on the beach, but on the riverfront they encountered the black troops from Paine's

XV Corps. These soldiers, who had not even disembarked from their transports during Butler's expedition, held their line, and Bragg recalled Hoke. The disgruntled Confederates marched back to the Sugar Loaf, certain that, given a little more time, they could have broken through, attacked the Union troops from the rear, relieved Fort Fisher, and driven Terry into the sea.[33]

As the sun began to set, Evans remembered, "The scene on the beach . . . was a pitiful one—dead and wounded officers and men as far as one could see. As a rule, they lay quiet on the sand and took their punishment like the brave lads they were, but occasionally the thirst brought on by loss of blood was more than they could bear, and a sound-save would drift along, 'Water, water, water!' and then all would be quiet again. It was one of the worst of the awful features of war."[34]

It seemed that squads of Confederate riflemen on the parapets were deliberately firing at the wounded as they tried to crawl away. "Now and then a wounded man would raise his head," Bartlett wrote. "A dozen bullets would fly toward him in an instant."[35]

Evans saw Assistant Surgeon William Longshaw, Jr., of the *Minnesota* working among the wounded. He called for the surgeon to lie down, but Longshaw, who had served with distinction on the monitor *Lehigh* during the bombardment of the Charleston batteries, took a canteen from a dead marine and gave a sip of water to Evans and another man. "We will have you all off the beach to-night," he said, and continued with his work.

Longshaw was tending a mortally wounded sailor when a Confederate bullet struck him in the head. His body was found side by side with the sailor's the next morning. Both bodies had been stripped. Parker speculated, "Some ghouls from our own forces had done this foul deed, for no Confederate had been near the spot."[36]

Many ignored the Confederate fire to do whatever they could to aid and comfort the wounded on the beach. Breese noted the gallantry of "a young lad of the *Wabash,* named Myers," who three separate times left the shelter of a deep hole in the sand to dash out, retrieve wounded men, and carry them back to his hole, "and this within a hundred yards of Fort Fisher."[37]

At Terry's request, the fleet resumed fire to clear the parapets of Confederates so the troops could advance. Army signalmen sent coordinates to Porter, who passed them on to the *New Ironsides*. The giant ironclad adjusted her guns away from the sea face and began pounding the land-face gun chambers just ahead of the Union forces. The 11- and 15-inch shells exploding among the Confederates drove them from the parapets. The only ones spared were those so close to the Union assault force that firing on them would have brought slaughter to both sides.[38]

The ships were anchored so that the trajectory was almost a right angle to the parapets; if they overshot, the shells generally fell among the defenders inside the fort rather than near the Union men. Fort Fisher's massive construction now was actually working against the Confederates, because the parapets were so wide that the traverses sheltered the attackers from the naval bombardment. As each gun chamber was knocked to pieces and its defenders killed or driven out, the blue-coated soldiers poured into it.[39]

This precision fire was coordinated by Lieutenant Clements, the army signal officer assigned to Porter's staff. The admiral later expressed his gratitude in a special report that he asked Welles to pass on to Secretary of War Stanton for attachment to Clements's file "as a slight evidence of my appreciation of him."[40]

Although bombardment helped the Union soldiers fighting on the parapets, it trapped the navy men still crouched by the palisade.[41] Most of the gunfire was on target, but there were enough near misses to undermine the already low morale. "We were now in a rather tight place, as some of the shells burst close to us, and we began to think of a surrender, but intended to hold out tho a shell did land directly among us," Lieutenant Bartlett wrote his sisters. "They landed everywhere but just where we lay." It was nerve-racking as bullet- and shell-ridden splinters of the palisade showered down on him, and he began wishing he were somewhere else.

A little after 6 P.M., the sailors and marines in the angle of the palisade decided it was dark enough to make a break. In small groups, they started up the beach to rejoin their brigade, carrying their wounded and their colors. There was still enough light for the Confederates on the parapet, though, and bullets began churning the sand around them. Many were "shot down like sheep as they ran," and over fifty now lay dead at the foot of the palisade. This discouraged any further attempts for the time being.[42]

The incoming tide began washing over the dead and wounded. Many called for help, but it would have been suicidal for the men behind the palisade to leave their shelter. Bartlett spotted Lieutenant Porter lying on the beach about a hundred yards away, and wondered if he were still alive. Finally, he could stand it no longer, and dashed out and dove into the sand beside Porter. Finding he was dead, Bartlett removed his sword, belt, and gloves.

Bullets were flying all around, and Bartlett decided to keep going. A few hundred yards up the beach, he found a wounded master's mate from the *Tuscarora* and helped him to a temporary field hospital, where he turned the man over to the surgeons. After that he helped carry wounded to the boats, until a boat from the *Susquehanna* pulled in and took him back to his ship. Arriving on board, Bartlett found Commodore Gordon surprised to see him. He had been reported killed at the palisade.[43]

A fireman from the gunboat *Chicopee* found Evans, but he was shot down after hauling him only a few feet. After dark, two of Cushing's sailors found him and carried him in turns on their backs the mile and a half up the beach to the field hospital.[44]

With the darkness, the wounded Lt. Comdr. Charles Cushman managed to assemble his division and post it in lines to cover the rear in case Bragg should again try to send a relief force.[45]

The assault was stalled. Quite simply, the Federals and Confederates had fought each other to exhaustion. Ames and Curtis were arguing vehemently. Ames wanted to entrench for the night and resume the fight the next day, while Curtis believed he could carry the fort. A short time earlier, Ames had sent Curtis entrenching tools, and Curtis had thrown them over the top of the traverse to the Confederates. He was almost to the Northeast Bastion, and he ordered Capt. David Magill of the 117th New York to gather the first men he saw and take the next traverse. Then Curtis mounted one of the traverses and was considering angles of attack when a shell exploded overhead. One fragment destroyed his left eye, and the other tore out part of the frontal bone of his skull. Unconscious and barely alive, he was carried off.[46]

Up the beach at his headquarters, General Terry was worried. He had Ames's report, and was seriously considering calling off the assault and digging in for a siege. Before deciding, however, he consulted Colonel Comstock, who advised sending in Abbott's and Paine's reserves. These troops were fresh, and the Confederates had no one to match them. Terry ordered Abbott into the fort, with Paine standing by outside under fire.

As Comstock anticipated, this marked the end. Although fighting continued inside the fort, the Union could press on and take it.[47]

Active command of Fort Fisher had devolved on Major Reilly, who led a third counterattack. This time, the erstwhile timid South Carolinians came into the fight, and very briefly the Federal assault was thrown back. But by 8 P.M. the Confederates' ammunition was virtually exhausted and Lt. John Kelly, Lamb's aide, came to the hospital and advised surrender. Remembering his promise to the women of Wilmington, as well as General Lee's dependence on Fort Fisher, Lamb replied that as long as he was alive the fort would hold. Because of the heavy loss of blood, Lamb's wound did, in fact, appear mortal; the less wounded General Whiting pledged to continue the fight if Lamb died.[48]

By 9 P.M., Union troops had occupied so much of Fort Fisher that further bombardment was dangerous and Porter ordered a cease-fire. The sudden end of the heavy gunfire brought a strange sort of silence to the fleet. "With the exception of an occasional volley and a desultory discharge of musketry in the farther end of the fortifications, all was quiet," one officer of the *Malvern* noted.[49]

The Confederate situation was hopeless. From Battery Buchanan, Maj. William Saunders, Lamb's chief of artillery, telegraphed General Hebert in Smithville: "The fort will be surrendered. We can get no help."[50]

For General Bragg, whose reasoning was growing cloudier by the moment, this was unbelievable and unacceptable. With Union soldiers mopping up the remaining resistance, he ordered Col. Robert Graham at Fort Anderson to take his command to reinforce Fort Fisher. "Reports of enemy's carrying any portion of that place [are] unfounded," the order stated. Although earlier Bragg had instructed Graham to bring out wounded, the colonel was now told, "Order to bring out any portion of garrison from Fisher is countermanded."[51]

Major Reilly was under no such illusions. Fort Fisher was lost. His only hope was Battery Buchanan, which Lamb had constructed in part as a refuge where the garrison could retreat and be carried off by boat if the fort fell.[52] Gathering up the wounded Lamb and Whiting, and assembling a handful of soldiers and marines, Reilly led them to the battery. "When we left the hospital," Lamb remembered, "the men were fighting over the adjoining traverse and the spent balls fell like hailstones around us."[53]

Battery Buchanan was deserted, its guns spiked and boats gone. Isolated at the battery, but with the hopeless fight at Fort Fisher in plain view, Chapman and his officers had begun drinking. Then Major Saunders arrived, sent his telegram to General Hebert, and suggested it was time to abandon the battery. The well-lubricated Chapman needed no prodding. He took his men across the river to Battery Lamb, where he rested them for half an hour before starting them toward Wilmington.[54]

As the last remnants of Fort Fisher's garrison waited for the inevitable, a rowboat drew up to the wharf near Battery Buchanan. It carried Gen. Alfred H. Colquitt, sent by Bragg to assume command in one last slap at Lamb and Whiting. Encouraged despite the insult, Lamb believed even now that if Bragg attacked from the rear and sent a fresh brigade to Battery Buchanan, the fort could be retaken. Colquitt was unconvinced. As he prepared to depart in his rowboat, someone suggested he take Lamb, but the colonel refused on the grounds that his duty was to his men. Instead, Lamb asked that Whiting be carried out because he had come to Fort Fisher as a volunteer with no official responsibility. At that point, however, approaching Union soldiers were spotted and Colquitt beat a hasty retreat, leaving Lamb and Whiting to their fate.[55]

Shadows could be seen advancing through the darkness. Major Reilly went out to meet them. For him, it was doubly humiliating. Almost four years before, he had been forced to surrender a Federal fort to North Carolinians. Now, just across the river from that same spot, he handed over North Carolina's greatest fort to Federals.

After Reilly returned with the Union soldiers, Whiting asked for their commanding officer. When General Terry stepped forward and introduced himself, Whiting said, "I surrender, sir, to you the forces under my command. I care not what becomes of myself." Terry accepted the surrender graciously, and then, mounting a horse that had been brought to Battery Buchanan by the Confederates, hurried back to Fort Fisher to send the news to General Grant.[56]

It was 10 P.M., January 15, 1865. The battle of Fort Fisher was over, and the Cape Fear River was effectively closed. An hour later, Bragg was still ordering Colonel Graham at Fort Anderson to take his troops to Fisher.[57]

15

AFTERMATH

ADMIRAL PORTER WAS IN HIS STATEROOM smoking his pipe, awaiting the outcome of the fight. All the bluster was gone. He was physically ill but too anxious to rest. Whether or not he consciously acknowledged it, he had much to answer for. He had boasted to Fox that his "webfooters" would show the army how to take a fort. Now, preliminary estimates showed as many as 250 dead because of his arrogance. The list included familiar names like Preston and Ben Porter. So far there was no attempt to reckon the number of wounded.[1]

While the admiral sat alone, the other officers were in the flagship's wardroom quietly discussing the day's events and recalling friends who had fallen. The *Malvern's* bell had just finished striking 10 P.M. when Lieutenant Clements was called on deck to answer an army signal from shore. His counterpart was waving a torch in Union code from atop Fort Fisher's Northeast Bastion. About that time a rocket was fired from within the fort, and the men on the ships heard cheering. The decoded message was sent to Porter, who rushed on deck and ordered three cheers for the fall of Fort Fisher.[2]

"The Admiral never before gave an order which was as heartily obeyed," Ensign Grattan wrote. "Everyone appeared to be wild with joy. All discipline was relaxed and the cheers of the officers and sailors could be heard far and wide over the smooth water . . . lights began to flash in all directions. The flag ship signalled the fleet and repeated the Admiral's order, and in a few seconds thousands of voices were united in tremendous cheering. All the vessels were quickly illuminated, rockets and signal lights were flashing in the air, bells were rung and steam whistles were screaming forth the glad tidings."[3]

On board the *Susquehanna,* Lieutenant Bartlett was glad to be alive. He took charge of the whistle, "and made it express my sentiments in many a loud blast."[4]

Henry Rogers of the *Wilderness* scribbled a quick note to his parents: "The Wilderness to 4 Kingston Street. Greeting! Fort Fisher is Ours! Illuminate and cheer as the Fleet is now doing, for a death-blow has this day been given to Secession. Your affectionate son is pretty well tired out but jubilant!"[5]

"Such . . . noise you never hered," William Cobb wrote to his father, "of men huzaying, Steam whistles Screaming, Rocketts, the air was a live with rocketts of all Collars. . . . [I]t done me more good to See it for I had an active part on gaining the Fort."[6]

The waiting over, Porter collapsed and had to be assisted to his cabin. Meanwhile, boats started for shore for the long, grim task of retrieving the navy dead and wounded.[7]

The significance of the rockets was not lost on the Confederates at nearby installations. At 10:30 P.M., Lieutenant Bright at Battery Lamb telegraphed General Hebert: "All at once firing has ceased; also signals; and the whole fleet are now throwing rockets up—all colors. It is fully believed that the fort has surrendered. I will telegraph you again in a few moments."[8]

At 11:15 P.M., Bright again contacted Hebert, advising that men "are constantly arriving from Battery Buchanan: they report the fort surrendered."[9] Five minutes later he reported that Chapman had come in from Battery Buchanan and confirmed the news. Fort Fisher had surrendered, and Whiting and Lamb were prisoners. Bright's own position at Battery Lamb was becoming untenable.[10]

Despite their loss, even the Confederates found the Union fireworks display impressive. Seaman Robert Watson, one of the refugees from Battery Buchanan, grudgingly admitted to his diary, "The sight was magnificent."[11]

January 16 was Acting Ensign Francis Sands's birthday. At 5 A.M. he slipped away from his *Gettysburg* men and retraced the line of the charge along the beach to the fort, noting the appalling death and destruction. The ground was littered with bodies. Reaching the breach in the palisade, he found the body of the sailor who had gone farthest in the charge, stretched out on the ground with his head toward the fort. The slope "had been torn and beat out of shape" by the bombardment. Inside the fort, Sands "went from casemate to casemate which were filled with dead and wounded. Out in the open, where could be seen the burned frames of the barracks and quarters which had been fired by the shells from the fleet, I saw numbers of dead. . . . On the traverses were the bodies of the fallen, showing how desperately but vainly the gallant Confederates under Lamb and Whiting had defended the works."

Sands wandered along the interior of the sea face, pausing to sketch the intact Armstrong rifle and the Mound, then returned to the Northeast Bastion. Inside the casemate, he found one of the electric storage batteries that was to have fired the torpedoes. Going back out, he climbed over the slope, where he located a strand of wires leading from the battery to the torpedoes. It had been cut by a shell, and the ends of the wires were welded together by the heat of the explosion. Sands cut off a piece as a souvenir and, after gathering up pieces of grape and canister as mementos, returned to the landing. There he was met by an officer from the *Gettysburg* with orders to return to the ship. As he boarded the launch, he met Acting Ensign A. S. Laighton and Assistant Paymaster R. H. Gillette, who were coming ashore. It was the last time Sands saw them alive.[12]

Immediately after the capture of Fort Fisher, General Ames ordered Lt. Col. Samuel M. Zent to post a guard on all the magazines and bombproofs. Zent toured the fort, placing sentries as he went along, but failed to notice the main magazine, sheltered behind its protective wall to the rear of the traverses, and still containing, according to Colonel Lamb's estimate, about thirteen thousand pounds of powder.

Lamb called the magazine "an artificial mound, covered with luxuriant turf, a most inviting bivouac for wearied soldiers." A large number of Federal soldiers did bivouac on it, and exhausted Confederates were resting in the galleries inside.[13]

During the night, Union soldiers, sailors, and marines wandered about the fort, plundering and collecting souvenirs. Some had run across a cache of liquor and were drunk. They were carrying open lights and discharging their muskets indiscriminately. About 7:30 A.M., some of them apparently touched off the powder in the magazine.[14]

The men on the ships felt the shock and saw a "great pall of smoke spreading umbrella-like over the fort."[15] Standing on the deck of the *Malvern,* Porter witnessed the explosion. "The earth-works seemed to be in motion, the light was obscured by smoke and sand, amid which I could see the bodies of many people carried up in the air, and I heard a great explosion which shook the earth."

The devastating effect of the explosion convinced Porter that the powder boat would have demolished Fort Fisher "if it could only have been got near enough to the fort or inside, and *all* the powder [in the *Louisiana*] had exploded." Despite his personal hatred for Butler, Porter was convinced that the failure of the idea "was not General Butler's fault."[16]

The exact number of dead and wounded that the explosion added to the already heavy Union casualty list has never been exactly determined. Later that morning, Seaman Cobb wrote that so far 150 bodies had been recovered from the sand. Among the dead were Acting Ensign Laighton and Assistant Paymaster Gillette of the *Gettysburg,* who had gone up to the fort from the landing, and had just reached the parapet opposite the magazine when it blew up.[17]

A subsequent court of inquiry convened by order of General Terry absolved the defeated Confederates of any blame for the explosion, attributing it instead "to carelessness on the part of persons . . . unknown."[18]

The gruesome task of cleaning up, sorting out the wounded, and burying the dead began. The dead were piled up between the traverses, sometimes a dozen deep. "It was a terrible sight," Lieutenant Bartlett recalled. "Too horrible to describe."[19]

Henry Rogers agreed, but tried to describe it anyway: "The dead and wounded, the fragments of shells, dismounted guns, splintered carriages, earth works ploughed in furrows, devastation, ruin, death in every attitude and every form, these are things that I have looked upon to-day."[20]

It took a long time to find the bodies of Preston and Ben Porter. Grattan noted the "calm, peaceful smile" on Porter's face, "but Preston wore a look of agony as his sufferings must have been terrible."[21]

Losses were heavy. On the Union side alone, the army listed 664 killed, wounded, or missing. Naval and marine casualties came to 309 killed, wounded, or missing. Confederate losses—always a vague area—were estimated at 500 killed and wounded, as well as the entire garrison taken prisoner.[22]

Welles learned "the glorious news" on the morning of Tuesday, January 17. He mourned the losses of Preston and Lieutenant Porter, but chortled that the victory would be "severe for Butler." As for his admiral, Welles wrote, "It is a great triumph for Porter,—greater since the first failure and the difference with Butler."[23]

Butler himself had just finished testifying before the Joint Committee on the Conduct of the War about the impregnability of Fort Fisher when the Navy Yard guns began booming in salute. A messenger entered the committee room and handed a piece of paper to committee chairman B. F. Wade.

Navy Department, Jan. 17, 1865

Fire a national salute in honor of the capture on the 15th instant of the rebel works on Federal Point (Fort Fisher), near Wilmington, N.C., by a combined attack of the army and navy.

Gideon Welles, Secretary of the Navy

Wade read it and passed it along to the members. When they had finished reading, it was handed over to Butler. He stared at it and said nothing.[24]

Although Porter was victorious, he needed someone to blame for the failure and heavy casualties of the naval assault. The obvious target was the marines. In his report to Welles, he wrote that the Naval Brigade

had succeeded in getting up to within a short distance of the fort and laid securely in their ditches. We had but very few killed and wounded to this point. The marines were to have held the rifle pits and cover the boarding party, which they failed to do. On rushing through the palisades . . . the head of the column received a murderous fire of grape and canister, which did not, however, check the officers and sailors who were leading; the parapets now swarmed with rebels, who poured in a destructive fire of musketry. At this moment, had the marines performed their duty, everyone of the rebels on the parapets would have been killed.[25]

The report infuriated Captain Dawson, who wrote his own version of the affair to Col. Jacob Zeilin, Commandant of the Marine Corps. After pointing out that Porter was nearly a mile offshore, he commented that

> the fort was defended by 2,000 muskets behind a parapet, with but 350 [marine] muskets opposed on an open beach; having to run under fire before reaching a point where they could return their fire . . . a wholly unorganized force of 1,400 men rushed along an open beach for 600 yards under fire by the flank, armed with pistols and cutlasses; and . . . that the naval party assaulted *before* the army, instead of *after,* thereby not only drawing the whole fire of the rebels upon themselves, but acting in direct violation of the admiral's express written order.[26]

This was not quite true, for the army had moved simultaneously with the Naval Brigade. Nevertheless, it summarized the basic facts of the assault. Dawson placed most of the blame for the fiasco on Breese, who he contended sent the brigade out from cover onto the exposed beach before it was properly organized, failed to assign the marines before ordering the charge, and ordered the charge before the Naval Brigade was organized.[27]

At home and nearing retirement, Admiral Du Pont had mixed emotions. He called the fall of Fort Fisher "glorious news" but berated Porter for "that silly storming party of sailors and marines, in order to have 'a share in the assault' . . . which was repulsed," and cost the lives of his young protégés, Preston and Porter. As more news arrived in the North, however, Du Pont reconsidered and wrote a friend: "The morning papers give better reasons for the sailor assault than I had supposed and, though unsuccessful, may have aided the soldiers by occupying the garrison on that side very materially."[28]

General Terry and Colonel Lamb, who were in the best position to know, agreed. In his official report to General Grant, Terry said: "The assault of the sailors and marines, although it failed, undoubtedly contributed somewhat to our success, and certainly nothing could surpass the perfect skill with which the fleet was handled by its commander. Every request which I made to Admiral Porter was most cheerfully complied with, and the utmost harmony has existed between us from the outset."[29] Several years later Lamb wrote, "The magnificent charge of the American navy upon the centre of our works, enabled the army to effect a lodgment on our left with comparatively small loss."[30]

With Fort Fisher in Union hands, the positions at Forts Caswell and

Campbell at Old Inlet were untenable. On January 16, the garrisons were marched out and demolition teams placed charges. That night, the forts were blown up.[31]

Unaware of these events, the government blockade-runner *Chameleon* (ex-*Tallahassee*), Lt. John Wilkinson commanding, cleared Nassau on January 19 for Wilmington with a load of provisions and a passenger list of important Confederate officers returning from Europe. After a rough crossing, the *Chameleon* approached New Inlet on a dark, rainy night. Unable to see the Mound clearly or get an answer to his signal, Wilkinson presumed he had miscalculated his position and put to sea again. The following night he tried again. The Mound Light was burning, range lights were in place, and Wilkinson was preparing to drop anchor and light the deck lamps when the signalman communicating with the Mound remarked, "No Confederate there. He can't read my signals."

Wilkinson didn't wait for an explanation. Ordering the screws run in opposite directions, he pivoted the *Chameleon* 180 degrees, dashed out of the river, and escaped into the night. Two other blockade-runners following the *Chameleon* into New Inlet missed the false signal and were captured.[32]

"This is the kind of blockading that I like, where the prizes come to us, instead of our going out for them," Henry Rogers wrote his parents. "The more the merrier: let them come on, for our capacity is large."[33]

Federal gunboats entered the Cape Fear River and, on February 11, began bombarding Fort Anderson. Eight days later it was abandoned, sealing the fate of Wilmington.[34] Among the casualties of the Confederate evacuation was the partially completed ironclad *Wilmington,* once touted as the ship that would be able "to go in and out of the harbor at all times [and] greatly relieve the port of Wilmington from the blockading vessels." She was destroyed on the ways to prevent her capture.[35]

The news could not have arrived in Richmond at a worse time. Confederate commissioners were preparing to meet with President Lincoln and U.S. Secretary of State William H. Seward in the hopes of negotiating an armistice. The Union leaders were already aware that morale was low in the Confederate capital, and that a strong anti-Davis movement had seriously divided both houses of Congress. Although the Confederate government still did not comprehend the depth of Lincoln's determination to have total surrender, Davis realized that the loss of Fort

Fisher would encourage his counterpart to impose much harsher terms for peace.[36]

Even before he left Fort Fisher for prisoner-of-war detention, Whiting prepared a report for General Lee in which he charged Bragg with the loss of the fort. Bragg, he said, had been negligent in failing to attack the Union forces when he had the opportunity, and made no effort to create a diversion once the fort was under attack. "I desire that a full investigation be had of this matter and these charges which I make," he wrote.[37]

The report was delayed pending General Grant's approval of its transmission through enemy lines. Whiting postponed submission until February, when he sent it from the hospital at Fort Columbus, New York, where he had been taken for treatment and internment. With it he sent a cover letter, restating his position more strongly. "I demand, in justice to the country, to the army, and to myself, that the course of this officer [Bragg] be investigated," he wrote. "I do not know what he was sent to Wilmington for."[38]

Whiting received yet another opportunity to officially disparage Bragg, this time through the offices of Ben Butler. In an effort to justify himself before the Joint Committee, Butler sent Whiting a long questionnaire concerning conditions in and around Fort Fisher at the time of the December expedition. Whiting replied at length, summing up his position in his answer to Butler's twenty-fourth and final question: "Neither attack was practicable in the presence of the supporting force, provided that had been under a competent officer. The first landing ought assuredly to have been captured entirely; and as for the second, although deriving much greater advantages from the different mode of attack by the fleet, and though pressed with great vigor, it is due to the supineness of the confederate general that it was not destroyed in the act of assault."[39]

Based on this and other testimony, the committee adjourned after concluding that Butler's decision against assaulting the fort was "fully justified by all the facts and circumstances then known or afterwards ascertained."[40]

The Joint Committee's conclusion notwithstanding, there is some disagreement as to how strong Fort Fisher really was. Admiral Porter, who was an observer in Sevastopol during the final assault on the Malakoff Tower in the Crimean War, wrote Welles after Fisher's capture: "These works are tremendous. I was in Fort Malakoff a few days after it surrendered to the French and English; the combined armies of the two nations were many months capturing that stronghold, and it won't compare, either in size or strength, to Fort Fisher."[41] Porter was writing as the victor, and victors sometimes enhance their own achievement by exaggerating the strength of the defeated enemy. The Malakoff Tower held out during almost eleven months of sustained siege before it fell. From the explosion of the *Louisiana* in December until the successful Union assault in January, Fort Fisher faced only three weeks of sporadic attack.

William Lamb, the man most responsible for Fort Fisher's construction and defense, was never totally satisfied with it. Although he believed it could "withstand the heaviest bombardment," he also remarked: "The fort was far from complete when it was attacked, especially as against an assault by land, the sides exposed to the sea being first constructed, on the theory that the Army of Wilmington would prevent an investment."[42] As it turned out, the Army of Wilmington did not prevent an investment, and Terry hit the fort at a point which, in addition to its inherent weakness, had already been substantially reduced by naval bombardment.

Augustus Charles Hobart-Hampden, a Crimean War veteran who toured the fort while waiting to depart from the Cape Fear on his first blockade run, agreed with Lamb that the fort could have been stronger. Hobart commented:

> We were much struck by the weakness of Fort Fisher, which, with a garrison of merely 1200 men, and only half finished, could have been easily taken at any time since the war began by a resolute body of 5000 men making a night-attack. It is true that at the time of its capture it was somewhat stronger than at the time I visited it, but even then its garrison was comparatively small, and its defences unfinished. I fancy the bold front so long shown by its occupiers had much to do with the fact that such an attack was not attempted till just before the close of the war.[43]

The truth no doubt lies somewhere between Porter's assertion that Fort Fisher was stronger than the Malakoff and Hobart's belief that its supposed impregnability involved a certain amount of bluff.

There is no question that Fort Fisher was strong. And had it been defended by supporting troops (i.e., Bragg and Hoke's Division), both Weitzel and Terry would have been pushed into the sea. But denied that defense, and regardless of indifferent naval gunnery during the first bombardment, it is very likely that the fort would have fallen on Christmas Day had Weitzel shown the same resolve that Terry would three weeks later. The fort, as Lamb himself noted, was built to withstand a naval bombardment; its defenses were not designed against a land attack.[44]

Weitzel's judgment, as he himself admitted, was affected by his memories of the slaughter at Battery Wagner. Yet Battery Wagner, in its design and compactness in relation to terrain, in armament, and in the strength of its garrison, was a stronger work than Fort Fisher.

Whatever the strengths or weaknesses of Fort Fisher, its fall closed the last port through which the Confederate armies could be supplied. Nevertheless, hope—or perhaps a refusal to face reality—persisted in Southern hearts. From London, Confederate commissioner J. M. Mason wrote to Secretary of State Judah Benjamin: "We have heard with great concern of the capture of Fort Fisher and other defenses protecting the port of Wilmington, but our troops made a gallant and great defense, and whatever the loss to us, its conquest has been at great cost to the enemy. Yet, beyond the disaster, we are cheered and elevated here by the defiant tone of the South, with renewed declaration of Congress that the war will be prosecuted to independence, at whatever cost or hazard."[45]

Brave words from a man who had no firsthand knowledge of actual conditions in the South, or that Congress itself was living in almost a dreamworld. Certainly, the conquest of Fort Fisher involved great cost to the North, but Northern losses could be replaced. Southern losses could not, and the closure of the only seaport available to Lee's army was irreparable. The war itself was now an exercise in futility, and the existence of the Confederacy as a sovereign nation could be reckoned in months.

EPILOGUE

FORT FISHER WAS to the Union navy what Appomattox was to the Union army. It was the last great maritime action of a war in which the navy had operated by sea and river, and had learned to work jointly—if not always harmoniously—with the army. Even if the generals did not realize it at the time, the great Napoleonic set-piece battles between massed armies were a thing of the past whenever naval support was available. Indeed, it is not unreasonable to state, as Howard Nash did in his *Naval History of the Civil War*, that from a tactical standpoint, the best the Union army could hope for without naval support was a draw. As the war progressed, the army relied increasingly on naval support, particularly in the closing months around Richmond and the Atlantic Coast.[1]

Federal troops marched into Wilmington on February 22, 1865. True to his nature, Terry was not a vindictive conqueror. He shook hands with Mayor John Dawson, and side by side they mounted the steps of city hall to formalize the surrender. The city was not burned, and the local population went about its business with the grim knowledge that the Confederate cause was doomed. Terry himself was preoccupied with the pursuit of Hoke's Division and left Maj. Gen. Jacob D. Cox in command of the city. Cox ordered his troops into camp around Wilmington and established a provost guard in town. It was all academic because the city no longer had any military value.[2]

Today, Wilmington is one of the most vibrant cities of the mid-Atlantic coast, a growing metropolis and center of the North Carolina film industry. But thanks to Terry's magnanimity, as well as the care of subsequent generations, it is also a time capsule of the past. Many buildings along Market Street and near the riverfront today would be familiar to Lamb, Whiting, Bragg, and countless blockade-runners and speculators.

General Whiting's wounds, though serious, were far from mortal, and he began to recover. In early March 1865, however, he contracted dysentery, the killer of so many prisoners on both sides. He died in the Fort Columbus hospital on March 10 and was buried in Greenwood Cemetery in Brooklyn. In January 1900 his remains were reinterred in Oakdale Cemetery in Wilmington. No action was ever taken against General Bragg, and today the U.S. Army honors him with Fort Bragg, North Carolina.[3]

Lamb, though more seriously wounded, fared better. Through the efforts of Lt. James Parker, he was put ashore at Fortress Monroe and treated in Chesapeake Hospital, where he was close to home and could be attended by his family. Upon his release he joined Daisy with her family in Rhode Island, where he underwent surgery to remove the bullet from his hip. Although he spent the next seven years on crutches, he became active in Republican politics, serving three terms as mayor of Norfolk. As time passed, Lamb developed a close friendship with General Curtis, who recovered from his near-fatal head wounds, and the two often visited Fort Fisher, discussed the battle, and lobbied for the fort's preservation.[4]

Robley Evans recovered from his wounds, and one of his first acts was to make certain James Flannigan's box was delivered to his sister in Philadelphia. He later assisted her in getting a survivor's pension.[5] With most of his life still ahead of him, Evans made the transition to the modern steel navy, and commanded the battleship *Iowa* during the Battle of Santiago de Cuba in the Spanish-American War. He was promoted to rear admiral, became Commander-in-Chief Asiatic, and later was selected to take President Theodore Roosevelt's Great White Fleet around the world. Ill health forced his retirement before that voyage was completed. A national hero, he lived until 1912.

Like Evans, George Dewey served into the modern era. In 1898 he was approaching retirement as commodore of the Asiatic Squadron in Hong Kong when he received word that war had broken out with Spain. He was ordered to the Philippines, where he won the navy's first victory with the destruction of the Spanish squadron in Manila Bay. For that he was awarded the unique rank of Admiral of the Navy.

Joe Danels was invalided back to Baltimore, where his tuberculosis claimed him soon after the battle of Fort Fisher. The terrible day on the beach probably hastened the end, but he died knowing that his effort had not been wasted; the Senate had confirmed his reinstatement in the Regular Navy, and his commission was in the mail. When the document arrived, less than an hour after his death, his wife took it to his room and placed it in his hands.[6]

In 1866 the War Department reactivated the ruined Fort Caswell, although the 205-man garrison was eventually reduced to a caretaker who drew his supplies monthly from Fort Johnston. In 1895, however, Congress appropriated funds to begin reconstruction of the post, and two years later the contract was awarded. Several large reinforced concrete emplacements for coastal-defense guns were constructed along a mile and a half of river- and oceanfront. One of these, designated Battery Caswell, was built within the old antebellum casemate structure. Extensive quarters and support buildings were erected, and the old casemate walls were totally surrounded by a modern military post.

The garrison was substantially reduced after World War I. In 1924 the remaining troops were removed, and the post reverted back to caretaker status. The following year, most of the reservation was sold and ultimately converted into a resort. On November 17, 1941, however, the navy purchased the reservation from the corporation that owned it, and the fort was designated a section base for various coastal functions, including antisubmarine patrol. With the close of World War II, the reservation was certified to the War Assets Administration for disposal and sold to the North Carolina Baptist Convention for $86,000. Today it is a church retreat and summer camp.[7]

The martial plan of the reservation is still evident, although much subdued by subsequent conversion and new construction for religious purposes. Some effort is required to find the original casemate, although a portion remains that was not destroyed by the magazine explosion when the Confederates abandoned the site. Over the last 130 years, blowing sand and remnants of the Confederate earth facing have covered the lower half of the old scarp wall so that the gun slits that originally were high over the moat are now almost at ground level. Part of the interior is covered by the turn-of-the-century gun emplacement. No real effort has been made to maintain or stabilize the overgrown ruins. The only indication of its past is a stone plaque over one of the old sally ports, giving its name and date of construction.

Fort Johnston is a dominant feature of Southport (formerly Smithville). It consists of several colonial-style buildings set back on a wide lawn that apparently was the former parade ground. It is maintained by the Department of the Army for recreational purposes made obvious by tennis courts. Southport itself retains the character of a quaint Atlantic fishing village, and much of old Smithville is recognizable. The small maritime museum is worth a stop; well-versed docents use a wall-size satellite photo to orient visitors to the history of the entire Cape Fear region, from Fayetteville to the Atlantic.

Upriver, on the west side of the Cape Fear by Orton Plantation, are the remarkably well preserved remains of Lamb's first project, Fort Anderson. The land-face works run past the bare, roofless walls of St. Philip's Church, where the yard contains tombs of notable early North Carolinians, including at least one governor. The fort partially encloses the ruins of Old Brunswick, the first capital of colonial North Carolina. There is an excellent museum at the visitors center, but most of the displays are devoted to Old Brunswick rather than the fort.

Federal troops began altering Fort Fisher almost immediately after its fall. With the war still on, Admiral Porter was afraid the Confederates would counterattack and try to retake it. "It is too important a place for the rebels to give up without a struggle for it," he told Fox.[8]

Given the condition of the Confederacy, and particularly the incoherent military command in North Carolina, Porter's fears were groundless. Nevertheless, army engineers reduced its size and strengthened the part that remained. Hundreds of men pulled down old earthworks and erected new ones. By the second week of February, the appearance of the fort was substantially changed.[9]

When the war ended, however, so did the need for the fort. It became an odd relic still littered with debris from the battle. Over the years, erosion wore down the works and the bombproofs caved in. In 1881 the Corps of Engineers constructed a weir to enclose New Inlet and improve navigation on the main channel of the Cape Fear. This changed the flow of the river as it emptied into the Atlantic, and shifted the currents running around Smith Island and up the beach along Federal Point. The beach rapidly eroded, and by the time it stabilized the sea face was dangerously close to the surf.

As the decades passed, survivors from both sides, drawn together by the terrors of January 15, 1865, visited the fort and became alarmed by the erosion of the works and the shoreline. In 1909 the Fort Fisher Survivors Association requested of the House Committee on Military Affairs a $40,000 appropriation to make the site into a national park. Although some old soldiers testified on behalf of the bill, a snowstorm prevented the more prominent veterans—Lamb and Curtis among them—from making the trip to Washington for the hearings. The bill died in committee, and the deaths of Lamb and Curtis during the next twelve months removed the most influential support for the project.[10]

It is interesting that 1909, the year in which the Fort Fisher bill was introduced and Lamb died, was also the year my father was born near the Black River, a tributary of the Cape Fear. He recalled that during his childhood in Wilmington his family often boarded a steamer for the trip down the river to picnic on the old earthworks and have a day at the beach. In school he wrote a paper about the fort, using much material that was available locally and talking to old veterans of the battle. I never saw that paper, but whenever he mentioned Fort Fisher I reached for an ashtray, pushed my chair back, and got comfortable, because I knew he would go on for at least two hours. To him, the peninsula was "Confederate Point"; he had grown up hearing the old vets call it that, and he never made the readjustment to "Federal Point." He spoke of Lamb and Whiting as if he had known them, and took Bragg's inaction as a personal affront. Fort Fisher remained one of his favorite subjects until his death in 1980.

No amount of sentiment could stop the erosion of the fort itself. The critical point came in the 1920s. With the fort becoming a popular tourist attraction, and with resort development up the point at Carolina and Kure Beaches, New Hanover County dredged up tons of the coquina rock from just offshore to crush into material for hard-surface roads down Federal Point. The rock had formed a natural sea wall, and once it was gone the surf undermined the sea face. Within a few years, the Northeast Bastion and the Pulpit Battery were gone.

Federal Point was remilitarized for antiaircraft artillery training during

SHEPPERD'S BATTERY TODAY, WITH RESTORED LAND-FACE TRAVERSES IN THE
BACKGROUND. THE PHOTO DOES NOT ADEQUATELY CONVEY THEIR SUBSTAN-
TIAL HEIGHT. THE GUN WAS SALVAGED FROM THE WRECKED UNION
BLOCKADER *Peterhoff* AS REPRESENTATIVE OF THE PERIOD.
Author's photo

World War II. Part of the land face was bulldozed for an airstrip. Much of
the Mound Battery and the upper works of Battery Buchanan were
removed to provide fill for ammunition bunkers along what was left of the
sea face.[11]

· The lower works of Battery Buchanan still exist at the end of Federal
Point, and can be easily identified by anyone who has seen the photographs taken in 1865, immediately after the battle. The best view is from
the car ferry that crosses the Cape Fear between the point and Southport.

I first saw Fort Fisher as an eight-year-old during a visit to my grandparents in Wilmington in August 1957, the year before North Carolina finally
obtained the site for a state park. The day was unseasonably cool and gray
and bleak, and I had to wear a jacket. I remember that the monument,
built in 1932 on a site called Battle Acre, stood in front of an embankment—the remains of the sea face—that blocked the view of the Atlantic.
I could not see the ocean, but I could hear the waves breaking on the other

side. I did not visit the fort again for more than thirty-eight years, until December 1995. Although I was aware that the sea face had washed away, I nevertheless got a shock when I saw Battle Acre again. Nothing was how I remembered it. The monument was right on the beach, only a few yards from the surf. The embankment had washed away.[12]

A road now cuts through the land face where the World War II runway was built, and the land face itself from the road to Shepperd's Battery by the river has been stabilized and restored. The gun chamber at Shepperd's Battery is reconstructed and armed with a 32-pounder pivot gun raised from the sunken Union blockader *Peterhoff*. There is a visitors center with excellent exhibits and friendly people. Part of the land face also remains between the road and the beach, but the traverses are eroded and overgrown with trees. In 1996 a multimillion-dollar erosion-control structure of heavy stone finally was emplaced along the line of the vanished sea face to prevent further erosion.[13] Nevertheless, to see Fort Fisher as it was, one must go to the Cape Fear Museum in Wilmington and view the giant diorama of the battle.

It has been said that soldiers have monuments, because their battles are fought on land; a sailor's only monument is the sea. Such is the case with Fort Fisher. The traverses and gun chambers where so many Union and Confederate soldiers fought and died have been preserved. But the Northeast Bastion, the palisade, and the beach where the sailors and marines fought and died are washed away. Although they, too, fought this battle on land, the jealous ocean has claimed that land for its own. Their monument is the gray Atlantic.

APPENDIX
The Naval Brigade at Fort Fisher

IN HIS REPORT to Admiral Porter, Lt. Comdr. Thomas O. Selfridge, who commanded the Third Division of the Naval Brigade, admitted "my entire unacquaintance with any of the officers or crews of my division."[1] It is, perhaps, for this reason that little if any effort has been made to detail the organization of the Naval Brigade, although exhaustive lists of the ships, military units, and aggregate manpower at Fort Fisher have been published many times.

Most of the problem is caused by the bureaucracy of an earlier era, which required less information. Not until well into the twentieth century did the army or navy require the encyclopedic paperwork that today is taken for granted. Nineteenth-century paperwork, when and if submitted, was often little more than a brief summary of a ship's involvement in a particular action. This problem becomes apparent when trying to determine the makeup of the Naval Brigade at Fort Fisher, for there seems to be no single list of ships involved, nor of the commanders of their landing parties, where those landing parties were assigned, or how many men were involved.

The larger ships sent over a hundred men each, and the reports of their landing officers are generally the most detailed. On the opposite extreme, some of the little gunboats and auxiliaries sent only a handful in a single boat, and their action reports are simply an acknowledgment that they were represented in the brigade. Some did not submit reports from their assault parties, or if they did, these are not available. This is particularly true of the ironclads.

The haphazard organization of the Naval Brigade also poses a problem. Although in theory the brigade was divided into divisions matching those of the fleet, and each ship's landing party was supposed to work in conjunction with others of its fleet division, this was not always the case. Some of the larger landing parties were divided among more than one division, and the parties from the ironclads had no divisional representation. It is also obvious from the action reports that even the divisional commanders were unsure of who was in their divisions, and the commanders of the parties from some of the ships had no idea of where they were supposed to be.

The following list, which does not pretend to be complete, was compiled from various reports in the *Official Records of the Union and Confederate Navies,* series 1, volume 11, that were reprinted on pages 442 to 575. Information was so scattered and incomplete that it was drawn not only from action reports but from casualty lists as well. Figures for each ship include officers and sailors, and, where relevant, engine room personnel, marines, surgeons, and nurses.

The commanders of the landing parties from individual ships could not always be determined. In some cases, the ship's commander did not bother to report who was in charge of the landing party. More often, however, the reports named several officers, these being the commanders of the boats as they were sent ashore. Once ashore, presumably the senior boat officer took charge during the assault, but this cannot be determined for certain. In the case of the *Powhatan,* command of the landing party was disputed at the time between Ensign Robley Evans, Lt. George M. Bache, and Acting Ensign Ira Harris, Jr. In his action report, Commodore Schenck made no effort to resolve it, and Evans was accepted here because no one has since argued with his claim.

THE NAVAL BRIGADE
Brigade Commander, Lt. Comdr. K. Randolph Breese

First Division
Lt. Comdr. Charles H. Cushman
USS *Colorado,* Lt. H. B. Robeson, 130.
USS *Iosco,* Acting Ensign W. Jameson, 44.
USS *Malvern,* Lt. Benjamin Porter, number not available.
USS *Monticello,* Lt. Comdr. W. B. Cushing, 40.

USS *Nereus,* Acting Ensign E. G. Dayton, 58.

USS *Susquehanna,* Lt. Comdr. F. B. Blake, 75.

USS *Ticonderoga,* Acting Ensign George W. Coffin, 41.

USS *Vanderbilt,* Acting Volunteer Lt. Comdr. Joseph D. Danels, number not available.

USS *Wabash,* Acting Ensign G. T. Davis, 188.

Second Division

Lt. Comdr. James Parker

USS *Gettysburg,* Lt. R. H. Lamson, 70.

USS *Kansas,* Acting Ensign George C. Williams, 19.

USS *Mackinaw,* Acting Master Abraham J. Louch, 44.

USS *Minnesota,* Lt. Comdr. James Parker, 241.

USS *Mohican,* commander unspecified, 52.

USS *Montgomery,* commander unspecified, 34.

USS *Osceola,* commander unspecified, 37.

USS *Rhode Island,* Lt. Fred R. Smith, number not available.

USS *Santiago de Cuba,* Lt. N. H. Farquhar, 49.

USS *Seneca,* Lt. Comdr. Montgomery Sicard, 28.

USS *Tacony,* commander unspecified, 30.

USS *Tuscarora,* Lt. Comdr. W. N. Allen, 60.

Third Division

Lt. Comdr. Thomas O. Selfridge

USS *Brooklyn,* Acting Ensign Douglas Cassel, number not available.

USS *Chippewa,* Acting Ensign George H. Wood, 20.

USS *Huron,* Lt. Comdr. Thomas O. Selfridge, number not available.

USS *Maratanza,* Acting Master J. B. Wood, 50.

USS *Powhatan,* Ensign R. D. Evans, 100.

USS *Shenandoah,* Lt. Smith W. Nichols, 54 and unnumbered marine sergeant's guard.

Marine Division

Capt. L. L. Dawson, USMC

Marines were drawn from various ships and are included with the ship figures, where available. Captain Dawson was from the *Colorado.*

Landing Crews Whose Divisions Could Not Be Determined

USS *Canonicus,* commander unspecified, number not available.

USS *Fort Jackson,* Lt. Symmes H. Hunt, 48 and unnumbered marine sergeant's guard.

USS *Juniata,* commander unspecified, 65.

USS *Pawtuxet,* Acting Ensign Slamm, number not available.

USS *Pequot,* Acting Ensign George Lamb, 42.

USS *Pontoosuc,* commander unspecified, number not available.

USS *Sassacus,* Acting Ensign William H. Mayer, 36.

USS *Saugus,* commander unspecified, number not available.

USS *Tristram Shandy,* commander unspecified, 22.

USS *Yantic,* commander unspecified, 42.

NOTES

PROLOGUE

1. "Terry's Fort Fisher Expedition," 304.

I. NORTH CAROLINA AND SECESSION

1. Lamb, *Colonel Lamb's Story,* 38.
2. Ibid., 32.
3. In 1860, the population of Wilmington was 9,552, including whites, free blacks, and slaves. See Kennedy, *Population of the United States,* 359.
4. Lincoln, Proclamation, April 19, 1861, in Richardson, *Messages and Papers,* 5:3215–16; Anderson, *By Sea and by River,* 33.
5. Anderson, *By Sea and by River,* 33–34; Wise, *Lifeline of the Confederacy,* 12; Anderson, "1861: Blockade vs. Closing the Confederate Ports," 191; Reed, *Combined Operations,* 4–5; Still, "A Naval Sieve," 38.
6. Reed, *Combined Operations,* 3–5; Anderson, *By Sea and by River,* 16.
7. Barrett, *Civil War in North Carolina,* 3; Wood, "Port Town at War," 2.
8. Barrett, *Civil War in North Carolina,* 4–5.
9. Quoted in ibid., 5 n.
10. Ibid., 5–6.
11. Smithville is now known as Southport.
12. Wood, "Port Town at War," 1–2. Fort Caswell is discussed in Herring and Williams, *Fort Caswell.* The construction of Fort Johnston is mentioned in Honeycutt, "Fort Fisher," 34, while Fort Macon is covered in Barry, "History of Fort Macon."
13. Wood, "Port Town at War," 2; Trotter, *Ironclads and Columbiads,* 7.
14. Barry, "History of Fort Macon," 180–81; Herring and Williams, *Fort Caswell,* 25–26; Trotter, *Ironclads and Columbiads,* 7.
15. Reilly to Col. S. Cooper, Adjutant General, U.S. Army, January 9, 1861, and Dardingkiller to Cooper, January 11, 1861, both in U.S. Department of War,

The War of the Rebellion: A Compilation of the Official Records of the Union and Confederate Armies, series 1, 1:474–76 [hereinafter cited as *ORA,* with all references to series 1]; Sprunt, *Chronicles,* 277; Trotter, *Ironclads and Columbiads,* 8–9; Herring and Williams, *Fort Caswell,* 26; Wood, "Port Town at War," 45.

16. Ellis to Buchanan, January 12, 1861, and Holt to Ellis, January 15, 1861, both in *ORA,* 1:484–85; Wood, "Port Town at War," 46–47; Barry, "History of Fort Macon," 181–83; Trotter, *Ironclads and Columbiads,* 9.

17. T. L. Clingman to Ellis, March 19, 1861, *ORA,* 1:486.

18. Lincoln, Proclamation, April 15, 1861, in Richardson, *Messages and Papers,* 5:3214–15.

19. Barrett, *Civil War in North Carolina,* 13.

20. Ellis to Cameron, April 15, 1861, *ORA,* 1:486.

21. Sprunt, *Chronicles,* 272; Trotter, *Ironclads and Columbiads,* 10.

22. Lincoln, Proclamation, April 27, 1861, in Richardson, *Messages and Papers,* 5:3216.

23. Trotter, *Ironclads and Columbiads,* 2.

24. Pollard, *Lost Cause,* 122; Barrett, *Civil War in North Carolina,* 14–16.

25. Warner, *Generals in Gray,* 334; Johnson and Malone, *Dictionary of American Biography,* 20:136.

26. Mrs. B. F. Butler to Mrs. Heard, November 27, 1863, in Butler, *Private and Official Correspondence,* 3:164.

27. Trotter, *Ironclads and Columbiads,* 2; Barrett, *Civil War in North Carolina,* 14.

28. Trotter, *Ironclads and Columbiads,* 2.

29. Wise, *Lifeline of the Confederacy,* 27.

30. Roberts, *Never Caught,* 12.

31. Wise, *Lifeline of the Confederacy,* 25.

2. THE NORTHERN THRUST

1. Boynton, *History of the Navy,* 1:331–32. The board consisted of Captains Samuel F. Du Pont and Charles H. Davis of the navy (both of whom became rear admirals during the war), Maj. John G. Barnard of the army, and Prof. Alexander Bache of the Coast Survey.

2. Scharf, *Confederate States Navy,* 368–69; Barrett, *Civil War in North Carolina,* 31–32; Wise, *Lifeline of the Confederacy,* 15.

3. Barrett, *Civil War in North Carolina,* 35–36.

4. Hawkins, "Early Coast Operations," 633. This is one of several notable works about the assault on Hatteras Inlet, some others being Boynton, *History of the Navy,* vol. 1; and Barrett, *Civil War in North Carolina.*

5. Barrett, *Civil War in North Carolina,* 47.

6. Du Pont's actions are detailed in H. A. Du Pont, *Rear-Admiral Samuel Francis Du Pont.* Port Royal was a U.S. Navy coaling station before the war.

7. Not to be confused with Beaufort, South Carolina, which is beyond the scope of this work.

8. Reed, *Combined Operations,* xviii.

9. McClellan, *Report,* 83; Anderson, *By Sea and by River,* 15. The railroad between Charleston and Virginia followed a circuitous route through Columbia, South Carolina.

10. McClellan, *McClellan's Own Story,* 203–4.

11. Wise, *Lifeline of the Confederacy,* 15.

12. Barry, "History of Fort Macon," 188–91.

13. Ibid., 207–8.

14. *Richmond Dispatch,* January 3, 1865, quoted in Jones, *War Clerk's Diary,* January 3, 1865, 2:375.

15. Macon Bonner to "My dear, darling Wife," August 15, 1862, Bonner Papers; Johns, "Wilmington during the Blockade," 35; Roberts, *Never Caught,* 35.

16. Trotter, *Ironclads and Columbiads,* 9, 11; Herring and Williams, *Fort Caswell,* 27–29.

17. Charles P. Bolles to *Wilmington Star,* August 12, 1903, Bolles Papers.

18. U.S. Congress, *Report of the Joint Committee on the Conduct of the War, at the Second Session Thirty-eighth Congress. Fort Fisher Expedition,* i [hereinafter cited as *Joint Committee Report—Fort Fisher*]; Browning, *From Cape Charles to Cape Fear,* 271.

19. McClellan to Burnside, January 7, 1862, in McClellan, *Report,* 85–86.

20. Burnside, "Burnside Expedition," 663–68.

21. Barrett, *Civil War in North Carolina,* 86–89; Browning, *From Cape Charles to Cape Fear,* 31.

22. Browning, *From Cape Charles to Cape Fear,* 31–34.

23. Ibid., 35; Barrett, *Civil War in North Carolina,* 108–9; Hawkins, "Early Coast Operations," 652; Trotter, *Ironclads and Columbiads,* 55–56.

24. Barry, "History of Fort Macon," 216.

25. Ibid., 224–27.

26. Ibid., 228, 230–33.

27. Ibid., 239–40; Hawkins, "Early Coast Operations," 653–54.

28. Du Pont to Gustavus Vasa Fox, May 31, 1862, in Hayes, *Samuel Francis Du Pont,* 2:91.

29. Browning, *From Cape Charles to Cape Fear,* 275.

30. Price, "North Carolina Railroads," 306.

31. Browning, *From Cape Charles to Cape Fear,* 275.

32. Gustavus Vasa Fox to Du Pont, June 3, 1862, in Hayes, *Samuel Francis Du Pont,* 2:96; Browning, *From Cape Charles to Cape Fear,* 275.

33. Price, "North Carolina Railroads," 306; Burnside, "Burnside Expedition," 669.

34. Gustavus Vasa Fox to Du Pont, June 3, 1862, in Hayes, *Samuel Francis Du Pont,* 2:96–97.

35. Price, "North Carolina Railroads," 307.

36. Butler to S. P. Chase, April 27, 1863, in Butler, *Private and Official Correspondence,* 3:62.

37. Reed, *Combined Operations,* xix.

38. McClellan, *McClellan's Own Story,* 204.

39. Fox to Du Pont, June 3, 1862, in Hayes, *Samuel Francis Du Pont,* 2:97.

40. McPherson, *Battle Cry of Freedom,* 620–25.
41. Roberts, *Never Caught,* 1; Semmes, *Service Afloat,* 792.
42. Wise, *Lifeline of the Confederacy,* 195; Peery, "Clandestine Commerce," 104–6.
43. Lee to Capt. C. S. Boggs, April 16, 1863, in U.S. Department of the Navy, *Official Records of the Union and Confederate Navies in the War of the Rebellion,* series 1, 8:810 [hereinafter cited as *ORN,* with all references to series 1 unless otherwise noted]. A Virginian who remained loyal to the Union, Lee was the third cousin of Robert E. Lee. His life is covered in Cornish and Laas, *Lincoln's Lee.*
44. Johns, "Wilmington during the Blockade," 36.
45. Lebergott, "Through the Blockade," 882, 884. The number of bales is compiled from a table of Southern cotton inventories and exports on page 882.
46. The accusation against Butler regarding Wilmington was made in a letter from Levi R. Greene, first assistant engineer of the USS *Massasoit,* to Senator H. B. Anthony on January 14, 1865. Greene said that on December 31, 1864, an Englishman named William Howard advised him that he (Howard) was to oversee the shipment of three thousand bales of cotton from Wilmington, and that Butler was "to work the thing through" for 50 percent of the proceeds. This, according to Greene, was the reason for Butler's failure to take Fort Fisher a week earlier. The letter was referred to the Joint Committee for the Conduct of the War. Upon Butler's vehement denial, committee chairman B. F. Wade called the matter "entirely hearsay," and the allegation was not pursued. Nevertheless, Greene's letter was reprinted twice in the Joint Committee's report on Fort Fisher, on pages 208–9, and together with Butler's response and Wade's comments on pages 257–59. Butler did not directly mention the accusation in his own memoirs, although he devoted several pages to claiming that he superintended the *legal* shipment of Southern cotton to the North, and otherwise wiped out corruption in the contraband business, always to the benefit of the Federal government (*Butler's Book,* 844–48). The Federal attitude toward the cotton trade is discussed in Nash, *Stormy Petrel,* 174–75, which specifically considers Butler's involvement, and in Johnson, "Northern Profit and Profiteers." It should be noted that Butler controlled textile mills in his hometown of Lowell, Massachusetts.
47. Price, "North Carolina Railroads," 307.

3. FORT FISHER

1. Friend to Catherine McGeachy, April 19, 1863, Buie Papers.
2. Adjutant and Inspector General's Office, Special Orders No. 262:VI, November 8, 1862, T. S. Rhett to Vance, November 10, 1862, and Jefferson Davis to Vance, November 11, 1862, all in *ORA,* 18:770.
3. Warner, *Generals in Gray,* 334–35; Johnson and Malone, *Dictionary of American Biography,* 20:136–37; Freeman, *Lee's Lieutenants,* 1:119–20.
4. Whiting to Maj. Gen. Gustavus W. Smith, November 18, 1862, *ORA,* 18:780; Whiting to Vance, December 6, 1862, Battle Papers. Before the development

of modern methods of food preservation, salt was essential to armies in the field and ships at sea.

5. Whiting to George W. Randolph, Secretary of War, November 18, 1862, *ORA*, 18:774.

6. Whiting to Smith, November 18, 1862, ibid., 773.

7. Whiting to Randolph, November 18, 1862, ibid., 774–76.

8. Smith, endorsement to ibid., November 20, 1862, ibid., 776–77; Jones, *War Clerk's Diary*, November 22, 1862, 1:195–96.

9. Bolles to *Wilmington Star*, August 12, 1903, and William L. DeRosset, letter in undated (1906) clipping from *Wilmington Messenger*, both in Bolles Papers; Browning, *From Cape Charles to Cape Fear*, 229.

10. Lamb, "Defense of Fort Fisher," 643 n.

11. Honeycutt, "Fort Fisher," 54–57; Gragg, *Confederate Goliath*, 14–16. Fort St. Philip was apparently so named because it encloses the ruins of St. Philip's Church, the only remaining structure of Brunswick Town.

12. Gragg, *Confederate Goliath*, 16.

13. Lamb, *Colonel Lamb's Story*, 1–2.

14. The bombardment of Fort Brown is recounted in many books, the most detailed probably being N. C. Brooks's *Complete History of the Mexican War*.

15. The modern transliteration from Cyrillic is "Malakhov." I have opted to use the nineteenth-century spelling for the sake of consistency with contemporary texts.

16. Honeycutt, "Fort Fisher," 57. In 1906, William DeRosset discussed the construction of Fort Fisher in a letter to Bolles. Among other things, DeRosset said, "I always understood from Whiting and Lamb that there was no plan made for Fort Fisher but that it was a gradual growth from Bolles Battery as development called for additional works" (DeRosset to Bolles, September 21, 1906, Bolles Papers). In view of this statement, as well as comments by Lamb (*Colonel Lamb's Story*, 1–5), it may be inferred that, rather than start over again, Lamb simply strengthened and expanded existing works based on his study of Malakoff and his own experience with Fort Anderson, not according to a specific plan.

17. Lamb, *Colonel Lamb's Story*, 2.

18. Ibid., 3.

19. Lamb, "Defense of Fort Fisher," 643 n.

20. Macon Bonner to "My dear, darling wife," August 15, 1862, Bonner Papers.

21. G. H. Scott to Rear Adm. S. P. Lee, October 11, 1862, *ORN*, 8:127.

22. William A. Parker to G. H. Scott, November 17, 1862, W. H. C. Whiting to Headquarters, Department of South Carolina and Georgia, November 19, 1862, and J. D. Warren to G. H. Scott, November 17, 1862, all in ibid., 214–16.

23. Taylor, *Running the Blockade*, 56.

24. Thomas, *Letters from the Colonel's Lady*, 44.

25. Ibid., 45.

26. Lamb, "Defense of Fort Fisher," 643.

27. Gragg, *Confederate Goliath,* 53–54.

28. Lt. Col. J. F. Gilmer, Chief of Engineer Bureau, to Capt. C. R. Collins, Corps of Engineers, Smithville, October 11, 1862, *ORA,* 18:756; Herring and Williams, *Fort Caswell,* 32, 45.

29. Lee to Fox, December 11, 1862, in Thompson and Wainwright, *Confidential Correspondence,* 2:238; Browning, *From Cape Charles to Cape Fear,* 277–78.

30. Browning, *From Cape Charles to Cape Fear,* 278.

31. Ibid.; Du Pont to Sophie Du Pont, January 6, 1863, in Hayes, *Samuel Francis Du Pont,* 2:348.

32. Lee to Fox, December 11, 1862, in Thompson and Wainwright, *Confidential Correspondence,* 2:237–38. The word "torpedo" describes a primitive mine, either subterranean or marine. The Confederates pioneered the concept, and the first known use was in a failed attempt against the Federal squadron in the Potomac on July 7, 1861. The search for a more efficient device continued, and marine torpedoes were successfully tested in January 1862. The following October, Congress created the Torpedo Service, which was responsible for research and development. Although under the jurisdiction of the War Department, it was a cooperative effort between the army and the navy, and "torpedoes" soon became very practical weapons. Several types of subterranean and marine mines were developed, some detonated by contact/impact and others by electricity. The "spar torpedo," mounted on a spar extending from the bow of a vessel, was a favorite of both Confederate and Union navies because of its effectiveness against ironclads. When the torpedo boat approached an enemy ship, it either rammed, detonating the torpedo by direct impact, or ran the lowered spar under the armor, then pulled a lanyard to release an impact trigger. The latter system was used on the spar torpedo that sank the Confederate ironclad *Albemarle.* The subterranean and marine mines installed at Fort Fisher were designed to be fired by electricity. Torpedoes are described in detail in Scharf, *Confederate States Navy,* 750ff., and photographs of different types appear in Time-Life, *Echoes of Glory: Arms and Equipment of the Confederacy,* 302–3.

33. Fox to Lee, December 15, 1862, in Thompson and Wainwright, *Confidential Correspondence,* 2:243–44.

34. Johnson and Malone, *Dictionary of American Biography,* 6:568–69; Hayes, "Captain Fox," 64–67; Welles, *Diary,* January 30, 1864, 2:233; Anderson, *By Sea and by River,* 5.

35. Fox's comments were recorded in a letter from Admiral Du Pont to his wife, January 25, 1863, in Hayes, *Samuel Francis Du Pont,* 2:379. In some accounts the *Nashville* is called by other names, most notably *Rattlesnake.*

36. Browning, *From Cape Charles to Cape Fear,* 280.

37. Ibid., 283

38. Seddon to Vance, January 11, 1863, *ORA,* 18:840.

39. B. W. Frobel, Chief of Artillery, to Lamb and Gwathmey, January 12, 1863, ibid., 842.

40. Whiting to Beauregard, January 13, 1863, Whiting to Gwathmey, January 13, 1863, and Whiting to Lamb, January 13, 1863, all ibid., 842–44; Herring and Williams, *Fort Caswell*, 44–45; Fox to Du Pont, January 6, 1863, in Hayes, *Samuel Francis Du Pont*, 2:353.

41. Du Pont to Sophie Du Pont, January 25, 1863, in Hayes, *Samuel Francis Du Pont*, 2:379.

4. THE CHARLESTON EFFECT

1. Lee to Fox, February 27, 1862, in Thompson and Wainwright, *Confidential Correspondence*, 2:248; Welles, *Diary*, January 5, 1864, 1:216.

2. Fox to Lee, December 15, 1862, in Thompson and Wainwright, *Confidential Correspondence*, 2:245.

3. Musicant, *Divided Waters*, 371–72; Du Pont, *Rear-Admiral Samuel Francis Du Pont*, 163–65.

4. Wise, *Lifeline of the Confederacy*, 122.

5. D. D. Porter, *Naval History*, 75, 432.

6. Ibid., 75–76, 433; Du Pont, *Rear-Admiral Samuel Francis Du Pont*, 146–49; Musicant, *Divided Waters*, 371.

7. Beauregard, "Defense of Charleston," 2.

8. Musicant, *Divided Waters*, 371–72; Du Pont, *Rear-Admiral Samuel Francis Du Pont*, 163–65; Welles to Du Pont, January 6, 1863, *ORN*, 13:503; D. D. Porter, *Naval History*, 434. In a subsequent letter to Abraham Lincoln, General Hunter, who apparently was unaware of Welles's involvement, blamed Du Pont for the plan to attack without army support, claiming that had he been included, the Charleston defenses could have been taken. See U.S. Congress, *Report of the Joint Committee on the Conduct of the War, at the Second Session Thirty-eighth Congress. Miscellaneous*, 12–13 [hereinafter cited as *Joint Committee Report—Miscellaneous*].

9. Du Pont to Fox, March 2, 1863, in Hayes, *Samuel Francis Du Pont*, 2:463.

10. Fox to Du Pont, March 11, 1863, ibid., 486–87.

11. Anderson, *By Sea and by River*, 163–65; Ammen, *Atlantic Coast*, 100–103. Much to the U.S. Navy's chagrin, the *Keokuk's* two guns were retrieved by Confederate military salvors working over several weeks at night, against heavy waves breaking over the wreck and inside the ironclad's water-filled turrets. One gun was mounted on Fort Sumter and the other on Sullivan's Island.

12. Gillmore, *Engineer and Artillery Operations*, 15; Musicant, *Divided Waters*, 395; Reed, *Combined Operations*, 299; Schneller, *Quest for Glory*, 254.

13. Musicant, *Divided Waters*, 395; Reed, *Combined Operations*, 299.

14. Gillmore, *Engineer and Artillery Operations*, 22 n, 37–38; Reed, *Combined Operations*, 300.

15. Gillmore, "Army before Charleston," 64; Gillmore, *Engineer and Artillery Operations*, 43–44; Emilio, *Brave Black Regiment*, 69; Beauregard, "Defense

of Charleston," 23; *Joint Committee Report—Miscellaneous,* 2; Garth W. James, quoted in Time-Life, *Charleston,* 70.

16. Schneller, *Quest for Glory,* 252.

17. Gillmore, *Engineer and Artillery Operations,* 35; Musicant, *Divided Waters,* 395; Emilio, *Brave Black Regiment,* 68.

18. Ammen, *Atlantic Coast,* 125–26; Musicant, *Divided Waters,* 397–98; *Joint Committee Report—Miscellaneous,* 2.

19. Emilio, *Brave Black Regiment,* 70; D. D. Porter, *Naval History,* 436.

20. Emilio, *Brave Black Regiment,* 78.

21. Ibid., 79; Ammen, *Atlantic Coast,* 128; *Joint Committee Report—Miscellaneous,* 2.

22. Emilio, *Brave Black Regiment,* 80–82.

23. Ammen, *Atlantic Coast,* 128–29; Schneller, *Quest for Glory,* 259.

24. Musicant, *Divided Waters,* 398; Emilio, *Brave Black Regiment,* 84; Time-Life, *Charleston,* 91. This assault was the climactic scene of the 1989 film *Glory.*

25. Schneller, *Quest for Glory,* 261–64; Gillmore, *Engineer and Artillery Operations,* 62–65 n. Musicant (*Divided Waters,* 400–401) makes a good case that Sumter was still vital because the Union could occupy it and bombard Charleston while the navy cleared the channel of obstructions, then steamed in to take the city. Schneller, however, contrasts the intense buildup of Confederate inner defenses—shore-based and underwater—with the progressive deterioration of the monitors from long service and minimal maintenance. Because the Confederates had salvaged the *Keokuk's* codebook and were reading the Union signals, they undoubtedly were aware of the situation with the monitors.

26. Gillmore, "Army before Charleston," 65; Schneller, *Quest for Glory,* 264–65.

27. The abortive assault on Fort Sumter is recalled in detail in Stevens, "Boat Attack," 47–51; Dahlgren quoted, ibid., 50; Schneller, *Quest for Glory,* 265.

5. LOST OPPORTUNITIES AND NEW HEROES

1. Lee to Fox, March 29, 1863, in Thompson and Wainwright, *Confidential Correspondence,* 2:253.

2. Lee to Welles, April 17, 1863, *ORN,* 8:812.

3. Lamb, "Defense of Fort Fisher," 643, and *Colonel Lamb's Story,* 2; Gragg, *Confederate Goliath,* 19.

4. Wilkinson, *Narrative of a Blockade-Runner,* 152.

5. Lamb, "Defense of Fort Fisher," 643, and *Colonel Lamb's Story,* 2; Gragg, *Confederate Goliath,* 19.

6. D. D. Porter, *Naval History,* 683.

7. Cornish and Laas, *Lincoln's Lee,* 118; Lee to Fox, March 29, 1863, in Thompson and Wainwright, *Confidential Correspondence,* 2:253.

8. Welles, *Diary,* May 20, 1863, 1:306–7.

9. Wise, *Lifeline of the Confederacy,* 124.

10. Grattan, "Under the Blue Pennant," 107, Grattan Papers.

11. Benjamin to John Slidell, September 2, 1863, *ORN*, series 2, 3:885.

12. Wilkinson, *Narrative of a Blockade-Runner*, 199.

13. Ibid., 200–201.

14. Ibid., 202–3.

15. West, *Gideon Welles*, 269–70.

16. Wood, "Port Town at War," 82–83; Whiting to S. Cooper, Adjutant Inspector General, December 21, 1863, Cooper Papers.

17. Quote from U.S. Department of the Navy, *Dictionary of American Naval Fighting Ships*, 2:221–22. Cushing's life is the subject of *Lincoln's Commando* by Ralph J. Roske and Charles Van Doren.

18. Jacksonville is now the location of Camp Lejeune Marine Corps Base.

19. Cushing, "War Experiences," 950–51; Roske and Van Doren, *Lincoln's Commando*, 134–39.

20. Cushing, "War Experiences," 952–56; Roske and Van Doren, *Lincoln's Commando*, 145–46.

21. Stephen R. Mallory, Secretary of the Navy, to Jefferson Davis, November 30, 1863, *ORN*, series 2, 2:528, 532; Wood, "Port Town at War," 102–3; *Dictionary of American Naval Fighting Ships*, 2:553, 577. The armament is from Mallory and the *Dictionary*. Sprunt (*Chronicles*, 479) wrote that the *North Carolina* mounted a 10-inch pivot gun forward and six 8-inchers in broadside.

22. Wood, "Port Town at War," 103; Sprunt, *Chronicles*, 487.

23. John L. Porter, Chief Constructor, to Mallory, November 1, 1864, *ORN*, series 2, 2:752. Porter did not mention the *Wilmington* by name in his report, but she was the only other ironclad ship under construction in Wilmington in that time frame and resembling that description.

24. *Dictionary of American Naval Fighting Ships*, 2:559; Sprunt, *Chronicles*, 480.

25. Sprunt, *Chronicles*, 480–81.

26. Ibid., 481; Scharf, *Confederate States Navy*, 414.

27. Scharf, *Confederate States Navy*, 414–415; Sprunt, *Chronicles*, 481–83; Donnelly, *Confederate States Marine Corps*, 74–76.

28. "Report of the Court of Inquiry," June 6, 1861 [1864], *ORN*, series 2, 2:74. The report, with the correct date, is also quoted in Scharf, *Confederate States Navy*, 415 n. Interestingly, as late as November 5, Secretary Mallory still listed both the *Raleigh* and the *North Carolina* as "in commission" (Mallory to Davis, November 5, 1864, *ORN*, series 2, 2:743).

29. Cushing, "War Experiences," 966–69; Roske and Van Doren, *Lincoln's Commando*, 8–13.

30. Cushing, "War Experiences," 969–70; Roske and Van Doren, *Lincoln's Commando*, 16–17.

31. Cushing, "War Experiences," 970–71; *New York Herald*, July 8, 1864.

32. Cushing, "War Experiences," 972–74; Ammen, *Atlantic Coast*, 211; *New York Herald*, July 8, 1864.

33. *New York Herald*, July 8, 1864.

34. Whiting to Gen. S. Cooper, July 4, 1864, *ORN*, 10:715.

6. "THERE SEEMS TO BE SOME DEFECT IN THE BLOCKADE"

1. Welles to Stanton, January 2, 1864, *Joint Committee Report—Fort Fisher,* 211.
2. Halleck to Stanton, January 6, 1864, *ORN,* 10:387.
3. Lamb, *Colonel Lamb's Story,* 3–5; Gragg, *Confederate Goliath,* 18–19.
4. Lamb, *Colonel Lamb's Story,* 8.
5. Taylor, *Running the Blockade,* 72; Wilkinson, *Narrative of a Blockade-Runner,* 153.
6. Wilkinson, *Narrative of a Blockade-Runner,* 153.
7. Cushing, "War Experiences," 966.
8. Taylor, *Running the Blockade,* 167.
9. Jones, *War Clerk's Diary,* January 3, 1865, 2:374–75.
10. *New York Herald,* August 5, 1864; Sprunt, *Chronicles,* 487; Wood, "Port Town at War," 103–4; *Dictionary of American Naval Fighting Ships,* 2:553. As early as April 30, 1864, Secretary of the Navy Mallory reported that the *North Carolina* had been dismantled as unserviceable (Mallory to Davis, April 30, 1864, *ORN,* series 2, 2:634).
11. Reed, *Combined Operations,* xix–xx.
12. *New York Herald,* August 2, 1864. The cotton ring is examined in Johnson, "Northern Profit and Profiteers."
13. West, *Gideon Welles,* 288.
14. Welles, *Diary,* August 30, 1864, 2:127.
15. Taylor, *Running the Blockade,* 46–47; Grattan, "Under the Blue Pennant," 42.
16. Cushing, "War Experiences," 966.
17. Grattan, "Under the Blue Pennant," 42.
18. Cushing, "War Experiences," 966.
19. Taylor, *Running the Blockade,* 49–50; Grattan, "Under the Blue Pennant," 107.
20. Cushing, "War Experiences," 966.
21. Taylor, *Running the Blockade,* 4; Grant, *Personal Memoirs,* 662.
22. Welles, "Lincoln's Triumph," 459.
23. Ibid., 459–60; Welles, *Diary,* August 30, 1864, 2:127–28. The encirclement of Petersburg in August 1864 disrupted the supply route through the Wilmington and Weldon, so that railroad was no longer critical; the main line to the front now ran inland via the Piedmont Railroad from Charlotte to Richmond. Assuming that Northern business interests were involved with blockade-running, the disruption of direct rail traffic between Wilmington and Richmond substantially reduced the Cape Fear's economic viability. Nevertheless, Wilmington remained the principal entrepôt for supplies to General Lee, and even now there was some resistance in the War Department to an expedition against the city. General Grant, once he accepted Welles's position, had to urge it on his superiors. Ibid., September 15, 1864, 2:146; Price, "North Carolina Railroads," 307.
24. Welles, *Diary,* September 1, 1864, 2:133.
25. Ibid., September 15, 1864, 2:146; Welles to Lincoln, October 28, 1864, *ORN,* series 2, vol. 1, pt. 1:3; Grattan, "Under the Blue Pennant," 103.

26. *Joint Committee Report—Fort Fisher,* i; Reed, *Combined Operations,* 332.

27. *Joint Committee Report—Fort Fisher,* i; Welles, *Diary,* September 15, 1864, 2:146.

28. Cornish and Laas, *Lincoln's Lee,* 139.

29. Ibid., 135–36. After two years of government inaction, Wilmington appeared to weigh heavily on Welles's mind. By August 1864 his diary entries show an uncharacteristic sensitivity to public opinion, and comments on Admiral Lee's real or imagined deficiencies grow in direct proportion to criticism of the navy's failure to close Wilmington. Welles himself did not attend the meeting between Grant, Fox, and Gillmore, but heard of Grant's objections to Admiral Lee from Fox, who openly advocated Farragut for command of the Wilmington expedition. Perhaps Welles accepted Fox's report at face value because it eased his conscience in making Lee a scapegoat for the failure of the Cape Fear blockade. In his own writings, Grant does not mention any preferences or reservations concerning admirals, nor does his aide, Gen. Horace Porter, whose memoirs provide much insight into the lieutenant general's thinking. Considering that Grant's objections to Gillmore as commander of the land forces were a matter of public record (see *Joint Committee—Fort Fisher,* i), it is reasonable to surmise that if Grant actually did oppose Admiral Lee, the record would not be limited to a diary entry by Welles.

30. Cornish and Laas, *Lincoln's Lee,* 137; Welles, "Lincoln's Triumph," 465–66. Fox's connection with the Blairs was more remote, Montgomery Blair being an in-law of his wife. Thus he was able to adjust to political realities without alienating the Blairs. On the other hand, Lee's wife, Elizabeth, was the sister of Frank and Montgomery Blair, and Lee identified his own interests with theirs. The needs of the government also disrupted a political alliance between Preston Blair, the family patriarch, and Gideon Welles that dated back to the Jackson era, but their personal friendship continued.

31. Welles, *Diary,* September 15, 1864, 2:146.

32. Ibid., October 1, 1864, 2:165; Cornish and Laas, *Lincoln's Lee,* 137.

33. Lee to Welles, September 6, 1864, *ORN,* 10:432.

34. Welles to Farragut, September 5, 1864, ibid., 430–31; Lee to Welles, September 8, 1864, ibid., 441–44.

35. Welles to Dahlgren, September 9, 1864, ibid., 449; Welles to Lee, September 17, 1864, ibid., 467.

36. Cornish and Laas, *Lincoln's Lee,* 136–38.

37. *New York Herald,* October 8, 1864.

38. Cornish and Laas, *Lincoln's Lee,* 136–37. The memorandum is in *ORN,* 10:554–56.

39. Welles to Farragut, September 22, 1864, *ORN,* 10:473; Welles to Farragut, October 1, 1864, ibid., 512–13; Welles, *Diary,* September 15, 1864, 2:146–47, and October 1, 1864, 2:164.

40. Reed, *Combined Operations,* 332.

41. Welles to Farragut, September 22, 1864, *ORN,* 10:473; Welles, *Diary,* September 15, 1864, 2:146–47.

42. There are several biographies of Porter. The classic is Soley's *Admiral Porter*, from which most of this sketch was drawn.
43. Nash, *Naval History*, 261–62; Musicant, *Divided Waters*, 226–28.
44. Butler, *Butler's Book*, 360.
45. *Joint Committee Report—Fort Fisher*, 88; Welles, *Diary*, September 17, 1864, 2:148.
46. *Joint Committee Report—Fort Fisher*, 88.
47. Ibid.; Welles to Porter, September 22, 1864, *ORN*, 10:473–74; Soley, *Admiral Porter*, 408–9; D. D. Porter, *Naval History*, 684.
48. Cornish and Laas, *Lincoln's Lee*, 137; Welles, *Diary*, September 15, 1864, 2:146; Lee to Welles, October 12, 1864, *ORN*, 10:554; Abstract of log, USS *Malvern*, October 12, 1864, ibid., 557.

7. THE UNION PREPARES

1. Soley, *Admiral Porter*, 409–10.
2. Porter to Fox, October 19, 1864, in Merrill, "Fort Fisher and Wilmington Campaign," 466.
3. Soley, *Admiral Porter*, 410.
4. Ibid., 411–12.
5. *Joint Committee Report—Fort Fisher*, 88.
6. Ibid., 88–89.
7. Soley, *Admiral Porter*, 414.
8. Porter to Fox, October 15, 1864, in Merrill, "Fort Fisher and Wilmington Campaign," 464.
9. Reed, *Combined Operations*, 333; *Joint Committee Report—Fort Fisher*, 3.
10. Grant to Butler, December 6, 1864, *ORA*, 42, pt. 1:971–72; Reed, *Combined Operations*, 333.
11. Butler (*Butler's Book*, 774) stated Grant was only willing to send 3,000. The actual number of troops embarked for the first Fort Fisher expedition was 6,500.
12. *Joint Committee Report—Fort Fisher*, ii; Butler, *Butler's Book*, 774.
13. Grant to Fox, September 19, 1864, *Joint Committee Report—Fort Fisher*, 216.
14. *Joint Committee Report—Fort Fisher*, 51.
15. Butler's life and career are covered in several works, the most important of which are Richard S. West's *Lincoln's Scapegoat General* and Howard Nash's *Stormy Petrel*. Dick Nolan's *Benjamin Franklin Butler, the Damndest Yankee* expands on some of the material but offers little new information, particularly concerning the Fort Fisher campaign.
16. D. D. Porter, *Naval History*, 692.
17. D. D. Porter, *Incidents and Anecdotes*, 262.
18. *Joint Committee Report—Fort Fisher*, 11; Reed, *Combined Operations*, 333–34, 434.
19. D. D. Porter, *Incidents and Anecdotes*, 262; Reed, *Combined Operations*, 334.

20. Browning, *Cape Charles to Cape Fear,* 289; Butler, *Butler's Book,* 819.

21. Grant, Report, July 22, 1865, *ORA,* 44, pt. 1:42; Grant quoted in *Joint Committee Report—Fort Fisher,* 51.

22. Reed, *Combined Operations,* 434. Butler (*Butler's Book,* 774) contended he sent Weitzel, while Welles ("Lincoln's Triumph," 461) maintained that Weitzel's reconnaissance was not undertaken until the navy suggested it.

23. *Joint Committee Report—Fort Fisher,* 68.

24. Ibid.

25. Ibid., 89. Rowena Reed (*Combined Operations,* 337–38) contends that the powder boat idea probably originated in the Navy Department, and perhaps even with Admiral Porter (who was equally fond of gadgets). Most primary sources, however, give credit to Butler. Decades later, Butler still claimed to have originated the idea, insisting it would have worked if handled properly (*Butler's Book,* 775). In his testimony before the Joint Committee on the Conduct of the War (*Joint Committee Report—Fort Fisher,* 51), Grant pointed out that the idea was not new, and that Butler initially had proposed using a powder boat against Charleston several months earlier.

26. Reed, *Combined Operations,* 338; Beard, "Fort Fisher 'Volcano,'" 1152.

27. *Joint Committee Report—Fort Fisher,* 4.

28. Quotes from D. D. Porter, *Incidents and Anecdotes,* 269–70; *Joint Committee Report—Fort Fisher,* 89.

29. Ammen, *Atlantic Coast,* 216; Welles to Lincoln, October 28, 1864, *Joint Committee Report—Fort Fisher,* 120–21 (also published in *ORN,* 11:3, and in Boynton, *History of the Navy,* 2:569–70).

30. Welles to Lincoln, October 28, 1864, *Joint Committee Report—Fort Fisher,* 120–21.

31. Ammen, *Atlantic Coast,* 216.

32. Butler, *Butler's Book,* 775.

33. Delafield to Assistant Secretary of War Charles A. Dana, November 18, 1865, *Joint Committee Report—Fort Fisher,* 217–23. It should be remembered that Delafield was applying the technology of his era. Twentieth-century ordnance produces far greater concussion.

34. Jeffers to H. A. Wise, Chief of Ordnance, November 23, 1864, ibid., 224–25.

35. Benton to Wise, ibid., 223–24.

36. H. Porter, *Campaigning with Grant,* 337.

37. Welles, *Diary,* December 26, 1864, 2:209.

38. H. Porter, *Campaigning with Grant,* 337.

39. Price and Sturgill, "Shock and Assault," 28–30.

40. Memorandum, *Joint Committee Report—Fort Fisher,* 225–26.

41. Ibid., 227.

42. Ibid., 244. For a description of the *Louisiana's* wartime service, see Blanding, *Recollections.*

43. Blanding, *Recollections,* 330.

44. Beard, "Fort Fisher 'Volcano,'" 1152; Blanding, *Recollections,* 329.

8. "GOODBYE WILMINGTON!"

1. *Richmond Dispatch,* October 7, 1864, reprinted in *New York Herald,* October 10, 1864.
2. Jones, *War Clerk's Diary,* October 28, 1864, 2:317.
3. Ibid., October 30, 1864, 318–19.
4. Strode, *Jefferson Davis,* 47–48; Gragg, *Confederate Goliath,* 57–58. Years later, with Whiting long dead and his own rancor dimmed by time, Davis would describe the general as a "brave and highly accomplished soldier" (Davis, *Rise and Fall,* 2:645).
5. Mallory to Davis, April 30, 1864, *ORN,* series 2, 2:633; Joseph Fernald to "My Dear Wife," August 30, 1864, Fernald Papers. The *Tallahassee's* exploits are covered in Shingleton, "Cruise of the CSS *Tallahassee.*"
6. Honeycutt, "Fort Fisher," 122.
7. Bragg's character is examined in *Braxton Bragg and Confederate Defeat,* 1:27–29.
8. Ibid., 136–39.
9. Warner, *Generals in Gray,* 30–31; Gragg, *Confederate Goliath,* 26–27.
10. *Braxton Bragg and Confederate Defeat,* 1:137, 327; Strode, *Jefferson Davis,* 16. Strode thoroughly analyzes Davis's problems in dealing with egotistical generals and disloyal politicians. Jones (*War Clerk's Diary*) is a good contemporary source, especially the second volume, written as the Confederacy was failing. Davis (*Rise and Fall*) is strangely silent about Bragg, giving him no particular mention following the Battle of Chickamauga.
11. *Braxton Bragg and Confederate Defeat,* 1:325–26, 2:221–22.
12. Quoted in Gragg, *Confederate Goliath,* 27, and in Sprunt, *Chronicles,* 492.
13. Jones, *War Clerk's Diary,* October 18, 1864, 2:310; *Braxton Bragg and Confederate Defeat,* 2:220–21.
14. Lamb, *Colonel Lamb's Story,* 11–12.
15. Lamb, Diary, October 24, 1864, Lamb Papers.
16. Ibid., October 25, 1864.
17. Ibid., October 26, 1864.
18. Ibid.; Lamb, "Defense of Fort Fisher," 643, and *Colonel Lamb's Story,* 2.
19. Lamb, *Colonel Lamb's Story,* 4–5, and Diary, October 27–28, 1864.
20. Quoted in Scharf, *Confederate States Navy,* 418.
21. Lamb, Diary, memoranda.
22. Ibid., November 5, 7–8, 1864.
23. Ibid., November 9, 1864.
24. Gragg, *Confederate Goliath,* 24; Lamb, Diary, various entries.
25. Lamb, Diary, November 10, 1864.
26. Ibid., November 13, 1864.
27. Ibid., November 24, 1864; Lamb, *Colonel Lamb's Story,* 8–9.
28. Lamb, Diary, November 24, 1864.
29. Sands, "Last of the Blockade," 12.

30. Read to "Dear Father and Mother," November 1864, Read Papers.
31. Evans, *Sailor's Log,* 75.
32. Grattan to "Dear Pa and Ma," December 1, 1864, Grattan Papers.
33. D. D. Porter, *Incidents and Anecdotes,* 263.
34. Ibid., 263–67.
35. Butler to George H. Powers, November 28, 1864, in Butler, *Private and Official Correspondence,* 5:367.
36. E. F. Jones to Butler, November 29, 1864, and Peter Lawson to Butler, November 30, 1864, both in Butler, *Private and Official Correspondence,* 5:370–71; D. D. Porter, *Incidents and Anecdotes,* 267.
37. H. Porter, *Campaigning with Grant,* 336; Lamb, Diary, November 22, 1864.
38. *Joint Committee Report—Fort Fisher,* 52; H. Porter, *Campaigning with Grant,* 346; Price and Sturgill, "Shock and Assault," 31.
39. *Joint Committee Report—Fort Fisher,* 52; Grant to Butler, November 30, 1864, *ORA,* 42, pt. 1:970–71.
40. *Joint Committee Report—Fort Fisher,* 11.
41. Ibid., 52, 74; H. Porter, *Campaigning with Grant,* 361.
42. Price and Sturgill, "Shock and Assault," 31.
43. Grant to Butler, December 4, 1864, *ORA,* 42, pt. 1:971.
44. "Story of the Powder-Boat," 79–80. All contemporary accounts state the *Louisiana* was painted white, although in all probability this actually indicated more of a haze gray, the standard blockade-runner color scheme.
45. *Joint Committee Report—Fort Fisher,* 244–50; Beard, "Fort Fisher 'Volcano,'" 1153. Initially the *Louisiana* was to have carried three hundred tons, but navy planners feared this would give her too heavy a draft for the shoals approaching Fort Fisher. See Browning, *From Cape Charles to Cape Fear,* 289.
46. Quoted in Beard, "The Fort Fisher 'Volcano,'" 1153, and in Rhind, "The Fort Fisher Powder-Boat," 232.
47. "Story of the Powder-Boat," 80; Rhind, "The Fort Fisher Powder-Boat," 233; Musicant, *Divided Waters,* 390.
48. Gragg, *Confederate Goliath,* 143; Du Pont to William Whetten, January 19, 1865, in Hayes, *Samuel Francis Du Pont,* 3:428.
49. Parker, "Navy in the Capture of Fort Fisher," 113–14; Gragg, *Confederate Goliath,* 143.
50. "Story of the Powder-Boat," 81; Beard, "The Fort Fisher 'Volcano,'" 1153; D. D. Porter, *Incidents and Anecdotes,* 271.

9. THE LAST VOYAGE OF THE LOUISIANA

1. Lamb, Diary, December 3, 1864; weather in various entries beginning November 23.
2. Ibid., December 4–9, 12, 1864; *New York Times,* December 24, 1864.
3. D. D. Porter, *Incidents and Anecdotes,* 271.
4. Turner, "Rocked in the Cradle," 73–74.

5. Butler, *Butler's Book,* 785–86; Turner, "Rocked in the Cradle," 74.

6. Grattan, Journal, December 13, 1864, and "Under the Blue Pennant," 149, Grattan Papers; *New York Times,* December 16, 22, 1864.

7. "Opposing Forces at Fort Fisher," 662; editor's note to Selfridge, "Navy at Fort Fisher," 655 n.

8. Dewey, *Autobiography,* 112.

9. *New York Times,* December 22, 1864.

10. Ibid.

11. Butler, *Butler's Book,* 786; Turner, "Rocked in the Cradle," 74; Butler to Grant, December 20, 1864, *ORA,* 42, pt. 1:964.

12. Grant to Butler, December 6, 1864, *ORA,* 42, pt. 1:971–72; *Joint Committee Report—Fort Fisher,* 52,

13. Grant, Report, July 22, 1865, *ORA,* 44, pt. 1:42.

14. Grattan, Journal, December 14–15, and "Under the Blue Pennant," 151; Sands, "Last of the Blockade," 13; "Story of the Powder-Boat," 83–84; Browning, *From Cape Charles to Cape Fear,* 289.

15. Rhind, "Fort Fisher Powder-Boat," 232; Rhind to Porter, February 2, 1865, *ORN,* 11:230.

16. Read to "Dear Parents," December 17, 1864, Read Papers.

17. Porter to Watmough, December 17, 1864, *ORN,* 11:220–21; "Story of the Powder-Boat," 84–85.

18. "Story of the Powder-Boat," 84.

19. Porter to Watmough, December 17, 1864, Porter to Senior Officer off Western Bar, December 17, 1864, and Porter to Rhind, December 17, 1864, all in *ORN,* 11:220–23; D. D. Porter, *Incidents and Anecdotes,* 271.

20. Gragg, *Confederate Goliath,* 46; Turner, "Rocked in the Cradle," 74; Butler, *Butler's Book,* 786–87; Lockwood, "Capture of Fort Fisher," 625.

21. Turner, "Rocked in the Cradle," 74.

22. Lamb, Diary, December 18, 1864. Northern reports referred to Battery Gatlin as Half Moon Battery.

23. Lockwood, "Capture of Fort Fisher," 626; Butler, *Butler's Book,* 787; Porter to Butler, December 18, 1864, *ORN,* 11:223–24.

24. "Story of the Powder-Boat," 85.

25. Grattan, Journal, December 18, 1864.

26. Butler to Grant, December 20, 1864, *ORA,* 42, pt. 1:965; "Story of the Powder-Boat," 85; Porter to Butler, December 18, 1864, and Porter to Welles, January 11, 1865, both in *ORN,* 11:223–28. Why the explosion was expected to flatten Fort Fisher—as well as houses in Smithville and Wilmington—but leave a Union landing party unscathed was never explained and apparently never considered.

27. Porter to Butler, December 18, 1864, Breese to Porter, January 11, 1865, Porter to Rhind, December 19, 1864, and Porter to Welles, January 11, 1865, all in *ORN,* 11:223–28; "Story of the Powder-Boat," 85.

28. Turner, "Rocked in the Cradle," 74.

29. Grattan, "Under the Blue Pennant," 154; Butler to Grant, *ORA,* 42, pt. 1:965.

30. Turner, "Rocked in the Cradle," 75.
31. Grattan, "Under the Blue Pennant," 153–54.
32. *New York Times,* December 22, 1864.
33. Ibid. The timing of this incident and the one following concerning the monitor *Monadnock* is ambiguous. The *Times* correspondent and a private letter from Comdr. Enoch Parrott of the *Monadnock* to his wife (January 11, 1865, Parrott Papers) indicate there were two gales—one off Cape Hatteras en route from Hampton Roads to Beaufort, and a second after the fleet arrived off Fort Fisher—and that these incidents occurred during the gale off Hatteras. However, virtually every other account, official and private, indicates smooth sailing from Hampton Roads to Beaufort and from Beaufort to Fort Fisher, and that the only rough weather came after the arrival off Fisher. In deference to the majority, particularly the daily journals, I have chosen to treat it as single gale that blew up after the arrival off the fort.
34. Parrot to "My dear Susan," January 11, 1865, Parrott Papers.
35. "Story of the Powder-Boat," 86–87.
36. Lamb, Diary, December 20, 1864, and *Colonel Lamb's Story,* 11.
37. Lamb, *Colonel Lamb's Story,* 11; Whiting, "Answers (numbered) to questions propounded by Benjamin F. Butler," *ORA,* 42, pt. 1:979; Donnelly, *Confederate States Marine Corps,* 85.
38. R. T. Chapman to Flag Officer R. F. Pinkney, December 29, 1864, and F. M. Roby to Lamb, December [?], 1864, *ORN,* 11:372–73; Clarence Cary, Diary, undated through December 20, 1864, ibid., 375; Scharf, *Confederate States Navy,* 422; Donnelly, *Confederate States Marine Corps,* 85. No accommodations for van Benthuysen are mentioned. As commanding officer of the marines in that district, he presumably would have bunked with Lieutenant Chapman.
39. Cary, quoted in Scharf, *Confederate States Navy,* 422.
40. Lamb, Diary, December 22, 1864, and *Colonel Lamb's Story,* 12.
41. Lamb, Diary, December 23, 1864, and *Colonel Lamb's Story,* 12. In his memoir, Lamb's figures on the strength of the reinforcements are not totally consistent with those in his diary, and Whiting contradicts both. In response to Butler's inquiry, Whiting ("Answers . . . to questions," *ORA,* 42, pt. 1:980) listed the reinforcements of December 23 as "110 men, veteran artillery of the Tenth Regiment North Carolina, 50 sailors, and the Seventh Battalion Reserves, about 250 strong." Whiting and Lamb's diary agree about the unit numbers, i.e., 10th North Carolina and 7th Reserves, while *Colonel Lamb's Story* gives them as 40th North Carolina and 17th Reserves, probably due to error in transcription when Lamb wrote the memoir years later. Lamb's diary places the arrival of Roby's naval detachment on December 21 and does not mention any sailors on December 23. But the papers originating with the detachment (*ORN,* 11:372–75) and Whiting both place its arrival on the twenty-third. This raises the possibility that Lamb was too busy preparing a defense to make complete daily entries and might have gone back and filled in the gaps of his diary after the fight of December 24–25, thus getting his dates confused.

42. Lamb, *Colonel Lamb's Story*, 12.
43. *Joint Committee Report—Fort Fisher*, 21; Porter to Rhind, December 23, 1864, and Porter to Watmough, December 23, 1864, both in *ORN*, 11:225; Price and Sturgill, "Shock and Assault," 33.
44. Browning, *Cape Charles to Cape Fear*, 290; Price and Sturgill, "Shock and Assault," 33–34; *Joint Committee Report—Fort Fisher*, 30–31.
45. Jeffers to Bureau of Ordnance, December 8, 1864, *Joint Committee Report—Fort Fisher*, 241; Price and Sturgill, "Shock and Assault," 32–33; "Story of the Powder-Boat," 85.
46. "Story of the Powder-Boat," 87.
47. Ibid., 87–88; Rhind to Porter, December 26, 1864, *ORN*, 11:226–27; Gragg, *Confederate Goliath*, 50–53.
48. Selfridge, "Navy at Fort Fisher," 655.
49. Grattan, Journal, December 24, 1865.
50. Lamb, Diary, December 24, 1864.
51. Cary, quoted in Scharf, *Confederate States Navy*, 422–23.
52. Rhind to Porter, February 2, 1865, *ORN*, 11:230; "Story of the Powder-Boat," 88.

10. "ENGAGE THE ENEMY"

1. Grattan, Journal, December 24, 1864; Dewey, *Autobiography*, 115.
2. Lanman to Porter, January 1, 1865, *ORN*, 11:301.
3. Cary, quoted in Scharf, *Confederate States Navy*, 423–24.
4. Grattan, Journal, December 24, 1864; Selfridge, "Navy at Fort Fisher," 655.
5. Sands, "Last of the Blockade," 14.
6. Rogers to his parents, December 24, 1864, in Rogers, *Memories of Ninety Years*, 91–92.
7. Lamb, *Colonel Lamb's Story*, 15; Dewey, *Autobiography*, 115; Selfridge, "Navy at Fort Fisher," 655; Gragg, *Confederate Goliath*, 64–65. Some accounts place the first shot at 12:45 P.M. Grattan's record of 12:53 P.M. is used here because it was the most immediate, being noted in his journal entry of December 24, 1864.
8. Sands, "Last of the Blockade," 15
9. Selfridge, "Navy at Fort Fisher," 4:657.
10. Parrott to "My dear Susan," January 11, 1865, Parrott Papers.
11. Ibid.
12. Cary, Diary, December 24, 1864, *ORN*, 11:376; Scharf, *Confederate States Navy*, 424.
13. Sands, "Last of the Blockade," 15; *ORN*, 11:277ff. Reaction of *Minnesota* crew in Joseph Lanman to Porter, January 1, 1865, ibid., 301. The reference to "Quaker" guns is in S. P. Crafts to Porter, December 31, 1864, ibid., 344. The reaction of the *Wabash* crew and the comment about "a cloud of thick black smoke" is in Read to "Dear Father and Mother," December 27, 1864, Read Papers.
14. Lamb, note to Selfridge, "Navy at Fort Fisher," 4:657 n; Lamb, *Colonel Lamb's Story*, 16–17.

15. Cary, Diary, December 24, 1864, *ORN*, 11:376; Lamb, *Colonel Lamb's Story,* 15; Scharf, *Confederate States Navy,* 424.

16. Read to "Dear Father and Mother," December 27, 1864, Read Papers.

17. Belknap to Porter, December 31, 1865, *ORN*, 11:277; Parrott to "My dear Susan," January 11, 1865, Parrott Papers; Scharf, *Confederate States Navy,* 424.

18. J. C. Beaumont to Porter, December 27, 1864, and Jefferson Young to Beaumont, December 24, 1864, both in *ORN*, 11:319–20.

19. Schenck to Porter, January 1, 1865, ibid., 305; Evans, *Sailor's Log,* 80.

20. Schenck to Porter, January 1, 1865, *ORN*, 11:305. The *Iosco* also claimed credit for shooting down the Mound flagstaff. At least two of the fort's several flagstaffs appear to have been shot down, with credit being claimed by the *Gettysburg, Minnesota,* and several other ships (John Guest to Porter, December 27, 1864, ibid., 330; Sands, "Last of the Blockade," 15–16; Parker, "Navy in the Capture of Fort Fisher," 109).

21. Sands, "Last of the Blockade," 15. Sands was the son of Capt. Benjamin Sands.

22. Grattan, Journal, December 24, 1864.

23. Harris to Porter, December 27, 1864, January 2, 1865, and H. K. Wheeler, Acting Assistant Surgeon, to Harris, December 24, 1864, *ORN*, 11:312–13.

24. Taylor to Porter, December 30, 1864, and Albert C. Gorgas, Surgeon, to Taylor, December 24, 1864, both in *ORN*, 11:321–22; Grattan, Journal, December 24, 1864.

25. Capt. Charles Steedman to Porter, December 30, 1864, *ORN*, 11:328. The printed version of the report in the *Official Records* says eleven men were wounded, but a manuscript copy gives the number as twelve, as does a letter from Steedman to his wife written December 27. Both letters are in the Perkins Library of Duke University.

26. Log, USS *Quaker City,* December 24, 1864, *ORN*, 11:331.

27. Clitz to Porter, December 27, 1864, ibid., 336.

28. Log, USS *Pawtuxet,* December 24, 1864, ibid., 323; Steedman to Porter, December 30, 1864, ibid., 328.

29. Scharf, *Confederate States Navy,* 424. For a description of Union and Confederate ordnance, see Time-Life, *Echoes of Glory.*

30. Cary, Diary, December 24, 1864, *ORN*, 11:376–77.

31. Scharf, *Confederate States Navy,* 425.

32. Lamb, *Colonel Lamb's Story,* 15–17.

33. Nash (*Naval History,* 269) contends that if Porter did not actually sabotage the expedition, he at least wanted it to fail. He is not alone in this supposition, and the possibility was discussed at length in conversations between the author and officials of Fort Fisher State Park and other historians in North Carolina.

34. The numerous reports are found in *ORN*, 11:275ff.

35. Porter to Fox, October 19, 1864, in Merrill, "Fort Fisher and Wilmington Campaign," 466.

36. Scharf, *Confederate States Navy,* 425.

37. *Joint Committee Report—Fort Fisher,* 21–22.

38. Ibid., 22, 30–31; Butler, *Butler's Book,* 791, 806–7; Weitzel to Brig. Gen. J. W.

Turner, Chief of Staff, December 31, 1864, *ORA,* 42, pt. 1:985; Gragg, *Confederate Goliath,* 73.
39. Whiting to Anderson, December 31, 1864, Whiting Papers.

11. THE GHOST OF BATTERY WAGNER

1. Gragg, *Confederate Goliath,* 76; Grattan, Journal, December 25, 1864 (first quote), and December 23, 1864 (second quote); Weitzel to Turner, December 31, 1864, *ORA,* 42, pt. 1:986.
2. E. S. Keyser to Porter, December 25, 1864, *ORN,* 11:378.
3. Log, USS *Monticello,* December 25, 1864, ibid., 341.
4. Joseph Fernald to Louise Fernald, December 25, 1864, Fernald Papers; O. S. Glisson to Porter, January 1, 1865, *ORN,* 11:333.
5. Porter to Welles, December 26, 1864, *ORN,* 11:258; Gragg, *Confederate Goliath,* 83–84.
6. Chapman to Flag Officer R. F. Pinkney, December 29, 1864, *ORN,* 11:373; W. T. Truxtun to Porter, December 27, 1864, ibid., 334; George Hopkins to Truxtun; December 27, 1864, ibid., 335; Porter to Welles, December 26, 1864, ibid., 258.
7. F. M. Roby to Lamb, December [?], 1864, *ORN,* 11:374; Cary, Diary, December 24, 1864, ibid., 377. In his account for Scharf's *Confederate States Navy* (page 425), written over twenty years later, Cary said at least one man died. However, neither his diary nor any other contemporary accounts mention deaths in the explosions, although wounded were noted.
8. Cushing, "War Experiences," 985; Asa Betham to "Dear Emma," December 25, 1864, Betham Papers; Roske and Van Doren, *Lincoln's Commando,* 258.
9. Porter to Welles, December 26, 1864, *ORN,* 11:258; Cushing, "War Experiences," 985.
10. O. S. Glisson to Porter, January 1, 1865, *ORN,* 11:333; Curtis to Capt. Charles A. Carleton, Assistant Adjutant General, December 28, 1864, *ORA,* 42, pt. 1:982.
11. Fernald to Louise Fernald, December 25, 1864, Fernald Papers; Glisson to Porter, December 25, 1864, *ORN,* 11:332–33; Huse to Porter, December 31, 1864, ibid., 351–52; log, USS *Britannia,* December 25, 1865, ibid., 352; Gragg, *Confederate Goliath,* 81–82.
12. *Joint Committee Report—Fort Fisher,* 24–25.
13. Curtis to Carleton, December 28, 1864, *ORA,* 42, pt. 1:982–84; Weitzel to Turner, December 31, 1864, ibid., 986; Lockwood, "Capture of Fort Fisher," 630–31; Gragg, *Confederate Goliath,* 82.
14. Weitzel to Turner, December 31, 1864, *ORA,* 42, pt. 1:986.
15. Lockwood, "Capture of Fort Fisher," 631.
16. Chapman to Pinkney, December 29, 1864, *ORN,* 11:373. Some Junior Reserves remained in the fort, cowering wherever they could find room in the bombproofs.
17. Cary, Diary, December 25, 1864, ibid., 377.
18. Beaumont to Porter, December 27, 1865, ibid., 319.
19. Schenck to Porter, January 1, 1865, ibid., 305; George M. Bache to Schenck, December 25, 1864, ibid., 306.

20. Smith to Porter, January 2, 1865, ibid., 306; Read to "Dear Father and Mother," December 27, 1864, Read Papers.
21. Lockwood, "Capture of Fort Fisher," 631.
22. Butler to Grant, January 3, 1865, *ORA,* 42, pt. 1:968; Harkness, "Expeditions against Fort Fisher," 160–61; *Joint Committee Report—Fort Fisher,* 24–25.
23. Hoke to Lee, December 25, 1864, *ORA,* 46, pt. 2:1026–27; Whiting, "Answers (numbered) to questions," ibid., 42, pt. 1:979.
24. Harkness, "Expeditions against Fort Fisher," 160; Ames, "Capture of Fort Fisher," 276; Butler to Grant, January 3, 1865, *ORA,* 42, pt. 1:968.
25. Cary, Diary, December 25, 1865, *ORN,* 11:377; Gragg, *Confederate Goliath,* 93.
26. Fernald to Louise Fernald, December 25, 1864, Fernald Papers.
27. Sprunt, *Chronicles,* 491.
28. Sicard to Porter, December 31, 1864, *ORN,* 11:315.
29. Glisson to Porter, January 1, 1865, ibid., 333; Curtis to Carleton, December 28, 1864, *ORA,* 42, pt. 1:983; *Joint Committee Report—Fort Fisher,* 92; Gragg, *Confederate Goliath,* 95.
30. Dewey, *Autobiography,* 117; log, USS *Colorado,* December 25, 1864, *ORN,* 11:296–97.
31. Fernald to Louise Fernald, December 25, 1864, Fernald Papers.
32. Chapman to Pinkney, December 29, 1864, *ORN,* 11:373; Cary, Diary, December 25, 1864, ibid., 377; Whiting to Anderson, December 31, 1864 (first quote), and Whiting to Bragg, December 26, 1864 (second quote), both in Whiting Papers; Gragg, *Confederate Goliath,* 95.
33. Whiting to Anderson, December 31, 1864, Whiting Papers; H. K. Thatcher to Porter, December 31, 1864, *ORN,* 11:295; Cary, Diary, December 26, 1864, ibid., 377.
34. J. C. Howell to Porter, January 3, 1865, George M. Smith to Howell, December 27, 1864, and Edward L. Haines to Howell, December 26, 27, 1864, all in *ORN,* 11:290–91; Poole to Acting Volunteer Lt. John MacDiarmid, ibid., 354.
35. Various letters and reports, ibid., 277ff.; Fernald to Louise Fernald, December 26–27, 1864, Fernald Papers.
36. Parker, "Navy in the Capture of Fort Fisher," 109.
37. Preston to Du Pont, January 3, 1865, in Hayes, *Samuel Francis Du Pont,* 3:424.
38. Parrott to "My dear Susan," January 11, 1865, Parrott Papers.
39. Grattan to "Dear Pa and Ma," January 4, 1865, Grattan Papers.
40. Whiting to Anderson, December 31, 1864, Whiting Papers; Lamb, Diary, memoranda.
41. Cary, Diary, December 27–28, 1864, *ORN,* 11:377.

12. REORGANIZATION

1. Porter to Benjamin F. Sands, December 26, 1864, and Porter to Glisson, December 26, 1864, both in *ORN,* 11:379.
2. Porter to Cushing, December 27, 1864, ibid., 384.
3. North Atlantic Squadron, General Order No. 75, December 30, 1864, ibid., 252–53.

4. The extensive reports are in *ORN,* 11:275ff.

5. Rogers to his parents, January 1, 1865, in Rogers, *Memories of Ninety Years,* 103.

6. North Atlantic Squadron, Special Order No. 8, January 3, 1865, *Joint Committee Report—Fort Fisher,* 198.

7. See various reports in *ORN,* 11:275ff.

8. Porter to Fox, January 7, 1865, in Merrill, "Fort Fisher and Wilmington Campaign," 467.

9. Steedman to "My Dear Sally," December 27, 1867, Steedman Papers. These papers also contain a copy of his official report of December 30, 1864, in which he also described the explosion.

10. Grant to Lincoln, December 28, 1864, in Grant, *Personal Memoirs,* 668.

11. H. Porter, *Campaigning with Grant,* 363.

12. Welles, *Diary,* December 29, 1864, 2:213–14.

13. Ibid., January 14, 1865, 2:215, 223; *New York Times,* January 13, 1865.

14. Turner, "Rocked in the Cradle," 79.

15. *New York Times,* January 13, 1865.

16. Grant, *Personal Memoirs,* 668.

17. Grant to Porter, December 30, 1864, quoted in Harkness, "Expeditions against Fort Fisher," 163.

18. Headquarters, Department of North Carolina, General Order No. 17, *ORA,* 42, pt. 1:999; Lamb, Diary, December 27–29, 1864.

19. Lamb, Diary, January 2, 1865; Gragg, *Confederate Goliath,* 140. Like Robert Capa, who was killed in Indochina, Vizetelly pushed his luck too far. On November 5, 1883, he was massacred with Hicks Pasha's ill-fated expedition during the Mahdist uprising in the Sudan.

20. Lamb, Diary, January 2, 1865.

21. Ibid., December 28, 1864–January 8, 1865; Lamb, *Colonel Lamb's Story.* 35; Whiting to Lamb, January 3, 1865, *ORA,* 46, pt. 2:1013.

22. Welles, *Diary,* January 6, 1865, 2:221–22.

23. Porter to Fox, January 7, 1865, in Merrill, "Fort Fisher and Wilmington Campaign," 467.

24. Preston to Du Pont, January 3, 1865, in Hayes, *Samuel Francis Du Pont,* 3:424.

25. Warner, *Generals in Blue,* 497.

26. Longacre, "Task before Them," 37; Terry to Brig. Gen. John A. Rawlins, Chief of Staff, January 25, 1865, *ORA,* 44, pt. 1:395.

27. Evans, *Sailor's Log,* 83; Dewey, *Autobiography,* 118.

28. Porter to Fox, January 7, 1865, in Merrill, "Fort Fisher and Wilmington Campaign," 467; Evans, *Sailor's Log,* 84.

29. Porter to Fox, January 7, 1865, in Merrill, "Fort Fisher and Wilmington Campaign," 467.

30. North Atlantic Squadron, General Order No. 81, January 4, 1865, printed copy in Grattan Papers.

31. Dewey, *Autobiography,* 120.

32. Terry to Rawlins, January 25, 1865, *ORA,* 44, pt. 1:395.

33. Ibid.; Adrian Terry to "My own darling wife," January 24, 1865, in Longacre, "Task before Them," 38.

34. Grant to Terry, January 3, 1865, *ORA*, 44, pt. 1:43.

35. D. D. Porter, *Naval History*, 711; Longacre, "Task before Them," 38.

36. D. D. Porter, *Naval History*, 711.

37. Soley, *Admiral Porter*, 426.

38. Porter to Welles, Special Report, January 17, 1865, *ORN*, 11:445.

39. Rogers to "Father and Mother," January 12, 1865, in Rogers, *Memories of Ninety Years*, 104.

13. "THEY'LL HAVE TO SWIM FOR IT"

1. Taylor, *Running the Blockade*, 136, 139; Lamb, *Colonel Lamb's Story*, 35; Gragg, *Confederate Goliath*, 216.

2. Strode, *Jefferson Davis*, 110.

3. Ibid., 138.

4. Whiting to Seddon, January 1, 1865, *ORA*, 46, pt. 2:1000–1001.

5. Endorsements to ibid., 1001–2.

6. Lamb, *Colonel Lamb's Story*, 22.

7. Bragg to Mallory, January 1, 1862, *ORA*, 46, pt. 2:1002. Bragg also ordered the army to give whatever assistance the navy might require to complete the ship (Archer Anderson, Assistant Adjutant General, Department of North Carolina, to Chief Constructor John L. Porter, CSN, January 1, 1865, ibid.).

8. Lipscomb to Maj. J. H. Hill, Assistant Adjutant General, January 12, 1865, ibid., 1043.

9. Lamb to Hill, January 12, 1865, ibid.; Lamb, Diary, January 12, 1865, and "Colonel Lamb's Story," 22.

10. Anderson to Whiting, January 12, 1865, *ORA*, 46, pt. 2:1043–44; Bragg to Vance, January 12, 1865, ibid., 1045; Anderson to Hebert, January 13, 1865, ibid., 1050.

11. Lamb, Diary, January 30, 1865, and "Defense of Fort Fisher," 647; Selfridge, "Navy at Fort Fisher," 658; Ammen, *Atlantic Coast*, 229.

12. Evans, *Sailor's Log*, 85; Dewey, *Autobiography*, 119; Grattan, "Under the Blue Pennant," 153.

13. Evans, *Sailor's Log*, 85; Grattan, "Under the Blue Pennant," 177.

14. Whiting, Special Order, January 13, 1865, *ORA*, 46, pt. 2:1048; Still, "Yankees Were Landing," 15.

15. Lamb to Hill, January 13, 1865, *ORA*, 46, pt. 2:1047.

16. Lamb, "Defense of Fort Fisher," 647.

17. Whiting to Bragg, January 13, 1865, *ORA*, 46, pt. 2:1048.

18. Anderson to Lamb, January 13, 1865, ibid., 1047.

19. Soley, *Admiral Porter*, 427.

20. Parker, "Navy in the Capture of Fort Fisher," 110–11.

21. Terry to Rawlins, January 25, 1865, *ORA*, 44, pt. 1:397; Curtis, "Capture of Fort Fisher," 307–8; Gragg, *Confederate Goliath*, 141.

22. Still, "Yankees Were Landing," 15.

23. Gragg, *Confederate Goliath,* 140.

24. Rogers to "Father and Mother," February 10, 1865, in Rogers, *Memories of Ninety Years,* 114.

25. Lamb, *Colonel Lamb's Story,* 23.

26. Ibid.

27. Bartlett to his sisters, January 18, 1865, *ORN,* 11:526.

28. Terry to Rawlins, January 25, 1865, *ORA,* 44, pt. 1:398; D. D. Porter, *Naval History,* 715.

29. Dewey, *Autobiography,* 119.

30. Evans, *Sailor's Log,* 86.

31. Dewey, *Autobiography,* 119.

32. Selfridge, "Navy at Fort Fisher," 659.

33. *Joint Committee Report—Fort Fisher,* 115, 117; Lamb, "Defense of Fort Fisher," 649.

34. Selfridge, "Navy at Fort Fisher," 659; Evans, *Sailor's Log,* 87; Parker, "Navy in the Capture of Fort Fisher," 111; Samuel Cobb to "Dear Father," January 16, 1865, Cobb Papers. Primary sources do not agree on the time of the landing order, with estimates ranging over a four-hour period from 9 A.M. to 1 P.M. Most accounts place it in the forenoon.

35. Parker, "Navy in the Capture of Fort Fisher," 111.

36. Evans, *Sailor's Log,* 91.

37. Parker, "Navy in the Capture of Fort Fisher," 113–14; Gragg, *Confederate Goliath,* 157; Du Pont to William Whetten, January 19, 1865, in Hayes, *Samuel Francis Du Pont,* 3:428.

38. Cushing, "War Experiences," 986.

39. Breese to Porter, January 16, 1865, *ORN,* 11:446; Parker to Porter, January 16, 1865, ibid., 498; Dawson to Col. Jacob Zeilin, Commandant of the Marine Corps, January 27, 1865 (first letter), Record Group 127, Records of the Commandant (Marine Corps), Letters Received, 1818–1915, National Archives [hereinafter cited as "Letters Received"]; Evans, *Sailor's Log,* 87.

40. Lamb, "Defense of Fort Fisher," 649.

41. Cushing, "War Experiences," 986. Figures on the number of men in the Naval Brigade range from 1,400 to 2,000. Breese gives 1,600 sailors in his report to Porter, January 16, 1865, *ORN,* 11:446; and Dawson says 350 marines in his first letter to Colonel Zeilin, January 27, 1865, "Letters Received." This makes 1,950 in aggregate.

42. Ammen, *Atlantic Coast,* 232; *Joint Committee Report—Fort Fisher,* 115.

43. Ammen, *Atlantic Coast,* 232–33.

44. Ibid., 233; Lanman to Porter, January 17, 1865, *ORN,* 11:494; Parker to Porter, January 16, 1865, ibid., 497; Breese to Porter, January 16, 1865, ibid., 446.

45. Gragg, *Confederate Goliath,* 142–43.

46. Selfridge, "Navy at Fort Fisher," 659; Breese to Porter, January 16, 1865, *ORN,* 11:446–47.

47. Curtis, "Capture of Fort Fisher," 311–12.

48. Parker, "Navy in the Capture of Fort Fisher," 116; Parker to Porter, January 16, 1865, *ORN,* 11:500.
49. Dawson to Zeilin, January 27, 1865 (two letters), "Letters Received."
50. Dawson to Zeilin, January 27, 1865 (first letter), "Letters Received." In his correspondence, Dawson refers to Cushman's group as the Second Division, when actually it was the First Division. Probably this was because it was suppose to form the second line, behind the marines, while Parker's Second Division formed the third line and Selfridge's Third Division formed the fourth.
51. Parker, "Navy in the Capture of Fort Fisher," 116.
52. Parker to Porter, January 16, 1865, *ORN,* 11:500.
53. Quoted in Lamb, "Defense of Fort Fisher," 649, and *Colonel Lamb's Story,* 26.
54. Lamb, "Defense of Fort Fisher," 650, and *Colonel Lamb's Story,* 26–27.

14. DISASTER AND TRIUMPH

1. Lamb, "Defense of Fort Fisher," 650, and *Colonel Lamb's Story,* 27.
2. Lamb, "Defense of Fort Fisher," 650.
3. Cobb to "Dear Father," January 16, 1865, Cobb Papers. Like that of many people of his era, Cobb's spelling was "original." No effort has been made to correct it in direct quotes.
4. Evans, *Sailor's Log,* 86.
5. Breese to Porter, January 16, 1865, *ORN,* 11:446; Barrett, *Civil War in North Carolina,* 276 n; Cobb to "Dear Father," January 16, 1865, Cobb Papers.
6. Evans, *Sailor's Log,* 89.
7. Cobb to "Dear Father," January 16, 1865, Cobb Papers. If the officer was, in fact, wounded at this early stage of the battle, he could not have been Lamb.
8. Evans, *Sailor's Log,* 89–90.
9. Parker to Porter, January 16, 1865, *ORN,* 11:498; Breese to Porter, January 16, 1865, ibid., 447; Lamson to Rhind, January 16, 1865, ibid., 450; Parker, "Navy in the Capture of Fort Fisher," 114; Evans, *Sailor's Log,* 90; Gragg, *Confederate Goliath,* 165.
10. Evans, *Sailor's Log,* 90–91.
11. Dewey, *Autobiography,* 120.
12. Ibid.
13. Evans, *Sailor's Log,* 90; Dawson to Zeilin, January 27, 1865 (second letter), "Letters Received."
14. Parker to Lanman, January 16, 1865, and Parker to Porter, January 16, 1865, both in *ORN,* 11:495–99.
15. Parker to Porter, January 16, 1865, ibid., 499.
16. Dawson to Zeilin, January 27, 1865 (first letter), "Letters Received."
17. Bartlett to his sisters, January 18, 1865, *ORN,* 11:528; Breese to Porter, January 16, 1865, ibid., 446–47; Breese to Porter, January 28, 1865, ibid., 451.
18. Bartlett to his sisters, January 18, 1865, ibid., 528.
19. Evans, *Sailor's Log,* 91.
20. Ibid., 92–93.

21. Dawson to Zeilin, January 27, 1865 (first letter), "Letters Received." Ever since the battle, the marines have been unfairly accused of starting the panic. One of the most recent to blame them has been Rod Gragg (*Confederate Goliath*, 167). These allegations are based largely on Admiral Porter's report to Secretary Welles (January 17, 1865, *ORN*, 11:439) and Breese's report to Porter (January 16, 1865, ibid., 446–48). Porter, whose order to assault a heavily defended fortress with cutlass and pistol made him as responsible as anyone for the fiasco, was looking for scapegoats. Breese, whose haphazard leadership contributed, was ready to provide them, although he qualified it by mentioning the general confusion of the assault. Certainly, individual marines did run, and others hid or buried themselves in the sand, too terrified to fight, but several primary sources indicate that, as a unit, the marines did good service throughout the battle. Most notable is Evans (*Sailor's Log*, 93), who remembered that following the rout of the Naval Brigade many Confederate sharpshooters had to remain on the Northeast Bastion while the army assaulted the opposite end of the land face, because "quite a number of marines were scattered about the beach wherever they could find cover, keeping up a steady fire." Lieutenant Commander Parker honestly stated that he could find no particular reason for the collapse of the assault, pointing out that the marines were at the front when the march began, and that during the entire advance under fire "not a man wavered" (Parker to Lanman, January 16, 1865, and Parker to Porter, January 16, 1865, both in *ORN*, 11:495–99). Even Breese (ibid., 446) admitted that the marines "most promptly occupied" the breastworks and rifle pits thrown up in advance by Preston's firemen. Perhaps the ultimate reason for the collapse of the naval assault at Fort Fisher was the same that a German admiral would give for the lost opportunity at Jutland fifty-one years later: "The thing just happened."
22. Lamb, *Colonel Lamb's Story*, 27.
23. Gragg, *Confederate Goliath*, 177; Curtis, "Capture of Fort Fisher," 313–14.
24. Curtis, "Capture of Fort Fisher," 314.
25. Ibid., 315; Lamb, *Colonel Lamb's Story*, 28.
26. Curtis, "Capture of Fort Fisher," 315–16; Gragg, *Confederate Goliath*, 264.
27. Lamb, *Colonel Lamb's Story*, 27–29.
28. Ibid.; Still, "Yankees Were Landing," 16.
29. Lamb, *Colonel Lamb's Story*, 33–34.
30. Harkness, "Expeditions against Fort Fisher," 174.
31. Evans, *Sailor's Log*, 93–94.
32. Bartlett to his sisters, January 18, 1865, *ORN*, 11:529.
33. Gragg, *Confederate Goliath*, 188–89; Carter, "Fourteen Months' Service," 175.
34. Evans, *Sailor's Log*, 95.
35. Parker to Porter, January 16, 1865, *ORN*, 11:500; Bartlett to his sisters, January 18, 1865, ibid., 528.
36. Parker to Porter, January 26, 1865, ibid., 500; Breese to Porter, January 16, 1865, ibid., 447; Evans, *Sailor's Log*, 96; Parker, "Navy in the Capture of Fort Fisher," 114. Evans, who was writing more than forty years later, remembered the surgeon as "Dr. Longstreet," but the only navy medical officer listed as killed was

Dr. Longshaw (see "List of officers killed and wounded during the attack upon Fort Fisher," *ORN*, 11:442). He is correctly identified by Parker and Breese.

37. Breese to Porter, January 28, 1865, *ORN*, 11:451.
38. Porter to Welles, Special Report, January 17, 1865, ibid., 445; Lamb, *Colonel Lamb's Story*, 33.
39. Lamb, *Colonel Lamb's Story*, 32; Barrett, *Civil War in North Carolina*, 278 n.
40. Porter to Welles, Special Report, January 17, 1865, *ORN*, 11:445.
41. Bartlett to his sisters, January 18, 1865, ibid., 528; Parker to Porter, January 16, 1865, ibid., 499.
42. Bartlett to his sisters, January 18, 1865, ibid., 528.
43. Ibid., 529.
44. Evans, *Sailor's Log*, 96–97.
45. Breese to Porter, January 28, 1865, *ORN*, 11:451.
46. Gragg, *Confederate Goliath*, 210–11; Curtis, "Capture of Fort Fisher," 319.
47. Terry to Rawlins, January 25, 1865, *ORA*, 44, pt. 1:399; Longacre, "Task Before Them," 43; Gragg, *Confederate Goliath*, 211–13.
48. Lamb, *Colonel Lamb's Story*, 35.
49. Grattan, "Under the Blue Pennant," 187.
50. Saunders to Hebert, January 15, 1865, *ORA*, 46, pt. 2:1073.
51. Archer Anderson, Assistant Adjutant General, Department of North Carolina, to Graham, January 15, 1865, 9:30 P.M., ibid., 1072. Bragg's haziness has never been adequately explained. Judith Lee Hallock (*Braxton Bragg and Confederate Defeat*, vol. 2) discusses in detail his complete and total failure to understand the situation at Fort Fisher, but makes no attempt to analyze it. One possibility is that Bragg, who suffered from very real and crippling migraines as well as hypochondria, was the victim of overmedication. The standard cure-all of the period was laudanum, a mixture of alcohol and tincture of opium, that was responsible for more than one military disaster during the Civil War. Most historians attribute Gen. John Bell Hood's failure at Franklin to the fact that he was in a narcotic stupor to relieve the excruciating pain of several war wounds. The likelihood that Fort Fisher fell for the same reason cannot be dismissed.
52. Lamb, *Colonel Lamb's Story*, 4–5.
53. Ibid., 36.
54. Ibid., 37; Gragg, *Confederate Goliath*, 218–19; Still, "Yankees Were Landing," 16.
55. Lamb, *Colonel Lamb's Story*, 37.
56. Adrian Terry to "My own darling wife," January 24, 1865, in Longacre, "Task before Them," 43.
57. Anderson to Graham, January 15, 1865, 11 P.M., *ORA*, 46, pt. 2:1072.

15. AFTERMATH

1. Grattan, "Under the Blue Pennant," 187–88; Gragg, *Confederate Goliath*, 220.
2. Grattan, "Under the Blue Pennant," 187–88; Sands, "Last of the Blockade," 25; Dewey, *Autobiography*, 122.
3. Grattan, "Under the Blue Pennant," 188.

4. Bartlett to his sisters, January 18, 1865, *ORN*, 11:529.

5. Rogers to his parents, January 15, 1865, in Rogers, *Memories of Ninety Years,* 108.

6. Cobb to "Dear Father," January 16, 1865, Cobb Papers.

7. Grattan, "Under the Blue Pennant," 189.

8. Bright to Hebert, January 15, 1865, 10:30 P.M., *ORA,* 46, pt. 2:1071.

9. Ibid., 11:15 P.M.

10. Ibid., 11:20 P.M. and 11:40 P.M.

11. Still, "Yankees Were Landing," 16.

12. Sands, "Last of the Blockade," 25–27.

13. Proceedings of a Court of Inquiry Constituted to Examine into the Cause of the Explosion of the Powder Magazine, January 20, 1865, *ORA,* 44, pt. 1:431 [hereinafter cited as "Proceedings"]; Lamb, *Colonel Lamb's Story,* 37–38.

14. "Proceedings," 430–31.

15. Sands, "Last of the Blockade," 27.

16. D. D. Porter, *Incidents and Anecdotes,* 272.

17. Sands, "Last of the Blockade," 27; Cobb to "Dear Father," January 16, 1865, Cobb Papers.

18. "Proceedings," 431.

19. Bartlett to his sisters, January 18, 1865, *ORN,* 11:528.

20. Rogers to "Father and Mother," January 17, 1865, in Rogers, *Memories of Ninety Years,* 109.

21. Grattan, "Under the Blue Pennant," 189.

22. Return of Casualties in the U.S. Forces Engaged in the Storming of Fort Fisher, N.C., January 15, 1865, *ORA,* 44, pt. 1:405; Bragg to Col. W. H. Taylor, Assistant Adjutant General, Army of Northern Virginia, ibid., 434; Porter to Welles, January 17, 1865, *ORN,* 11:444.

23. Welles, *Diary,* January 17, 1865, 2:226–27.

24. Parker, "Navy in the Capture of Fort Fisher," 117.

25. Porter to Welles, January 17, 1865, *ORN,* 11:439.

26. Dawson to Zeilin, January 27, 1865 (second letter), "Letters Received."

27. Ibid.

28. Du Pont to William Whetten, January 19, 1865, in Hayes, *Samuel Francis Du Pont,* 3:428–29.

29. Terry to Rawlins, January 25, 1865, *ORA,* 44, pt. 1:400.

30. Lamb, *Colonel Lamb's Story,* 27.

31. Barrett, *Civil War in North Carolina,* 280–81.

32. Wilkinson, *Narrative of a Blockade-Runner,* 231–33.

33. Rogers to "Father and Mother," January 20, 1865, in Rogers, *Memories of Ninety Years,* 113.

34. Barrett, *Civil War in North Carolina,* 282–83.

35. John L. Porter to Mallory, November 1, 1864, *ORN,* series 2, 2:751; *Dictionary of American Fighting Ships,* 2:582.

36. Strode, *Jefferson Davis,* 138.

37. Whiting to Lee, January 18, 1865, *ORA,* 44, pt. 1:440.

38. Whiting to Lee, February 19, 1865, ibid., 441–42.

39. Whiting to Butler, February 28, 1865, *Joint Committee Report—Fort Fisher*, 106–8. Butler's questions and Whiting's responses also appear in *ORA*, 42, pt. 1:977–80.
40. *Joint Committee Report—Fort Fisher*, viii.
41. Ibid., 184; Porter to Welles, January 16, 1865, *ORN*, 11:436; Boynton, *History of the Navy*, 2:570.
42. Lamb, "Defense of Fort Fisher," 643 n.
43. Roberts, *Never Caught*, 14.
44. Lamb, *Colonel Lamb's Story*, 32.
45. Mason to Benjamin, undated [February 1865], *ORN*, series 2, 3:1260.

EPILOGUE

1. Dewey, *Autobiography*, 122; Browning, *From Cape Charles to Cape Fear*, 308; Nash, *Naval History*, 301. Gettysburg may be considered a strategic victory because Confederate losses were such that (Early's diversionary move against Washington in 1864 notwithstanding) the South could never again mount a major offensive. Tactically, however, it was a draw because neither army gained an immediate advantage; they simply hammered each other to exhaustion.
2. Barrett, *Civil War in North Carolina*, 284; Gragg, *Confederate Goliath*, 246–47; Sprunt, *Chronicles*, 499. Gragg (246) says the city was placed under command of Gen. Joseph Hawley. Sprunt quotes an extract from Cox's diary of February 15–22, 1865.
3. Gragg, *Confederate Goliath*, 252–54.
4. Ibid., 268–71.
5. Evans, *Sailor's Log*, 86–87.
6. Parker, "Navy in the Capture of Fort Fisher," 116.
7. The complete history up to the present is in Herring and Williams, *Fort Caswell*.
8. Porter to Fox, January 20, 1865, in Merrill, "Fort Fisher and Wilmington Campaign," 469.
9. Rogers to "Father and Mother," February 10, 1865, in Rogers, *Memories of Ninety Years*, 115.
10. Page, *Ships versus Shore*, 102–3; Gragg, *Confederate Goliath*, 272–73.
11. Page, *Ships versus Shore*, 103; Gragg, *Confederate Goliath*, 273–74; E. Gehrig Spencer, manager, Fort Fisher Historic Site, to author, February 14, 1997. When I was in the Wilmington area in 1995, I heard a rumor that the Mound Battery was bulldozed to prevent German submarines from using it as a landmark. However, Mr. Spencer indicated that there is no evidence that the Mound was removed for that reason.
12. Spencer to author, February 14, 1997.
13. Ibid.

APPENDIX

1. Selfridge to Porter, January 17, 1865, *ORN*, 11:477.

BIBLIOGRAPHY

MANUSCRIPTS

Battle Family Papers. Southern Historical Collection, University of North Carolina Library, Chapel Hill.

Betham, Asa. Papers. Library of Congress, Washington, D.C.

Bolles, Charles Pattison. Papers. North Carolina Department of Cultural Resources, Division of Archives and History, Raleigh.

Bonner, Macon. Papers. Southern Historical Collection, University of North Carolina Library, Chapel Hill.

Buie, Catherine Jane (McGeachy). Papers. Special Collections Library, Duke University, Durham, North Carolina.

Cleer, James J. Papers. Special Collections Library, Duke University, Durham, North Carolina.

Cobb, William. Papers. North Carolina Department of Cultural Resources, Fort Fisher State Historic Site, Kure Beach.

Cooper, Samuel. Papers. Southern Historical Collection, University of North Carolina Library, Chapel Hill.

Fernald, Joseph. Papers. Southern Historical Collection, University of North Carolina Library, Chapel Hill.

Grattan, John W. Journal and Papers. Library of Congress, Washington, D.C.

———. "Under the Blue Pennant or Notes of a Naval Officer." John W. Grattan Papers. Library of Congress, Washington, D.C.

Lamb, William. Diary and Papers. Manuscripts and Rare Books Department, Swem Library, College of William and Mary, Williamsburg, Virginia.

Parrott, Enoch Greenleafe. Papers. Special Collections Library, Duke University, Durham, North Carolina.

Read, William, Jr. Papers. Special Collections Library, Duke University, Durham, North Carolina.

Steedman, Charles. Papers. Special Collections Library, Duke University, Durham, North Carolina.

Whiting, William Henry Chase. Papers. North Carolina Department of Cultural Resources, Division of Archives and History, Raleigh.

U.S. GOVERNMENT DOCUMENTS

Kennedy, Joseph C. G. *Population of the United States in 1860: Compiled from the Original Returns of the Eighth Census under the Direction of the Secretary of the Interior.* Washington, D.C.: Government Printing Office, 1864.

McClellan, George B. *Report on the Organization and Campaigns of the Army of the Potomac: To Which Is Added an Account of the Campaign in Western Virginia, with Plans of Battle-Fields.* 1864. Reprint, Freeport, N.Y.: Books for Libraries Press, 1970.

Richardson, James D., comp. *A Compilation of the Messages and Papers of the Presidents.* Vol. 5. Washington, D.C.: Bureau of National Literature and Art, 1910.

U.S. Congress. *Report of the Joint Committee on the Conduct of the War, at the Second Session Thirty-eighth Congress. Fort Fisher Expedition.* Washington, D.C.: Government Printing Office, 1865.

———. *Report of the Joint Committee on the Conduct of the War, at the Second Session Thirty-eighth Congress. Miscellaneous.* Washington, D.C.: Government Printing Office, 1865.

U.S. Department of the Navy. *Dictionary of American Naval Fighting Ships.* Vol. 2. 1963. Reprint, Washington, D.C.: Government Printing Office, 1977.

———. *Official Records of the Union and Confederate Navies in the War of the Rebellion.* 30 vols. Washington, D.C.: Government Printing Office, 1894–1927.

———. Record Group 127. Records of the Commandant (Marine Corps), Letters Received, 1818–1915. National Archives, Washington.

U.S. Department of War. *The War of the Rebellion: A Compilation of the Official Records of the Union and Confederate Armies.* 130 vols. Washington, D.C.: Government Printing Office, 1891–98.

BOOKS—PRIMARY

Ammen, Daniel. *The Atlantic Coast.* The Navy in the Civil War, vol. 2. 1883. Reprint, Wilmington, N.C.: Broadfoot, 1989.

Blanding, Stephen F. *Recollections of a Sailor Boy or the Cruise of the Gunboat Louisiana.* Providence: E. A. Johnson, 1886.

Butler, Benjamin F. *Butler's Book: Autobiography and Personal Reminiscences of Major-General Benjamin F. Butler.* Boston: A. M. Thayer, 1892.

———. *Private and Official Correspondence of Gen. Benjamin F. Butler during the Period of the Civil War.* 5 vols. Norwood, Mass.: Privately printed, 1917.

Davis, Jefferson. *The Rise and Fall of the Confederate Government.* 2 vols. Richmond: Garrett and Massie, 1881.

Dewey, George. *Autobiography of George Dewey, Admiral of the Navy.* 1913. Reprint, Annapolis, Md.: Naval Institute Press, 1987.

Emilio, Luis F. *A Brave Black Regiment: History of the Fifty-fourth Regiment of Massachusetts Volunteer Infantry, 1863–1865.* 3rd ed. Salem, N.H.: Ayer, 1990.

Evans, Robley D. *A Sailor's Log: Recollections of Forty Years of Naval Life.* New York: D. Appleton, 1908.

Gillmore, Quincy Adams. *Engineer and Artillery Operations against the Defences of Charleston Harbor in 1863: Comprising the Descent upon Morris Island, the Demolition of Fort Sumter, the Reduction of Forts Wagner and Gregg.* New York: D. Van Nostrand, 1865.

Grant, U. S. *Personal Memoirs of U. S. Grant/Selected Letters 1839–1865.* Memoirs, 2 vols. 1885–86. Letters (abridged), 14 vols. 1867–85. Reprint (one volume), New York: Library of America, 1990.

Hayes, John D., ed. *Samuel Francis Du Pont: A Selection from His Civil War Letters.* 3 vols. Ithaca, N.Y.: Cornell University Press, 1969.

Johnson, Robert Underwood, and Clarence Clough Buel, eds. *Battles and Leaders of the Civil War.* 4 vols. 1887–88. Reprint, New York: Thomas Yoseloff, 1956.

Jones, John B. *A Rebel War Clerk's Diary at the Confederate States Capital.* 2 vols. 1866. Reprint, Alexandria, Va.: Time-Life, 1982.

Lamb, William. *Colonel Lamb's Story of Fort Fisher: The Battles Fought Here in 1864 and 1865.* 1893. Reprint, Carolina Beach, N.C.: The Blockade Runner Museum, 1966.

McClellan, George B. *McClellan's Own Story: The War for the Union, the Soldiers Who Fought It, the Civilians Who Directed It, and His Relations to It and to Them.* New York: Charles L. Webster, 1887.

Pollard, Edward A. *The Lost Cause.* 1866. Reprint, New York: Gramercy, 1994.

Porter, David D. *Incidents and Anecdotes of the Civil War.* New York: D. Appleton, 1885.

———. *The Naval History of the Civil War.* 1886. Reprint, Secaucus, N.J.: Castle, 1984.

Porter, Horace. *Campaigning with Grant.* 1897. Reprint, Alexandria, Va.: Time-Life, 1985.

Roberts, Captain [Augustus Charles Hobart-Hampden]. *Never Caught: The Personal Adventures Connected with Twelve Successful Trips in Blockade-Running during the American Civil War, 1863–1864.* 1867. Reprint, Carolina Beach, N.C.: The Blockade Runner Museum, 1967.

Rogers, Henry Monroe. *Memories of Ninety Years.* Boston: Houghton Mifflin, 1928.

Selfridge, Thomas O., Jr. *Memoirs of Thomas O. Selfridge, Jr., Rear Admiral, U.S.N.* New York: Putnam, 1924.

Semmes, Raphael. *Memoirs of Service Afloat, during the War between the States.* Baltimore: Kelly, Piet, 1869.

Sprunt, James. *Chronicles of the Cape Fear River, 1660–1916.* 2nd. ed. 1916. Reprint, Wilmington, N.C.: Broadfoot, 1992.

———. *Tales of the Cape Fear Blockade.* 1902. Reprint, Winnabow, N.C.: Charles Towne Preservation Trust, 1960.

Taylor, Thomas E. *Running the Blockade: A Personal Narrative of Adventures, Risks, and Escapes during the American Civil War.* New York: Scribner, 1896.

Thomas, Cornelius M. Dickinson. *Letters from the Colonel's Lady: Correspondence of Mrs. (Col.) William Lamb Written from Fort Fisher, N.C., C.S.A., to Her Parents in Providence, R.I., U.S.A.* Winnabow, N.C.: Charles Towne Preservation Trust, 1965.

Thompson, Robert Means, and Richard Wainwright, eds. *Confidential Correspondence of Gustavus Vasa Fox, Assistant Secretary of the Navy 1861–1865.* 2 vols. New York: Naval Historical Society, 1919.

Welles, Gideon. *Diary of Gideon Welles, Secretary of the Navy under Lincoln and Johnson.* 3 vols. Boston: Houghton Mifflin, 1911.

Wilkinson, John. *The Narrative of a Blockade-Runner.* 1877. Reprint, Alexandria, Va.: Time-Life, 1984.

BOOKS—SECONDARY

Anderson, Bern. *By Sea and by River: The Naval History of the Civil War.* New York: Knopf, 1962.

Barrett, John G. *The Civil War in North Carolina.* Chapel Hill: University of North Carolina Press, 1963.

Boynton, Charles B. *The History of the Navy during the Rebellion.* 2 vols. New York: D. Appleton, 1868.

Braxton Bragg and Confederate Defeat. Vol. 1, *Field Command,* by Grady McWhiney. New York: Columbia University Press, 1969.

———. Vol. 2, by Judith Lee Hallock. Tuscaloosa: University of Alabama Press, 1991.

Brooks, N. C. *A Complete History of the Mexican War: Its Causes, Conduct, and Consequences: Comprising an Account of the Various Military and Naval Operations from Its Commencement to the Treaty of Peace.* Baltimore: Hutchinson & Seebold, 1849.

Browning, Robert M., Jr. *From Cape Charles to Cape Fear: The North Atlantic Blockading Squadron during the Civil War.* Tuscaloosa: University of Alabama Press, 1993.

Cornish, Dudley Taylor, and Virginia Jeans Laas. *Lincoln's Lee: The Life of Samuel Phillips Lee, United States Navy, 1812–1897.* Lawrence: University Press of Kansas, 1986.

Donnelly, Ralph W. *The History of the Confederate States Marine Corps.* Washington, N.C.: Privately printed, 1976.

Du Pont, H. A. *Rear-Admiral Samuel Francis Du Pont, United States Navy: A Biography.* New York: National Americana Society, 1926.

Freeman, Douglas Southall. *Lee's Lieutenants: A Study in Command.* 4 vols. New York: Scribner, 1942.

Gragg, Rod. *Confederate Goliath: The Battle of Fort Fisher.* 1991. Reprint, Baton Rouge: Louisiana State University Press, 1994.

Herring, Ethel, and Carolee Williams. *Fort Caswell in War and Peace.* Wendell, N.C.: Broadfoot's Bookmark, 1983.

Johnson, Allen, and Dumas Malone, eds. *Dictionary of American Biography.* 21 vols. New York: Scribner, 1928–44.

McPherson, James M. *Battle Cry of Freedom: The Civil War Era.* New York: Oxford University Press, 1988.

Musicant, Ivan. *Divided Waters: The Naval History of the Civil War.* New York: HarperCollins, 1995.

Nash, Howard P. *A Naval History of the Civil War.* A. S. Barnes, 1972.

———. *Stormy Petrel: The Life and Times of Benjamin F. Butler, 1818–1893.* Cranbury, N.J.: Associated University Presses, Inc., and Fairleigh Dickenson University Press, 1969.

Nolan, Dick. *Benjamin Franklin Butler, the Damndest Yankee.* Novato, Calif.: Presidio Press, 1991.

Page, Dave. *Ships versus Shore: Civil War Engagements along Southern Shores and Rivers.* Nashville, Tenn.: Rutledge Hill Press, 1994.

Reed, Rowena. *Combined Operations in the Civil War.* Annapolis, Md.: Naval Institute Press, 1978.

Roske, Ralph J., and Charles Van Doren. *Lincoln's Commando: The Biography of Commander William B. Cushing, U.S. Navy.* 1957. Reprint, Annapolis, Md.: Naval Institute Press, 1995.

Scharf, J. Thomas. *History of the Confederate States Navy from Its Organization to the Surrender of Its Last Vessel.* 1887. Reprint, New York: Fairfax Press, 1977.

Schneller, Robert J., Jr. *A Quest for Glory: A Biography of Rear Admiral John A. Dahlgren.* Annapolis, Md.: Naval Institute Press, 1996.

Soley, James Russell. *Admiral Porter.* New York: D. Appleton, 1903.

Strode, Hudson. *Jefferson Davis: Tragic Hero—The Last Twenty-Five Years, 1864–1889.* New York: Harcourt, Brace and World, 1964.

Time-Life Books. *Charleston.* Alexandrian, Va.: Time-Life, 1997.

———. *Echoes of Glory.* 3 vols. Alexandria, Va.: Time-Life, 1991.

Trotter, William R. *Ironclads and Columbiads.* 1989. Reprint, Winston-Salem, N.C.: John F. Blair, 1991.

Warner, Ezra J. *Generals in Blue: Lives of the Union Commanders.* Baton Rouge: Louisiana State University Press, 1964.

———. *Generals in Gray: Lives of the Confederate Commanders.* Baton Rouge: Louisiana State University Press, 1959.

West, Richard S., Jr. *Gideon Welles, Lincoln's Navy Department.* Indianapolis: Bobbs-Merrill, 1943.

———. *Lincoln's Scapegoat General: A Life of Benjamin F. Butler, 1818–1893.* Boston: Houghton Mifflin Company, 1965.

Wise, Stephen R. *Lifeline of the Confederacy: Blockade Running during the Civil War.* 1988. Reprint, Columbia: University of South Carolina Press, 1991.

ARTICLES—PRIMARY

Ames, Adelbert. "The Capture of Fort Fisher." In *Civil War Papers Read before the Commandery of the State of Massachusetts, Military Order of the Loyal Legion of the United States,* 1:271–95. Boston: The Commandery, 1900.

Beauregard, Pierre Gustave Toussaint. "The Defense of Charleston." In Johnson and Buel, *Battles and Leaders of the Civil War,* 4:1–23.

Burnside, Ambrose E. "The Burnside Expedition." In Johnson and Buel, *Battles and Leaders of the Civil War,* 1:660–70.

Carter, Solon A. "Fourteen Months' Service with Colored Troops." In *Civil War Papers Read before the Commandery of the State of Massachusetts, Military Order of the Loyal Legion of the United States,* 1:155–79. Boston: The Commandery, 1900.

Curtis, Newton Martin. "The Capture of Fort Fisher." In *Civil War Papers Read before the Commandery of the State of Massachusetts, Military Order of the Loyal Legion of the United States,* 1:299–307. Boston: The Commandery, 1900.

Cushing, William B. "Outline Story of the War Experience of William B. Cushing as Told by Himself." *Proceedings of the United States Naval Institute* 38 (September 1912): 941–91.

Dickinson, A. G. "Blockade Running from Wilmington." *Confederate Veteran* 3 (1895).

Gillmore, Quincy Adams. "The Army before Charleston in 1863." In Johnson and Buel, *Battles and Leaders of the Civil War,* 4:52–71.

Harkness, Edson J. "The Expeditions against Fort Fisher and Wilmington." In *Military Essays and Recollections: Papers Read before the Commandery of the State of Illinois, Military Order of the Loyal Legion of the United States,* 2:145–188. Chicago: McClurg, 1894.

Hawkins, Rush C. "Early Coast Operations in North Carolina." In Johnson and Buel, *Battles and Leaders of the Civil War,* 1:632–59.

Johns, John. "Wilmington during the Blockade." 1866. Reprint, *Civil War Times Illustrated* 13 (June 1974): 34–44.

Lamb, William. "The Defense of Fort Fisher." In Johnson and Buel, *Battles and Leaders of the Civil War,* 4:642–54.

Lockwood, H. C. "The Capture of Fort Fisher." *Atlantic Monthly,* May 1871: 622–36.

Longacre, Edward G., ed. "The Task before Them: Yanks Attack Fort Fisher." *Civil War Times Illustrated* 21 (February 1983): 36–43.

Parker, James. "The Navy in the Battles and Capture of Fort Fisher." In *Personal Recollections of the War of the Rebellion: Addresses Delivered before the Commandery of the State of New York, Military Order of the Loyal Legion of the United States,* ed. A. Noel Blakeman. Second series, 104–17. New York: Putnam, 1897.

Rhind, A. C. "The Last of the Fort Fisher Powder-Boat." *United Service* 1 (April 1879): 227–36.

Sands, Francis P. B. "The Last of the Blockade and the Fall of Fort Fisher." 1902. Reprint, Ann Arbor, Mich.: University Microfilms, 1968.

Selfridge, Thomas O., Jr. "The Navy at Fort Fisher." In Johnson and Buel, *Battles and Leaders of the Civil War,* 4:655–61.

Stevens, Thomas H. "The Boat Attack on Sumter." In Johnson and Buel, *Battles and Leaders of the Civil War,* 4:47–51.

Still, William N., Jr., ed. "'The Yankees Were Landing Below Us': The Journal of Robert Watson, C.S.N." *Civil War Times Illustrated* 15 (April 1976): 12–21.

"The Story of the Powder-Boat." *Galaxy* 9 (January 1870): 77–88.

"Terry's Fort Fisher Expedition." *Old and New* 11 (March 1875): 290–304.

Turner, Henry M. "Rocked in the Cradle of Consternation." 1865. Reprint, *American Heritage* 31 (October/November 1980): 70–79.

Welles, Gideon. "Lincoln's Triumph in 1864." *Atlantic Monthly,* April 1878, 454–68.

ARTICLES—SECONDARY

Anderson, Stuart. "1861: Blockade vs. Closing the Confederate Ports." *Military Affairs* (December 1977): 190–93.

Beard, William E. "The Fort Fisher 'Volcano.'" *Proceedings of the United States Naval Institute* (August 1932): 1151–56.

Hayes, John D. "Captain Fox—*He* is the Navy Department." *Proceedings of the United States Naval Institute* 91 (September 1965): 64–71.

Johnson, Ludwell H. "Northern Profit and Profiteers: The Cotton Rings of 1864–1865." *Civil War History* 12 (June 1966): 101–15.

Lebergott, Stanley. "Through the Blockade: The Profitability and Extent of Cotton Smuggling, 1861–1865." *Journal of Economic History* 41 (December 1981): 867–88.

Merrill, James M. "The Fort Fisher and Wilmington Campaign: Letters from Rear Admiral David D. Porter." *North Carolina Historical Review* 35 (October 1958): 461–75.

"The Opposing Forces at Fort Fisher." In Johnson and Buel, *Battles and Leaders of the Civil War,* 4:661–62.

Peery, Charles. "Clandestine Commerce: Yankee Blockade Running." *Journal of Confederate History* 4 (1989): 89–111.

Price, Charles L. "North Carolina Railroads during the Civil War." *Civil War History* 7 (September 1961): 298–309.

Price, Charles L., and Claude C. Sturgill. "Shock and Assault in the First Battle of Fort Fisher." *North Carolina Historical Review* 47 (January 1970): 24–39.

Shingleton, Royce Gordon. "Cruise of the CSS *Tallahassee.*" *Civil War Times Illustrated* 15 (May 1976): 30–40.

Still, William N., Jr. "A Naval Sieve: The Union Blockade in the Civil War." *Naval War College Review* 36 (May–June 1983): 38–45.

THESES AND DISSERTATIONS

Barry, Richard Schriver. "The History of Fort Macon." Master's thesis, Duke University, 1950.

Honeycutt, Ava L., Jr. "Fort Fisher, Malakoff of the South." Master's thesis, Duke University, 1963.

Wood, Richard E. "Port Town at War: Wilmington, North Carolina, 1860–1865." Ph.D. diss., Florida State University, 1976.

NEWSPAPERS

New York Herald
New York Times

INDEX

ABOUT THE AUTHOR

Charles M. Robinson III was born in Harlingen, Texas, and spent boyhood summers with his grandparents in Wilmington, North Carolina. He first saw Fort Fisher in 1957 when much of the sea face was still intact.

He has a bachelor's degree in history from St. Edward's University in Austin, Texas, and a master's degree from the University of Texas Pan-American. Most of his work focuses on the American West. His book *Bad Hand: A Biography of General Ranald S. Mackenzie* won the Texas Historical Commission's T. R. Fehrenbach Book Award, and *The Court Martial of Lieutenant Henry Flipper* was a finalist for the Spur Award, presented by the Western Writers of America. He is an instructor in U.S. history at South Texas Community College in McAllen, Texas.

The **Naval Institute Press** is the book-publishing arm of the U.S. Naval Institute, a private, nonprofit, membership society for sea service professionals and others who share an interest in naval and maritime affairs. Established in 1873 at the U.S. Naval Academy in Annapolis, Maryland, where its offices remain today, the Naval Institute has members worldwide.

Members of the Naval Institute support the education programs of the society and receive the influential monthly magazine *Proceedings* and discounts on fine nautical prints and on ship and aircraft photos. They also have access to the transcripts of the Institute's Oral History Program and get discounted admission to any of the Institute-sponsored seminars offered around the country.

The Naval Institute also publishes *Naval History* magazine. This colorful bimonthly is filled with entertaining and thought-provoking articles, first-person reminiscences, and dramatic art and photography. Members receive a discount on *Naval History* subscriptions.

The Naval Institute's book-publishing program, begun in 1898 with basic guides to naval practices, has broadened its scope in recent years to include books of more general interest. Now the Naval Institute Press publishes about 100 titles each year, ranging from how-to books on boating and navigation to battle histories, biographies, ship and aircraft guides, and novels. Institute members receive discounts of 20 to 50 percent on the Press's nearly 600 books in print.

Full-time students are eligible for special half-price membership rates. Life memberships are also available.

For a free catalog describing Naval Institute Press books currently available, and for further information about subscribing to *Naval History* magazine or about joining the U.S. Naval Institute, please write to:

Membership Department
U.S. Naval Institute
118 Maryland Avenue
Annapolis, MD 21402-5035
Telephone: (800) 233-8764
Fax: (410) 269-7940
Web address: www.usni.org